THE ULTIMATE DECISION

The President as Commander in Chief

By Ernest R. May

World War and American Isolation,
1914–1917 (1959)

THE ULTIMATE DECISION

The President as Commander in Chief

Edited with an introduction by

ERNEST R. MAY

GEORGE BRAZILLER

NEW YORK, 1960

ACKNOWLEDGMENTS:

The chapter on James K. Polk has been reprinted from *The Jacksonians* by
Leonard D. White, by permission of The Macmillan Company, Copyright ©
1954 by The Macmillan Company.

The chapter on Abraham Lincoln has been reprinted from *Lincoln and His
Generals* by T. Harry Williams, by permission of Alfred A. Knopf, Inc. Copyright 1952 by Alfred A. Knopf, Inc.

The President shall be Commander in Chief of the Army and Navy of the United States, and of the Militia of the several States, when called into the actual Service of the United States . . .

He shall have Power, by and with the Advice and Consent of the Senate, to make Treaties, provided two thirds of the Senators present concur . . .

from Article II, Section 2, of
The Constitution of the United States

CONTENTS

ILLUSTRATIONS

The illustrations will be found following page 142.

Introduction

O N THE BANK of the Potomac River, just south of the District of Columbia, stands the squat, five-sided Pentagon Building. Its aboveground floors enclose a neat grass courtyard dotted with small trees and crossed by wide, concrete footpaths. Each floor has five corridors or "rings," with offices on each side, only the outmost and inmost having windows. In the central corridors of one floor on the northern side are the double-guarded quarters of the Joint Chiefs of Staff.

There work officers from all the services, some civilians, and even a few enlisted men. Their business is preparing papers to inform, advise, or warn the chairman and the four service chiefs (including the Commandant of the Marine Corps) who collectively make up "the JCS." On Mondays and Wednesdays the chiefs themselves gather around a long mahogany table in a mustard-walled conference room and discuss, reject, amend, or accept the recommendations in these staff papers.

Once the chiefs have reached some kind of agreement, the resulting documents travel to the outmost bank of offices on the same floor, those occupied by the Secretary and the Assistant Secretaries of Defense. After scrutiny and possible revision by them, they go under the care of an armed messenger across Memorial Bridge, around the giant, brooding statue of Abraham Lincoln, and into a side door of the flamboyant Old State-War-Navy Building which stands on Pennsylvania Avenue just west of the White House.

There, in the offices of the Planning Board of the National Security Council, either the delegate of the Joint Chiefs or the member representing the Defense Department opens discussions with officials of the State and Treasury departments, the Central Intelligence Agency, the Bureau of the Budget, and other agencies. The problem may be restudied by the Council secretariat. Days, even weeks, may pass. Changed, rewritten, amplified, or just approved, the recommendations of the JCS then go into a paper numbered something like NSC 000/0000. It is circulated to members of the Council, and its title goes on the Council's agenda.

On a Thursday, the Council gathers in a sedate, early American study in the White House. The Secretaries of State, Defense, and the Treasury, the Director of Central Intelligence, the Director of the Bureau of the Budget, the Chairman of the Joint Chiefs, and invited specialists state their opinions. According to Boston banker Robert Cutler, who held the job under Eisenhower, the President's Special Assistant for National Security Affairs deliberately whips up debate and disagreement. Cutler speaks in his 1956 *Foreign Affairs* article, "The Development of the National Security Council," of "flashing interchange" among the members.

But the Council does not vote. It does not make decisions. The final word lies with one man, the man at the head of the table, the man toward whom all argument and exhortation is directed—the President of the United States. As in the motto on Harry Truman's desk, "The buck ends here."

This seems a far cry from the 1790's, when government under the Constitution had its beginnings. The War Department in 1793 consisted of a Secretary, six copy clerks, and a part-time messenger. There was no Navy Department. There were only 5,000 men in the whole military establishment. In Philadelphia, the temporary capital, General Henry Knox, the Secretary of War, could walk from his residence on Chestnut Street to the Morris House, where President Washington lived. If necessary, he might draft a letter and have his clerks copy it for circulation to the three other members of the cabinet—the Secretary of State, the Secretary of the Treasury, and the Attorney General. If they were not away in New York or Virginia on private business, Knox could have his answers almost immediately.

But the essentials were the same. Knox did not make the decisions; nor did the cabinet. The power rested only with the President, and the burden lay as heavily on Washington as later on Truman or Eisenhower. Washington could caution Knox as he did in a letter of August 13, 1792, that if war came "(which heaven avert) we must expect to encounter a powerful confederacy, and ought not to put any thing to hazard which can be avoided by military foresight." But he could not stop at exhortation. Washington himself had to approve all appointments of commanders, provisions for calling up militia, and even arrangements for recasting old cannon and laying up stores of powder and saltpeter.

These burdens have lain on every president because of the

simple words that begin Article II, Section 2 of the Constitution: "The President shall be Commander in Chief of the Army and Navy of the United States." In Britain, direction of the armed forces is shared by a cabinet. In the third and fourth French republics, it was actually divided between a ministry, a minister, and a parliamentary committee. In the U.S.S.R., it is at least theoretically the corporate business of a council of ministers and the party presidium. In fact, of course, there may often be one ruling personality—a Hitler, a Stalin, a Khrushchev, or even a Bismarck or a Churchill—to whom issues of national security are appealed and whose decisions are final. But the president of the United States, alone among the executives of major powers, has the daily duty of presiding over the armed forces.

The peculiar provision in the American Constitution has aroused some fear in the past. Presidents, beginning with Lincoln, claimed authority in time of war to suspend habeas corpus and establish controls over the civil population. Franklin Roosevelt went so far in September, 1942, as to warn Congress that if it failed to pass certain laws, he would enact them by fiat. "The President has the powers, under the Constitution . . . ," he declared, "to take measures necessary to avert a disaster which would interfere with the winning of the war." The potential menace in the commander-in-chief clause led Justice Jackson in *Woods vs. Miller Co.* in 1948 to label it "the most dangerous one to free government in the whole catalogue of powers."

With the serious onset of the Cold War came other fears. The military machine became increasingly big and unwieldy. At a cost running annually to tens of billions, men in the uniforms of four different services handled not only missiles, rockets, jet aircraft, and giant submarines and carriers, but also explosives capable of obliterating all life on the planet. When President Truman relieved General MacArthur in Korea and later when President Eisenhower admitted having authorized U-2 observation flights over the Soviet Union, Americans of quite different political faiths wondered anxiously if the command-in-chief had not become too great, too complex, and too terrible a job for any one man.

The following essays indicate why the constitutional clause was written as it was. They also show how successive wartime presidents managed their immense responsibilities. They suggest why Americans have not had the experience of peoples who imitated them—why the United States has never been ruled by a Batista, a Trujillo, or even a Frondizi. They also testify to the resiliency and durability that democratic, constitutional government has had and, we hope, will have.

ERNEST R. MAY

Cambridge, Mass.
July, 1960

I

"The President Shall Be Commander in Chief"

(1787–1789)

ERNEST R. MAY

DURING THE FIRST World War President Woodrow Wilson once found on his desk a letter from an artist. Enclosed was an etching that pictured him in military uniform. Instead of telling his secretary to send a note of thanks, Wilson sat down at his own little portable Corona and, in his sober, thoughtful, literal-minded way, pecked out:

"I warmly and sincerely appreciate the sentiment which led you to make the etching . . . , but I feel bound, in replying to your letter . . . to say that there is a sense in which putting me in uniform violates a very fundamental principle of our institutions, namely, that the military power is subordinate to the civil. The framers of the Constitution, of course, realized that the President would seldom be a soldier and their idea in making him the Commander-in-Chief of the Army and Navy of the United States was that the armed forces of the country must be the instruments of the authority by which policy was determined."

Wilson had been a professor of political science at Princeton and had written not only several notable books on American government but also a five-volume history of the United States. Yet he seemed to disregard the best known of all commentaries on the Constitution, *The Federalist Papers,* in No. 69 of which Alexander Hamilton had written that the commander in chief would have "the supreme command and direction of the military and naval forces, as first General and admiral of the Confederacy." Hamilton's words suggested that at least in time of war the distinction between civil and military would lapse.

The discrepancy does not necessarily show Wilson as a bad historian, for in stipulating that the president should be "Commander in Chief of the Army and Navy" the framers had anticipated Napoleon's maxim that constitutions should be short and obscure. The clause had been approved by the Philadelphia convention on August 27, 1787. Though Luther Martin of Maryland recalled later that some had wanted to forbid the president's commanding in person, James Madison, who jotted the fullest minutes of proceedings, made no record of any debate, nor did any other delegate who tried to keep notes.

Others besides President Wilson showed mystification later. In 1917 Charles Evans Hughes, who had served on the Supreme Court, suggested to the American Bar Association that perhaps the framers meant the country to have two instruments of government, one "a *fighting* constitution." Justice Burton, dissenting in *Duncan vs. Kahanamoku* in 1946, elaborated the same theory. The Constitution, he asserted, "was written by a generation fresh from war. The people established a more perfect union, in part, so that they might the better defend themselves from military attack. In doing so they centralized far more military power and responsibility in the Chief Executive than previously had been done. . . . In time of war the nation simply changes gears." Apt and interesting though these speculations were, they merely indicated, like Wilson's letter to the artist, that the real aim of the framers remained a mystery.

That this should be so is all the more surprising because the brief clause making the president commander in chief has proved to be one of the most important in the Constitution. Along with the provision that he "take care that the laws be faithfully executed," it has supplied the legal basis for most of the vast expansion in the presidency. Clinton Rossiter declares in *The Supreme Court and the Commander in Chief* that "of all his powers, the most basic, spectacular, and injurious to private rights" is that which the president holds as commander in chief.

Some Americans of the time saw possible dangers. In the Virginia ratifying convention, Patrick Henry warned, "If your American chief be a man of ambition and abilities, how easy is it for him to render himself absolute! The army is in his hands. . . . Can he not, at the head of his army, beat down every opposition?" In his *Observations on the New Constitution*, Elbridge Gerry of Massachusetts put it even more eloquently: "freedom revolts at the idea, when the Divan, or the Despot, may draw out his dragoons to suppress the murmurs of a few." Yet Henry, Gerry, William Miller in the North Carolina ratifying convention, and George Clinton in his letter as "Cato" to the *New York Journal* for November 8, 1787, were the only prominent men to protest the clause. George Mason, charging in the Virginia convention that the president would have exces-

5

sive power, still "admitted the propriety of his being commander-in-chief . . . ; but he thought it would be dangerous to let him command in person, without any restraint, as he might make a bad use of it." Miller was the only one to suggest that command should lie with Congress. No one at all proposed a separate office, a single chief of staff or committee of chiefs of staff, responsible to both executive and legislative branches.

Why were the framers and sponsors of the Constitution so sure that this power should lie solely with the president? In the Virginia convention, Madison asked Henry in wonderment, "Would the honorable member say that the sword ought to be put in the hands of the representatives of the people, or in other hands independent of the government altogether?" In North Carolina, Richard D. Spaight replied to Miller, saying, "He was surprised that any objection should be made." If we can get behind this attitude and find out why the drafters made such an assumption, perhaps we can guess how they intended the president to act in his separate capacity as commander in chief.

In part, no doubt, the men in Philadelphia were influenced by recent experience. The Revolutionary War had been fought successfully under a single commander in chief. In June, 1775, there was fighting around Boston. Members of the Continental Congress thought the patriots would only hold out if assured of support from the United Colonies, and they voted to raise reinforcements in Pennsylvania, Maryland, and Virginia. The delegates from these colonies did not want their troops under the Massachusetts commander, Artemas Ward. On the other hand, all the forces in the area needed one head, and the obvious solution was to place one man over all the colonial army. On John Adams' motion, George Washington of Virginia was appointed. The Congress reserved to itself and to the states the naming of subordinate generals, and Washington often lacked control over other commanders. Douglas Southall Freeman comments that in 1776 he was exercising almost no supervision over General Schuyler and hardly even communicating with General Wooster. Nevertheless, he had the title, and, looking back from 1787, the makers of the Constitution could see little reason for regretting the fact. Spaight in North Carolina remarked "that Congress had, in the last war, given the exclusive command of the army to the commander-in-chief, and that if they had not done so, perhaps the independence of America would not have been established." Memories of the Revolution certainly influenced the generation of 1787.

So did the fact that the former commander in chief was expected to be the first president. Mason in the Virginia convention tried to persuade his fellow delegates that they should forget the Revolutionary War. He called attention to "the extent of what the late commander-in-chief might have done, from his great abilities, and the strong attachment of both officers and soldiers towards him, if, instead of being disinterested, he had been an ambitious man." But most men were visualizing Washington not only in his old post but also in the new one. Pierce Butler, who had sat in the Philadelphia convention as a delegate from South Carolina, confessed in a letter of May 5, 1788, that he thought the presidential powers "full great, and greater than I was disposed to make them. Nor, Entre Nous, do I believe they would have been so great had not many of the members cast their eyes towards General Washington as President; and shaped their Ideas of the Powers to be given to a President, by their opinions of his Virtue."

Nor was it only Washington's experience, prestige, and personality that weighed with the framers. Former officers of his army had banded together in the Society of the Cincinnati. Judge Aedanus Burke of South Carolina immediately published *Considerations on the Society or Order of the Cincinnati, . . . Proving that it Creates a Race of Hereditary Patricians, or Nobility,* a pamphlet charging these officers with "fiery hot ambition, and thirst for power." Many members held state and local offices; many agitated for a stronger federal government, partly in order to get veterans' benefits that had been promised them. The Society was one of the few truly national organizations of the time, and it alarmed others besides Judge Burke. Edmund Randolph, for example, wrote to Jefferson on April 24, 1784, warning that ex-officers were gradually monopolizing posts in county government, and at the Philadelphia convention both Gerry and Mason expressed fear lest the Cincinnati control nationwide elections for the presidency. James Warren wrote John Adams on March 10, 1784, that nothing was more "a General Subject of Conversation than the Cincinnati Clubb." And Washington was not only the past general, he was also titular head of the Society. If he were commander in chief as well as president, he would be able to hold the Cincinnati in check. Respect for Washington's political as well as military capabilities thus had something to do with the framing of the commander-in-chief clause.

Nevertheless, neither the Revolutionary War experience nor the expectation that Washington would be president quite explains the assumption of the Constitution makers. Many were men of great learning. Their speeches and pamphlets brimmed with allusions to Roman generals, attempts at despotism in England, and military tyrannies in continental Europe. That the new central government would be able to have a standing army formed a major grievance of the Constitution's opponents. To understand why the commander-in-chief clause excited so little dispute, one needs also to go farther back into American experience and memory.

Before the Revolutionary War the colonists had had some experience with independent military commanders. In the aftermath of the Seven Years War, the English government had stationed forces in North America under an English commander in chief residing in New York. Though the generals holding this office endeavored to be discreet and to interfere in civil affairs as little as possible, their power and importance grew. By the mid-1770's, as Clarence E. Carter has pointed out in an essay in Richard B. Morris' *The Era of the American Revolution,* they had acquired great influence over trade, transportation, and Indian relations. Few merchants or politicians were unaware of the commander in chief's powers, and the incidents leading up to the Revolution made all colonists conscious of them. One of the grievances in the Declaration of Independence was that George III had "affected to render the military independent of, and superior to, the civil power." The example of a command-in-chief not subject to political control may have remained vivid in the minds of some of the Constitution's framers.

In addition, they had perhaps sharper recollections of the success which individual colonies had experienced in combining the command-in-chief with the governorship. In each colony, the governor or proprietor had been styled "captain-general" and controlled all provincial forces. Yet the colonists had found little cause for complaint. Assemblies claimed and asserted rights not only to vote money for troops but also to authorize their calling up. Under one or the other of these principles, they neutralized whatever pernicious power the executive might have had.

By the mid-eighteenth century, indeed, grievances seemed all on the side of the governors. Clinton in New York complained in 1752 that his assembly had not voted a militia law for four years. Pownal protested that Massachusetts forces in the French and Indian War were directed not by him but by a supervising committee of the General Court. Dinwiddie of Virginia described Pennsylvania's statutes as a "Joke on all military Affairs." And Governor Glen in his *Description of South Carolina* wrote, "The Governor is appointed by Patent, by the title of Governor in Chief, and Captain-General in and over the province; He receives also a Vice-Admiral's Commission: But alas! these high-sounding titles convey very little Power." The colonists were so pleased with this state of affairs that they never protested the governors' titles, and when state constitutions were framed, all put command of the militia back into the hands of the governors.

Under the Constitution, Congress was to have the colonial and state assemblies' rights of voting funds and legislating for the armed forces. It was also to have some voice in appointments and, in addition, exclusive power to declare war. In justifying the commander-in-chief clause, sponsors of the new instrument often felt that they needed to do little more than point to these other provisions and cite either colonial precedent or examples of the states. James Iredell in the North Carolina convention remarked in passing, "I believe most of the governors of the different states have powers similar to those of the President," and Hamilton in *The Federalist*, No. 69, compared the federal Constitution's provision and that of New York's, adding, "It may well be a question, whether those of New Hampshire and Massachusetts . . . do not, in this instance, confer larger powers upon their respective governors than could be claimed by a President of the United States." Colonial and state experience had much to do with making the commander-in-chief clause acceptable.

But part of the explanation for its presence in the Constitution still lies elsewhere—not in the Revolution or in the personality of Washington or in colonial and state precedent, but in the experience of Americans as Englishmen. It is often forgotten that the colonists were citizens of the Old World as well as the New. When creating their own institutions, they drew not only on English philosophical writings and legal commentaries but also on lessons they thought to be taught by English experience. The history of England made as deep an impress on American institutions as the history of Japan on Korea or the history of the United States on the Philippines.

It was with the unwritten English constitution that Americans were constantly comparing their own. Patrick Henry, Gerry, and George Clinton cited the commander-in-chief clause when protesting that the presidency resembled the English monarchy. Madison in Virginia, Iredell in North Carolina, Hamilton in *The Federalist,* Noah Webster in *An Examination into the Leading Principles of the Federal Constitution,* and Alexander Contee Hanson in *Remarks on the Proposed Plan of a Federal Government* all defended the provision on the ground that it simply gave the president a power historically held by the executive, the crown, in England. Hamilton quoted Blackstone's statement that the Long Parliament, in challenging the military powers of Charles I, had acted "contrary to all reason and precedent." He went on to cite a statute of Charles II which proclaimed, "The sole supreme government and command of the militia within his Majesty's realms and dominions, and of all forces by sea and land . . . EVER WAS AND IS the undoubted right of his Majesty." Hanson wrote, "The troops, continually kept up in Great Britain, are formidable to its neighbors, and yet no rational Englishman apprehends the destruction of his rights. . . . Ought then an American to have greater fears of a president, than an Englishman has of his king?" It is in English experience as much as in American that we can learn why the Constitution-makers dismissed the alternatives of vesting the supreme command in Congress or in some officer answerable to both branches. There, too, we can perhaps divine what the term, commander in chief, was supposed to mean.

The reasons for not entrusting the power to the legislature may be obvious. Iredell observed, "From the nature of the thing, the command of armies ought to be delegated to one person only," and Spaight remarked that "it was well known that the direction of an army could not be properly exercised by a numerous body of men." England had had one trial of legislative control. After the final breach with Charles in 1642, the Long Parliament marshalled forces and placed them under standing committees. Setbacks at Edgehill and elsewhere seemed to prove this system unworkable. Command was gradually centralized until, in the end, the victorious armies were all under one man, and that one man, Cromwell, eventually used his troops to overawe Parliament and uphold his own dictatorship. Like many other Englishmen, Americans in the eighteenth century had mixed memories of Cromwell. In spite of constant talk about dangers of despotism and tyranny, they scarcely mentioned him when debating the new Constitution. Nevertheless, recollection of the Protectorate was there, and this memory would explain why but one voice spoke out for investing in Congress the exclusive control of military forces.

The reasons for not dividing the power between executive and legislature are more obscure. The names of the Dukes of Marlborough and Cumberland are less well known now than in 1787, and it is necessary to recall what was then familiar. At the end of the Protectorate in 1660, Charles II was summoned to the throne. Among the virtual conditions of his restoration was the proviso that command over the armed forces remain with Monck, one of Cromwell's former generals. After Monck's death, it reverted to the crown. Charles held it; so did James II; so did William III after the Glorious Revolution of 1688. Parliament protected itself by ensuring that there should be little or nothing for these kings to command. William, for example, set £1,500,000 as a minimum essential military budget; the Commons voted £700,000. Parliament also took the precaution of passing annual Mutiny Acts, making the soldier's legal requirement to obey the king depend on a statute that could be repealed or simply not renewed. As Evarts B. Greene comments in *The Provincial Governor in the English Colonies*, the devices used by colonial assemblies were borrowed from the House of Commons. But in England these expedients suited only a brief period when the nation was not at war.

Once struggles with Louis XIV had begun in earnest, the question had to be faced more realistically. When William died in 1702, he was succeeded by Queen Anne. Fat, frowzy, and none too bright, she hardly seemed able to say, as Elizabeth had to the defenders of 1588, "I have the heart and stomach of a king. . . . I myself will be your general." The command-in-chief passed to her ablest general, John Churchill, the Duke of Marlborough.

More than any other example, that of Marlborough showed the makers of the American Constitution the peril that could come if command were separated from the crown. Marlborough was immensely successful. At Blenheim, Oudenarde, and elsewhere, he achieved victories ranking with those of Alexander and Napoleon. At home, he also employed his tactical talents. In alliance first with one set of politicians and then another, he came practically to govern England. The Tory, Bolingbroke, remarked in No. VIII of his *Letters on the Study and Use of History* that Marlborough, "a new, a private man, a subject, acquired by merit and by management a more deciding influence, than high birth, confirmed authority, and even the crown of Great Britain had given King William." When the Queen eventually turned against him, he was so armored by his successes in Europe and in the House of Commons that he proved almost as hard to depose as if he had been a monarch. Swift in his *Letter to a Whig-Lord* asserted that Marlborough's influence "did reach the Ministry at home as much as the Enemy abroad: Nay, his Rage against the former was so much the more violent of the two, that, as it is affirmed by skilful Computors, he spent more money here upon *Secret Service,* in a few Months, than he did for many Years in *Flanders.*" As presented by these hostile publicists, the case appeared to prove that a military commander serving crown and parliament could become a danger to both.

Marlborough's example seemed also to offer other lessons. Despite his victories, there was much to criticize in what he had done. In 1704 he suddenly marched his forces out of the low countries, up the Rhine, and then eastward. The battlefield of Blenheim lies in marshes between the Neckar and the Danube. British public opinion was already divided as to whether it was worthwhile to fight in the low countries instead of on the seas. Hardly anyone had suspected that England had vital interests in the heart of Central Europe. Even though Marlborough won a spectacular triumph, it was disturbing that for his own reasons and on his own initiative, he should have carried English forces off to so remote a theater. The case posed the question of whether even so technical an issue as the choice of a battlefield could be left to an independent commander.

Involved was also the issue of where responsibility should lie for determining military aims. Marlborough wanted to destroy France's armies, wherever they might be found. He has since been praised for thus anticipating the doctrines of Jomini and Clausewitz, but it was by no means clear at the time that England wanted or should have wanted the destruction of French power. And the issue came into even clearer focus late in the war when Marlborough and his cohorts cried "No peace without Spain!" Many patriotic Englishmen saw no reason at all why peace should not be made without Spain, and it seemed a great disadvantage to them that the question should have become the business of the commanding general rather than of civilians such as ministers of the crown or members of parliament.

Americans had special reasons for remembering the lessons of the Marlborough era. The general's preference for European battlegrounds meant that little was spared for projects nearer to American hearts, such as descents upon French Canada or the French or Spanish West Indies. An attack against Quebec was eventually planned and carried out, but only by ministers hostile to the Duke and on such a scale and under such command that it met instant disaster. Many Americans had reason for agreeing with Swift's comment in *The Conduct of the Allies*, that "It was the Kingdom's Misfortune that the Sea was not the Duke of *Marlborough's* Element, otherwise the whole Force of the War would infallibly have been bestowed there, infinitely to the Advantage of his Country."

The example fixed itself in American minds. Madison and others studied Bolingbroke's *Letters* in school. Many must have read Dean Swift despite his Tory principles. At the Philadelphia convention, Butler referred to "the artifices of the Duke of Marlbro' to prolong the war of which he had the management." Hamilton in *The Federalist*, No. 6, reminded his readers that Marlborough's ambition "protracted the war beyond the limits marked out by sound policy, and for a considerable time in opposition to the views of the court." England's experience seemed to show plainly the danger involved in a supreme command separate from the crown.

In their own early lives the Constitution-makers were reminded of this lesson. After Marlborough was finally brought down, British statesmen tried to ensure that no comparable mistake occurred again. Anne divided command among several generals. The Hanoverian monarchs served as commanders in chief even when they spoke little or no English. When the Austrian Succession war came in the 1740's, several senior generals were considered for the post but were all passed over in favor of William Augustus, the Duke of Cumberland. He had the disadvantages of being only twenty-four, obese, frivolous, and dissolute, but he had the compensating advantage of being George II's son and hence, presumably, accountable in a way in which another general might not be. For those with long memories, it may even have seemed some reassurance that Cumberland would be unlikely to achieve a Blenheim or an Oudenarde.

In his own way, however, Cumberland set as bad an example as Marlborough. To begin with, he began to collect glory, even from his defeats. He was credited with a gallant defense at Fontenoy against the great French marshal, Saxe. He was then acclaimed for turning back the Young Pretender at Culloden. Since it was his family's policy to defend Hanover, whatever the cost to England, he became identified, as Marlborough had, with a Europe-first strategy. Those who were more interested in the seas and the colonies found his growing prestige a nuisance. Americans, who also blamed him for sending them General Braddock, viewed him as a menace.

When the Seven Years War opened, Cumberland was still commander in chief. He departed with the largest part of the English army in order to defend Hanover. Trapped in a narrow between the Weser and the Elbe, he signed the humiliating Convention of Klosterzeven, promising that British forces would go home and not thereafter take part in the war. If his earlier career had suggested, like Marlborough's, that a commander in chief who was capable could be dangerous, his later days indicated that one who was not could be disastrous.

The multiple lesson was certainly heeded in England itself. The Klosterzeven agreement was broken, and fighting resumed. But no one replaced Cumberland. Pitt, the Earl of Chatham, who became the king's most powerful minister, wanted Field Marshal Ligonier to be commander in chief, but other ministers and members of parliament rebelled. Throughout that conflict and the War of the American Revolution, the office of commander in chief remained with the crown. Only much later, after George III had become unquestionably (though not undisputedly) mad, did it go to another royal son, Frederick, Duke of York. And even then, some doubt was cast on the wisdom of the expedient when it was learned that he permitted his mistress to sell commissions in the army.

At the time when the Constitution was written, the memory of Cumberland was fresh. Through Bolingbroke and Swift, if through no other sources, the recollection of Marlborough remained vivid. The men who met in Philadelphia in 1787 knew from the example of Cromwell that a supreme commander responsible only to the legislature was a potential dictator. From the instances of Marlborough and Cumberland, they could reason that the power should not be vested in any individual other than the executive himself. Among the many influences that shaped Article II, Section 2, none was stronger, probably, than the body of experience borrowed from the former mother country.

If so, then perhaps something more can be guessed about the meaning of the clause. The framers intended the president to perform certain military functions separate from those he had as chief civil magistrate. Hamilton said in *The Federalist*, No. 69, that as commander in chief the president's "authority would be nominally the same with that of the king of Great Britain, but in substance much inferior to it. It would amount to nothing more than the supreme command and direction of the military and naval forces." Chief Justice Taney in *Fleming vs. Page* spoke of the function as "purely military." Only gradually did it come to be construed in such terms as to justify James M. Carlisle's warning plea in *The Prize Cases:* "It makes the President, in some sort, the impersonation of the country, and invokes for him the power and right to use all the forces he can command to *'save the life of the nation.'* "

This is not to argue, of course, that the presidents treated in this volume usurped authority or that every justice since Taney has been in error. It is only to say that the framers of the Constitution probably had in mind something less than a grant of all the powers useful in waging war. The commander-in-chief clause was almost certainly intended, in the first place, to insure that control over the armed forces remained in politically responsible hands. Wilson C. Nicholas remarked in the Virginia ratifying convention that "The President, at the end of four years, was to relinquish all his offices. But if any other person was to have the command, the time would not be limited." In the second place, it was meant to insure that America's chief executive should make those decisions that Marlborough made for Anne. Once war had been declared, he was to determine where it was to be fought. He, though usually a civilian, was to make the choices between primary and secondary theaters. He was to assume responsibility for naming the officers to direct operations in each of these theaters and hence for their choice of subsidiary aims. He was expected, in other words, to make decisions on *priorities* and *command.* And it is with the performance of presidents in these and related areas that the following chapters are concerned.

II

MADISON

(1812–1815)

MARCUS CUNLIFFE

IF JAMES MADISON is esteemed as a Founding Father, and on the whole respected as a president, he is certainly not much praised for his performance as commander in chief in the War of 1812. Political opponents at the time alternated between denunciations of his folly in having led the country into war at all, and of his administration's mismanagement of the war once it was declared. Federalist critics in Congress charged that he had been pushed into the conflict by such Republican "war hawks" as Henry Clay and John C. Calhoun. Madison, they asserted, only *pretended* to be warlike during the summer of 1812 so that he could secure the Republican renomination as president. According to one of his senior generals, James Wilkinson, who writes with a heavy irony, the "meek and amiable republican," "the wise and virtuous President Madison," was dominated by the active members of his cabinet.[1]

Subsequent historians have developed the argument along

similar lines. Less heavy-handed than Wilkinson but no less ironical, Henry Adams explains Madison as a prim soul who was almost comically ill equipped for his belligerent role. Most of Madison's biographers agree. To Sydney Howard Gay he is a man who "plunged the country into an unnecessary war," and who when it was on his hands "neither knew what to do with it nor how to choose the right men who did know." Gay goes on to speak of "the remarkable incompetence which he showed in rallying the moral and material forces of the nation to meet an emergency of his own creation." Another biographer, Gaillard Hunt, more or less agrees:

In truth he was not an inspiring figure to lead in war. The hour had come, but the man was wanting. Not a scholar in governments ancient and modern, not an unimpassioned writer of careful messages, but a robust leader to rally the people and unite them to fight was what the time needed, and what it did not find in Madison.

Julius W. Pratt, a third student of Madison, concurs that "despite his admirable qualities," he was "not the man to lead the country through such an ordeal. . . ." A fourth biographer, Abbot Emerson Smith, reinforces the indictment: "the real shortcomings of Madison as a war president . . . lay not in his ignorance of military affairs, nor in the misfortunes of his early appointments, but in his failure to exert a powerful moral and political leadership." In this view Madison failed "because he did not understand either the necessity or the method of forcibly combining interests and ideals into a great national emotion. The War of 1812 was not a national crusade like that of 1917, but the difference lay not in the causes or justification, but in the manipulation of public opinion." In his administrative history, *The Jeffersonians,* Leonard D. White says of Madison:

As commander in chief, the President was irresolute, weak in his judgment of men, unaware of his proper function, and incapable of giving direction to the course of events.

And finally, an investigation of American civil-military relations leads Louis Smith to describe Madison as "a most inept wartime executive, who provided little energy or direction in the War of 1812."[2]

There is no need to give further citations. One voice, it is true, has been raised in Madison's defense—that of his latest biographer, Irving Brant, who has already done much to dispel criticisms of Madison's prewar career.[3] But there seems to be an almost unanimous conviction that little Jemmy Madison was a ludicrous commander in chief. Is this conviction justified?

My own verdict is neither "guilty" nor "not guilty," but "not proven." Even at its narrowest, as a narrative of battles and campaigns, military history seems to tempt us into too-positive assertions. How confidently we apportion praise and blame, how readily we pronounce upon the relative merits of a Grant or a Lee, how arrogantly we consign the defeated leaders to the dustbin of history and install the victorious ones in the halls of fame. But how do we *know?* How may we properly assess the part played by luck, superior numbers, better training, the talent of subordinates?

It may be answered that we must and do nevertheless make such judgments, and that by their admittedly conventional and approximate standards Madison must be deemed a bad commander in chief. Even if we give him the benefit of the doubt and refuse to blame him for the pitiful outcome of the 1812 campaigns along the Canadian border, when three American forces (under William Hull, Stephen Van Rensselaer, and Alexander Smyth) were routed, it may be argued that little improvement was discernible in 1813; and that in 1814, though some able American leaders came to the fore, Madison was fortunate to escape military disaster and the possible collapse of the Union.

This sort of evaluation still appears to me meaningless until we have taken into account the wider elements of the war. The first and most important point to stress is that it was an extremely unpopular war. We might construct a rough graph of the degree of national unity underlying the various wars discussed in this volume. On such an unpopularity-scale the War of 1812 would appear as the highest mark in the graph, which would thereafter run steadily downward through the Mexican War, the Civil War (if we consider only the scene within the Union), the Spanish War, the first World War, and so down to the almost complete unanimity of national sentiment brought about in World War II by the Japanese attack on Pearl Harbor on December 7, 1941. The very day after the attack, Congress declared war on Japan with only one dissenting vote.

Contrast the public reaction of December 8, 1941, to the spectacle in 1812. Madison sent his war message to Congress on June 1. It was wrangled over until June 18, and in the final vote the Senate responded with a hesitant majority of only 19 to 13, while the House split 79 to 49 in favor of the declaration. At the very outset "Mr. Madison's War" was resisted by some and disliked by many. For the next two and a half years, until the peace proposals reached America from Ghent in February, 1815, the progress of the war on the American side was attended with serious disunity and uncertainty. What were Madi-

son's war aims? To resist British maritime oppression? To wrest
Canada from the enemy, or East Florida from the Spanish? If
these aims were hard to define precisely, how could any exact
strategy be devised?

And on which side of the scale should this factor be placed?
Irving Brant sees it as an extenuating circumstance. "Open
sedition and silent resistance forced the United States to fight
the war with one arm—New England—tied behind her back.
That was more crippling than incompetent generals, raw militia, and an empty treasury."[4] Madison's supporters in Congress, naturally enough, used the same argument. Felix Grundy,
a "war hawk" from Tennessee, accused the Federalist bloc of
what he called "moral treason." New Englanders and New
Yorkers, or a Republican such as John Randolph of Roanoke
who also opposed the war, gave comfort to America's enemy
every time they rose to speak. They crippled the nation's war
effort, it was said, by advising their constituents not to enlist or
to subscribe money. They warped the direction of strategy.
Thus, if America were bent on seizing Canada, the obvious
major thrust should have been up Lake Champlain and on to
Montreal. But since the northeastern states were so dissident,
Madison was compelled to rely upon attempts at invasion via
Detroit or the Niagara front, which at best could only be
secondary campaigns.

On the other hand, Madison's critics have tended to echo
the complaint made by the Federalists. In the forceful language
of Daniel Webster, who was then a young Congressman from
Portsmouth, New Hampshire,

Quite too small a portion of public opinion was in favor of the
war, to justify it originally. A much smaller portion is in favor of the

mode in which it has been conducted. This is the radical infirmity. Public opinion . . . is not with you, in your Canada project. Whether it ought to be, or ought not to be, the fact that it is not should by this time be evident to all; and it is the business of practical statesmen to act upon the state of things as it is, and not to be always attempting to prove what it ought to be.

Mere party support, Webster went on, "is not the kind of support necessary to sustain the country through a long, expensive and bloody contest; and this should have been considered before the war was declared. The cause, to be successful, must be upheld by other sentiments, and higher motives." From this, "the radical infirmity," flowed all of Madison's major troubles— for instance, the poor response to his efforts to raise a sizeable army:

Unlike the old nations of Europe, there are in this country no dregs of population, fit only to supply the constant waste of war, and out of which an army can be raised, for hire, at any time and for any purpose. Armies of any magnitude can here be nothing but the people embodied—and if the object be one for which the people will not embody, there can be no armies.[5]

If we accept Webster's contentions, it would appear that Madison's great initial blunder was to take his country into war, and that the mishaps which followed all derived from or were affected by this primary mistake. One way or the other, it is clear that Madison faced a task of exceptional difficulty. Whether or not we hold him responsible, it also seems clear that—as a general rule—leaders of democracies are wise to make sure of the public's enthusiasm before they commit themselves to warfare. Despite the comment by Abbot Emerson

Smith, quoted above, there was a very considerable difference between the war spirit of 1812 and that of 1917—a far greater difference than could be eliminated by any amount of "manipulation of public opinion" on Madison's part.

A second complication in attempting to assess Madison's ability as commander in chief lies in the fact that his was, while an ill-defined, nevertheless a "limited," war. Perhaps it is wrong to apply the terminology of the twentieth century to Madison's era, except to remind ourselves that

a) his war was oddly traditional (and thus "limited") in style. It was diplomacy carried on by other means: a logical stage in a dispute, a final form of protest, resorted to in order to prove that America was in earnest and meant to have redress. The gigantic struggle going on in Europe at the same time, in contrast, was "unlimited": it could have no outcome except in the overthrow of Napoleon or else in the downfall of Britain and her allies. This very contrast made it hard for Madison to refute the accusation that he had allowed the United States to fall into the Napoleonic orbit. At worst, it exposed him to the charge of greed and cynicism; and even at best, it lent an odd air of pedantry and futility to his protestations;

b) in their wars, Americans have not responded readily to a fight for "limited" objectives. Even if there had been no dissension, Madison would probably have failed to convince his countrymen of the need for taking the War of 1812 seriously. The British Orders in Council, a major cause of friction, were revoked immediately before Congress declared war; and though this was not known at the moment of the declaration it was known soon after. A temporary and local armistice was agreed upon in 1812 by the British and American commanders on the Canadian front (Sir George Prevost and General Henry Dearborn). More ambitious efforts were initiated only a few weeks after the war began, though they came to nothing. A Russian offer of mediation was accepted by Madison in March, 1813. Although the British would not meet Madison's commissioners on that occasion, by the beginning of 1814 they were arranging with him for direct negotiations. The Anglo-American commissioners did not manage to sit down together, at Ghent in Belgium, until August, 1814, and did not sign the peace articles until Christmas of that year. But peace terms ran together with war aims; and while that might be a sensible way of conducting war, it hardly comported with the roaring oratory of the "war hawks."

Moreover, the War of 1812 was—inevitably—a peripheral war. Whatever Madison might have accomplished in the way of victories, in the eyes of Europe his war was a sideshow. His army and navy, even if they had been as big as the administration would have liked them to be, would have been tiny in comparison with the vast formations of the Napoleonic Wars. The War of 1812 therefore had little shape of its own. Whatever the Americans might say or do, the principal decisions— at any rate until the last few months of 1814—were reached in Europe. Even in American cartoons, let alone those drawn in England, Brother Jonathan or Uncle Sam were puny figures when set against burly John Bull or the Napoleon colossus. To an unsympathetic eye, the actual physique of little James Madison might seem to express all too accurately the symbolic and secondary stature of the United States in a conflict of giants.

A third problem makes it yet more difficult for us to arrive at a dispassionate appreciation of Madison as commander in chief. Once again, it may be counted on either side of the balance sheet according to taste.

The problem is that the Republicans claimed to be a party governed by principle. They had not always been consistent. Nevertheless they were associated with belief in a modest, minimal federal government, and so with opposition to a national debt or to anything that would produce a national debt or a swollen administration, including a standing army and navy. War involved debt, a regular army, a federal navy. True, an army and navy had existed under the peacetime administrations of Jefferson and Madison, but these were vestigial—a few thousand men and a handful of frigates, with a scatter of smaller craft. In theory the army had been augmented in 1808 to something over ten thousand men. But enlistment lagged; in 1809 the actual strength was still under three thousand.[6] The Republican heritage proved an acute embarrassment for Madison. His own supporters in Congress grumbled at his war measures and did not hesitate to scale down the administration's proposals. They were joined by the Federalists in dwelling upon the anomalies of Republican doctrine.

In his annual message to Congress of November 5, 1811— several months before the declaration of war—Madison tried to put the nation on a war footing. He recommended that "adequate provision be made for filling the ranks and prolonging the enlistments of the regular troops; for an auxiliary force to be engaged for a more limited term; for the acceptance of volunteer corps, whose patriotic ardor may court a participation in urgent services; for detachments . . . of other portions of the militia, and for such a preparation of the great body as will proportion its usefulness to its intrinsic capacities."[7] But when this was translated into a legislative proposal it offered an irresistible target to a soured Republican like John Randolph. Reminding his party of their resistance to the army of 1798–99, raised at the time of the French crisis and under the command of George Washington, the enraged Randolph cried out:

Republicans were then unwilling to trust a standing army even to his hands who had given proof that he was above all human temptation. Where now is the revolutionary hero to whom you are about to confide this sacred trust? . . . Sir, you may raise this army, you may build up this vast structure of patronage, this mighty apparatus of favoritism; but . . . you will never live to enjoy the succession; you sign your political death-warrant. . . .[8]

As to the outcome of this particular debate, Madison wrote ruefully to his mentor Jefferson in February, 1812:

The Newspapers give you a sufficient insight into the measures of Congress. With a view to enable the Executive to step at once into Canada they have provided after two months delay, for a regular force requiring 12 to raise it, and after 3 months for a volunteer force, on terms not likely to raise it at all for that object. The mixture of good & bad, avowed & disguised motives accounting for these things is curious eno' but not to be explained in the compass of a letter.

Jefferson replied sympathetically, though his letter could not have brought much comfort to the President:

I have much doubted whether, in case of a war, Congress would find it practicable to do their part of the business. That a body containing 100 lawyers . . . should direct the measures of a war, is, I fear, impossible. . . .[9]

A fourth problem in assessment is hinted at in such quotations: namely, the lack of precedents to guide even a more harmonious administration. All countries, no doubt, begin a new war by seeking to refight the previous one. So it was not surprising that Republicans and Federalists alike should invoke the Revolutionary memory of George Washington; or that the moves against Canada planned in 1812 should recall Montgomery's endeavor of 1775; or that naval tactics should also hearken back to the Revolutionary War. It was natural enough that Madison's Secretary of War, in summoning James Wilkinson north in 1813 to take up a command, should tell him: "If our cards be well played, we may *renew the scene of Saratoga.*"[10] Both men had been present at that victory of 1777. Perhaps it was natural, too, that when he headed away from Canada a year later in disgrace, to face a court-martial, Wilkinson should ask his old friend Van Rensselaer to join him in a last sentimental tour of the Saratoga battleground.[11] It was unfortunate, though, that these and other commanders were elderly men, past their prime.

It was still more unfortunate that the Revolutionary War and its aftermath yielded so few useful lessons. Or if there were lessons, they had not been learned. George Washington furnished orators with an easy inspiration but—as Randolph's speech reveals—with not much else. What *could* be learned, practically speaking, from one who was "above all human temptation?" There had been little serious discussion since the Revolution of military affairs. Some commentators have been unrealistic in condemning the Founding Fathers for their failure to establish a substantial regular army and navy.[12] These would have been a grievous financial burden for the infant nation. It would be hard to prove that they were indispensable in the early years of the republic. And though warnings against the dangers of a standing army became a piece of empty rhetoric after the War of 1812, they were not altogether baseless until the war was over. Artemas Ward of Massachusetts was not merely indulging in partisan prejudice when in March, 1814, he invited the House of Representatives

. . . to consider what has taken place in our time, and what they have read in the history of other times. We have seen the legislature of France, turned out of the Hall of Liberty by a military force which it had nurtured. . . . We have read in history that the same was done in England, in the days of Cromwell. However secure gentlemen may feel in their seats, it is not impossible that they may witness . . . the same scenes here, and that the military force which they now vote to raise, without being able to render any reason, may ere long put an end to their existence as legislators. Executive patronage and executive influence are truly alarming. . . .[13]

If this was a quite negative precedent, a handicap and not a guide for the perplexed Madison, it was an understandable attitude. Another negative precedent was less forgivable. This concerned the role of the militia. If nothing more than a skeleton standing army was to be tolerated, then (as all her orators told her) America's main reliance must be upon the militia. But to be effective the militia would have to be equipped and trained. It would have to be classified by age-group, with the main obligation falling upon the younger men. It would have to be available, in wartime, outside the borders of its particular state and for periods of longer than the usual ninety days.

34

These steps were never taken. They entailed a form of conscription, inconvenience, expense. Here, it must be said, Jefferson and Madison were fairly clear as to what was needed, and quite clear that an efficient militia was consonant with Republican doctrine. In message after message they reminded Congress of the importance of the militia, but without result except for the meager enactment of 1808, which allotted the annual sum of $200,000 for the arming of the "constitutional force" of a whole nation.[14] Jefferson was informing Madison and his cabinet colleague James Monroe of what they already knew, and of what they had certainly relearned during the war, when he wrote to Monroe in October, 1814, that

. . . we must prepare for interminable war. To this end we should put our house in order, by providing men and money to indefinite extent. The former may be done by classing our militia, and assigning each class to the . . . duties for which it is fit. It is nonsense to talk of regulars. They are not to be had among a people so easy and happy at home as ours. We might as well rely on calling down an army of angels from heaven. I trust it is now seen that the refusal to class the militia, when proposed years ago, is the real source of all our misfortunes in this war.[15]

Jefferson both exaggerated and oversimplified. *Some* professional soldiers were required, and some were raised. The Military Academy at West Point had been established in 1802, under his administration though not at his instigation. He and Madison approved of it, and though only about seventy cadets had graduated from it by 1812, Madison took steps in that year to fill it with 250 cadets.[16] In practice Madison depended upon a stiffening of regulars, enlisted for five years. But Jefferson was correct in saying that the solution did not rest with a regular army. Despite bounties and land grants, the regular ranks could not be filled during the war. Nor was it possible to improvise any large and reliable militia force. In between, therefore, came the curious and ambiguous troops known as the volunteers, who were neither regulars nor militia but something of both. Madison, in short, inherited a tangled and unsatisfactory military system which he could hardly be expected to reform overnight. It is also to be remembered that Polk inherited essentially the same system. But by 1846 the regular army was in better shape, and the militia as a field force yielded almost entirely to the volunteer regiments.

Nor was Polk confronted with the constitutional issue that faced Madison when some of the New England governors denied his authority to call out the militia of their states and the right of any subordinate of the president to prescribe the duties of these militia when they were called out. Not until the war had been over for a dozen years did the Supreme Court rule (in *Martin vs. Mott*, 1827) that the initial authority rested with the president. The issue was still not quite dead, as Jefferson Davis and even Lincoln to a lesser extent were to discover. There is no doubt, however, that Madison's tribulations in this matter as in others exceeded those of later commanders in chief.[17]

The authority of the commander in chief had not yet been defined in other areas. A minor uncertainty, for example, existed as to whether the president might in certain circumstances take command in the field. It could be argued that Washington had done so, or had been prepared to do so, during the Pennsylvania Whisky Rebellion of 1794.[18] Perhaps Madison had some such martial impulse when, immediately after the declaration of war, "he visited in person—a thing never known before

—all the offices of the departments of war and the navy, stimulating everything in a manner worthy of a little commander-in-chief, with his little round hat and huge cockade."[19] When the war arrived on his doorstep in the shape of a British raid on Washington in August, 1814, Madison rode out from the city to witness the fighting at Bladensburg. These instances cannot be taken to indicate any real clash of interests on Madison's part. His place was obviously at the center of affairs; though if the war had continued to be waged close to Washington, as it was for Lincoln, he might have anticipated Lincoln in occasionally directing operations.

A more complex and important uncertainty involved his relations with the Navy and War Secretaries. It was hard to distinguish them, in career and temperament, from some of the senior officers in the services, particularly where the army was concerned. Henry Dearborn, whom Madison appointed major general in February, 1812, and so to the army's senior post, had indeed been Jefferson's Secretary of War. His military experience in the field had been no greater than that of Madison's first Secretary of War, William Eustis, who had served as a surgeon in the Revolution. Eustis' successor, John Armstrong, who had likewise been a Revolutionary officer, held a brigadier general's commission for several months before coming to the War Department. Before that, he had acted as American minister to France. Another Revolutionary veteran and diplomatist, Thomas Pinckney, was appointed to the junior major-generalcy of the army in 1812. Madison's Secretary of State, James Monroe, had risen to a colonelcy during the Revolution; he eventually supplanted Armstrong at the War Department, while also remaining Secretary of State. A few other senior figures, notably James Wilkinson, had long years of continuous military service. But the majority, inevitably, had only civilian careers stretching between their memories of the Revolution and the new excitements of 1812.

In such a situation, no nice line had been drawn or could be drawn between the civil and the military. There was therefore nothing inherently absurd in Madison's suggestions to Monroe, in September, 1812, that he might be given a senior commission and the chance of leading the advance into Canada. In view of the dismal defeat of William Hull and the somnolence of Henry Dearborn, it did not seem silly to suppose that Monroe—a fiercely energetic man—might be made lieutenant general, and so commander of all the American armies.[20] As it happened, none of these plans was implemented. But the lines between civil and military duty and between the administrative and command functions of Madison's cabinet remained blurred. After William Eustis resigned his office in December, 1812, Monroe acted as Secretary of War *pro tempore*. He was immensely active in this part-time capacity, recommending a new organization for the army, drawing up plans for the 1813 campaigns, and not altogether relinquishing his dreams of personal military glory. When John Armstrong stepped into the War Department in February, 1813, he was equally ambitious. Within a short time he was proposing to go himself to the Canadian front. Later in the year Armstrong did so, arriving at Sackett's Harbor (at the eastern end of Lake Ontario) on September 5 and not returning to Washington until November.[21] It was far from being a mere tour of inspection; Armstrong assumed control of operations, issuing detailed and sometimes peremptory orders to Wilkinson, Wade Hampton, and other commanders.

This conduct was criticized at the time, by members of Congress and by Monroe. Monroe wrote to the President, on hearing of Armstrong's intended move, to question its constitutionality and propriety:

There ceases to be a check on Executive power as to military operations; indeed the Executive power, as known in the Constitution, is destroyed. The whole is transferred from the Executive to the General at the head of the army. It is completely absorbed in hands where it is most dangerous. It may be said that the President is Commander in Chief; that the Secry at War is his organ as to military operations, and that he may allow him to go to the army, as being well informed in military affairs, & act for himself. I am inclined to think that the President, unless he takes the command of the army in person, acts, in directing its movements, more as the Executive power than as Commander in Chief. . . .[22]

Madison himself later reprimanded Armstrong in detail for having exceeded his authority. But it is hard to determine how Madison felt in 1813. He had been ready to release his Secretary of State, Monroe, for a field command; and Monroe, though seemingly a stickler for constitutionality, never seemed to feel that his own ambitious schemes were open to criticism on similar grounds. We do know that Madison fell seriously ill in the early summer of 1813. During his long convalescence he could probably take no more than a languid interest in such problems. Yet he had long been aware of Armstrong's intentions, and he seems to have made no formal objection. Perhaps he shared the somewhat equivocal views of his Secretary of the Treasury, Albert Gallatin. In April, 1813, Gallatin wrote to Madison:

In a conversation with General Armstrong, he appeared disposed to make an excursion towards the scene of action on our northern frontier. I have, perhaps, more confidence in General Dearborn than almost any other person, and, for many reasons, have no wish to see General Armstrong unite the character of general with that of secretary.

From this beginning we would expect Gallatin to proceed to a denunciation of Armstrong. How does he continue, though?

Yet from my knowledge of both, I think that the success of the campaign may be secured by General Armstrong's presence for a few days at the army. His military views are generally more extensive, and for this year's operations appear to me more correct, than those of General Dearborn.[23]

Gallatin was a clear-witted man, acutely aware of the need to form American government on sound constitutional principles. But on this debatable ground of civil-military relations his thinking, like that of Madison, Monroe, Armstrong, and the rest, seems ambiguous. The precedents did not exist. It is anachronistic to measure Madison by rules which had not yet been thought out.

A fifth and final complexity must be mentioned: the clash of personalities within the armed forces and within Madison's administration. Here his difficulties differed rather in degree than in kind from those of later commanders in chief; but at any rate it is arguable that his difficulties were greater, and that only in part were they of his own making. Within the army, as we have already suggested, he had little initial choice, and the senior officers on whom he had to rely were often bitterly at odds. Unfortunately but perhaps inevitably, as Winfield Scott (himself a Republican) reminiscently testified,

Party spirit of that day knew no bounds, and, of course, was blind to policy. Federalists were almost entirely excluded from selection, though great numbers were eager for the field, and in New England and others—"fit for nothing else," which always turned out *utterly cans.* Hence the selections from those communities consisted mostly of coarse and ignorant men. In the other States, where there was no lack of educated men in the dominant party, the appointments consisted, generally, of swaggerers, dependants, decayed gentlemen, and others—"fit for nothing else," which always turned out *utterly unfit for any military purpose whatever.*[24]

Within the Republican ranks an intense antipathy developed between James Wilkinson and Wade Hampton, with their subordinates lining up on one side or the other. Since these two held senior commands on the northern frontier in 1813, and since the whole advance on Montreal depended upon their co-operation, the results were fatal. Each despised and blamed the other when the campaign collapsed. *"To General Hampton's outrage of every principle of subordination and discipline may be ascribed the failure of the expedition,"* Wilkinson told Armstrong in November, 1813; "and that I have not yet arrested him must be attributed to my respect for you, and my desire that the arrest should proceed from the highest authority."[25] Recrimination became universal. Relieved of command, Wilkinson poured out his abuse on Armstrong. No one held aloof from controversy, or seemed to wish to remain aloof. This was true even of relatively uncontroversial figures like William Henry Harrison, the governor of Indiana Territory, who from the vantage point of 1840 seemed enough of a respectable military hero to secure the Whig nomination for the presidency. But in 1813 he was less widely admired. "This man's talents have been greatly overrated," W. H. Crawford of Georgia wrote to Gallatin. "He flatters the Kentuckians, and they tell the government he ought to be made a major-general, and he is made one. His official communications . . . are the most vague and puerile productions which I have ever seen. . . . For God's sake, . . . endeavor to rid the army of old women and blockheads. . . ."[26]

The worst clash of temperament and ambition, however, occurred within the cabinet, between Armstrong and Monroe. Madison's first Secretary of War, William Eustis, resigned in December, 1812. We may assume that he was a mediocre figure, like Madison's first Navy Secretary, Paul Hamilton, who resigned at the same time. Jefferson described Eustis as "a pleasant, gentlemanly man in society" and said that "the indecision of his character rather added to the amenity of his conversation." Gallatin commented that "his incapacity and the total want of confidence in him were felt through every ramification of the public service."[27] Eustis appears to have been overwhelmed by his sudden heavy responsibilities. At the beginning of the war he had only eight clerks in his small department, and Congress rejected a proposal to provide him with two senior assistants. Like Simon Cameron in Lincoln's cabinet and Russell A. Alger in McKinley's, Eustis was made the scapegoat. His faults, like theirs, were exaggerated; or, as Josiah Quincy of Massachusetts stated it, Eustis was "hunted down."[28]

Gallatin, in the letter just quoted, went on to admit that "To find a successor qualified, popular, and willing to accept is extremely difficult." The main difficulty seems to have been that Monroe wished to be entrusted with the direction of strategy, either as Secretary of War or, preferably, at the head of the troops in the field. According to Josiah Quincy, who delivered a witheringly effective speech on the topic in January, 1813:

Mr. Speaker, when I assert that the present Secretary of State, who is now acting Secretary of War, is destined by a cabinet of which he himself constitutes one third for the command of this army, I know that I assert intentions . . . which have not yet developed themselves by an official avowal. . . . The cabinet must work along by degrees, and only show their cards as they play them. The army must first be authorized. The bill for the new Major Generals must be passed. Then, upon their plan, it will be found necessary to constitute *a Lieutenant General.* "And who so proper," the cabinet will exclaim, "as one of ourselves?"[29]

Quincy asserted that the scheme was in mind as early as June, 1812. Madison, Monroe, and Gallatin, he continued, "are about to raise an army of fifty-five thousand men, invest one of their own body with this most solemn command, and he the man who is the destined candidate for the President's chair! What a grasp at power is this!" Though Quincy's interpretation of Madison's and Monroe's motives was no doubt partisan and did less than justice to their patriotism, there seems little doubt that they did hope for some such outcome and that the criticisms voiced by Quincy and others discouraged them. Instead, Madison appointed John Armstrong of New York, a man whose ambitions were as strong and as militant as those of Monroe. Monroe was disappointed. "Had it been decided," he told Jefferson, "to continue the command of the army under Genl Dearborn [whom Armstrong relieved of active command in the summer of 1813], and the question been with me, would I take the dep^t of War, . . . I would not have hesitated a moment in complying. But it never assumed that form." Monroe was doubly disappointed when Armstrong proceeded to outmaneuver him. In his plans for an augmented army, drawn up while he was temporarily in charge of the War Department,

Monroe had recommended several new senior posts. These were approved by Armstrong and sanctioned by Congress:

On the day that the nomination of these officers was made to the Senate, the President sent for me, & stated that the Secretary at War, had placed me, in his list of Major Generals, at their head, and wished to know whether I would accept the appointment, intimating that he did not think I ought to do it, nor did he wish me to leave my present situation.[30]

On the face of it, Armstrong had paid the Secretary of State a considerable compliment. But Monroe declined to serve in a subordinate capacity. And by the time that Dearborn was discarded, Armstrong was decisively in control where Monroe had wished to be. "I suppose you are apprized," John Randolph wrote to Josiah Quincy in August, 1813,

of the deadly feud between [Monroe] and Armstrong. The partisans of the former keep no terms in speaking of the latter. There is no measure to their obloquy, if a great deal of truth mixed with some falsehood may pass by that name. It is however plain that the cabinet *dare* not displace Armstrong. He is now gone on to "organized victory" in Canada.[31]

The nature of the triangular relationship between Madison, Armstrong, and Monroe still puzzles historians. The President's two executive heads were men of exceptional ability. Armstrong was vigorous and decisive. Whatever his motives, he strengthened the war effort by ousting Dearborn and Wilkinson, and he was probably correct in getting rid of Harrison. Though he was self-seeking and sometimes disingenuous, the same might be said of Monroe, and his standing with the President was hardly improved by the angry accusations that

Monroe made against him in correspondence with Madison. As it happened, Armstrong ruined himself by failing to produce a successful invasion of Canada; then, in attempting to win favor with Andrew Jackson, by claiming the credit for promoting that warrior to a major-generalcy when the credit should have been at least shared with Madison; and finally, perhaps through pique, by doing almost nothing to prepare the defenses of Washington against the threat of a British raid. When the raid became a reality in August, 1814, Armstrong was hooted out of office without the need for a formal dismissal by Madison. Monroe at least had got what he wanted. By the test of success, in the remaining months of the war, he was the better man. But we should beware of any categorical statement about Madison and his war cabinet.

We have listed five factors that inhibit judgment of Madison's performance as commander in chief. They are:

a) the unpopularity of the War of 1812;

b) the limited, ill-defined, and peripheral nature of the war;

c) the nature of Republican party doctrine;

d) the lack of precedents to guide the nation or the president in war;

e) friction between the principal figures involved in the war effort.

These circumscribe our judgment. Indeed the first of them deserves a whole essay to itself: no wonder that contemporaries of Madison kept talking about the *reasons* for (or against) the war rather than about the *fact* of war. Nevertheless we can offer some tentative remarks on Madison's achievements and deficiencies as a war president.

What he achieved has to be seen in the context of what it was possible for him to achieve. In addition to the handicaps already outlined, Madison was unlucky. True, he might have expected to run into vehement opposition. But he knew that he could count on congressional majorities. It was not foolish to suppose that his war preparations would be approved by Congress. His own explanation of what he hoped for, written in September, 1813, accords well with what he had said earlier. He believed the war to be just and unavoidable. He gambled on a quick blow:

> As it was obvious that advantage ought to be taken of our chusing the time for commencing, or rather retorting, hostilities, and of the pains taken to make the British Government believe that they were not to be resorted to by the United States; and as it was foreseen that there would be great delay, if not impossibility, in raising a large army for a long term of service, it was thought best to limit our first attempts to such a force as might be obtained in a short time, and be sufficient to reduce Canada, from Montreal upwards, before the enemy would be prepared to resist its progress; trusting to the impression to be made by success, and to the time that would be afforded, for such an augmentation of the durable force as would be able to extend as well as secure our conquests.[32]

The British garrisons in Canada were small and could not be quickly reinforced. Neither Madison nor the overconfident "war hawks"—no matter how foolish their prophecies were soon to sound—was initially foolish in anticipating an easy victory. The British (and the Canadians) turned out to be far tougher and more enterprising than during the Revolutionary War. Even so, if any of the American senior commanders in

1812 had shown the energy or initiative that Andrew Jackson or Winfield Scott or Jacob Brown were to reveal a little later, the campaigns against Canada might have fared very differently. A good deal, though not all, of the unpopularity of Mr. Madison's War lay in its early setbacks. A successful start might have made it much less unpopular, even in New England. Under these considerations Madison's original scheme was sound enough. It acknowledged America's peculiar military situation. If he erred on the side of rash optimism, at any rate he himself—unlike Hull and the others—could not be convicted of timidity and inactivity.

Madison's administration asked Congress at the end of 1811 for a regular army to be built up to its existing establishment of 10,000 and for another 10,000 with a shorter enlistment, together with a force of volunteers. Congress thwarted him, in part through the malice of the Republican leader, William B. Giles of Virginia, who insisted on a larger army than the country could hope to provide. Madison asked also for the establishment of two new "vital Departments, the Commissary's and Quarter Master's," within the army.[33] But Congress reacted so reluctantly that these essential administrative services were organized too late, and never functioned properly during the war.

Despite these handicaps, Madison remained cool and yet determined. His new Secretary of War, John Armstrong, reflected this determination even if the appointment perhaps created more problems than it solved. Madison's new Secretary of the Navy, William Jones, seems to have been an altogether admirable choice.[34] He and Madison both understood the importance of naval supremacy on the Great Lakes (a point which General Hull had also emphasized, though in vain); and

Madison is entitled to much of the credit for the crucial victories on Lake Erie in 1813 and Lake Champlain in 1814.

The President and his Navy Secretary apparently saw eye to eye; they worked harmoniously with the House Naval Affairs Committee; and even Madison's sharpest critics paused in their diatribes to shower compliments upon the nation's seamen. They paid a somewhat more grudging tribute to Andrew Jackson for his bold operations in the Floridas against the Indians, and to the soldiers who fought so tenaciously on the Niagara front in the summer of 1814. Criticism was altogether silenced by his spectacular victory at New Orleans in January, 1815.

If Madison was held responsible for the ignominies of 1812–13, then by the same broad rule he must be held responsible for the accomplishments of 1814–15. The more so in that he was not a mere cipher. No one, even at the height of the feud between Monroe and Armstrong, took the President to be a weakling at the mercy of strong-willed associates. He allowed them more latitude than some presidents would have cared to do, just as he appeared to leave Congress more to its own devices than would subsequent presidents. In part these tendencies reflected his own and his time's view of the nature of the executive branch. Despite Federalist assertions that the President had been bullied into the war by Republican firebrands, they knew very well that it *was* Mr. Madison's War.

Strategy was evolved inside the cabinet. Learning as he went along, Madison developed an increasingly sharp picture of himself as commander in chief. To some extent the trend was an inevitable consequence of the character of the American federal government: in war, the president's powers grow almost despite himself. Madison's own conscious contribution can be seen in the long letter of rebuke which he addressed to Armstrong in August, 1814, which begins:

On viewing the course which the proceedings of the War Department have not unfrequently taken, I find that I owe it to my own responsibility as well as to other considerations, to make some remarks on the relations in which the Head of the Department stands to the President, and to lay down some rules for conducting the business of the Department which are dictated by the nature of those relations.

It is an incisive and not a petulant document. The same firmness and clarity are evident in a later communication discussing the Navy Department.[35]

So much for Madison's accomplishments. What of his deficiencies as commander in chief? We may feel that he was not a good judge of men. Anticipating war, as he did, he might have been wise to replace William Eustis and the ill-qualified Paul Hamilton with more aggressive figures, before war came. The appointment of Brigadier General William H. Winder to command the Washington district in 1814 seems to have been ill advised, and Madison's whole handling of the British descent on the capital is open to criticism—although he is not so culpable as some historians maintain. At least he foresaw the likelihood of the attack and ordered that steps be taken to meet it, even if the appointment of Winder was one of the steps and even if the chain of command became twisted at Bladensburg. We may feel that he created difficulties for himself in encouraging Monroe's dreams of military glory and then in not satisfying them. In view of his subsequent strictures on Armstrong, Madison might have been more sensible not to have appointed him at all, or at any rate to have kept a closer watch upon Armstrong's activities.[36]

In other respects he might well have been more ruthless. It is impossible not to feel a good deal of sympathy for Madison when one reads through the testimonies of Wilkinson, Armstrong, and the rest, with their sour flavor of recrimination and jealousy, their florid sentiments and hand-on-heart protestations of probity and zeal.[37] The road to Canada was paved with good intentions and bad faith. Madison could not but be perplexed by his far-off assortment of bickering, vain, ill commanders (half their letters are dictated from sickbeds; they are absorbed in their own symptoms). But one wonders why Madison did not lose his temper with them more often, and whether an occasional explosion might not have had some effect—for example, in making Wilkinson and Wade Hampton either cooperate or resign.

One has the same reaction to some of Madison's messages to Congress. True, such messages are almost always couched in a tone of pious generality; it would not be easy to gauge the temperament of, say, Andrew Jackson merely by studying his annual messages. True, also, there is no sign of defeatism in Madison's utterances. Nor did presidents in his era have the means or the inclination to arouse the nation by bursts of oratory. Even so, Madison's messages are a little cool, and perhaps a little evasive. Unwilling no doubt to provide ammunition for his enemies, he glossed over defeats and financial woes, expatiating on the wickedness of the enemy, the prowess of America's soldiers and sailors, and the beneficial effects of adversity upon the formulation of the American national character. This would not have mattered much if he had not simultaneously asked for large-scale and extremely expensive additions to the war establishment. His enemies pounced on the discrepancy. Elisha Potter of Rhode Island, in the House debate of January, 1814, on the administration's five-year enlistment bill, said:

The President, in his Message to Congress of November, 1812, after stating what progress had been made in the war . . . , mentions the capture of General Hull and his army, and the surrender of the whole Michigan Territory, as but a partial calamity; and that even that calamity had been converted into a source of invigorated effort, so that it had become more necessary to limit than to excite the patriotic zeal of the people. . . . And, in his Message [December 7, 1813] at the opening of the present session, . . . he seems to impute the failure of . . . the most sanguine . . . expectations, not to . . . the want of any human exertions, but to adverse weather. . . . Why then should we provide for raising more men, or giving such extraordinary encouragement to enlistments, not asked for nor recommended by the Executive authority?[38]

We are back again at the tantalizing problem of whether Madison, the good Republican who disliked military establishments as much as the next man, the mild and decent scholar whose logic carried him into a command for which neither his training nor his temperament fitted him—whether, given all the circumstances of disunity and ill-preparedness, this man's capacities can be calculated without an excess of qualifications.

It seems evident that he did not make an inspiring success of the task, though we may beg the question by saying that the task was impossible. It may also seem evident that in my view he did not disgrace the office. His weaknesses—personal insignificance, attachment to Republican principles, and a certain demureness and detachment—were also his strengths. If he was not a hero, he was not a bully either; there was no hint of a

Sedition Act under his administration, though his opponents might have been considered seditious. If he failed to arouse Congress and the nation by feats of oratory, he also kept calm in moments of black crisis. British troops set fire to the White House and the Capitol in August, 1814. When Madison summoned Congress to assemble, less than a month later, the legislators had to squeeze into the post-office building. His annual message of September, 1814, betrayed no sense of dismay. Its prose was as circumspect, as faintly old-fashioned as ever.

Whatever scorn they might reserve for his executive heads or for his generals, most of Madison's political opponents recognized this quality in him. Elisha Brigham of Massachusetts, after presenting the usual Federalist version of the war, went on to say of the President: "Indeed, he has not seen much service—he has not had the experience of Bonaparte; but there is no doubt but he is hearty in the cause, and has conducted the war according to the best of his ability."[39] Perhaps that does not tell us a great deal about Madison, but it is as good an assessment of his stature as commander in chief as we are likely to get.

After all, it is essentially the same statement as the one made by his political supporters. Charles Jared Ingersoll, though writing a generation afterward, was a Republican Congressman in the War of 1812. According to Ingersoll, Madison

went through the war meekly, . . . no doubt with anxious longing for the restoration of peace, but without ever yielding a principle to his enemies or a point to his adversaries; leaving a United States, which he found embarrassed and discredited, successful, prosperous, glorious and content. A constitution which its opponents pronounced incapable of hostilities, under his administration triumphantly bore their severest brunt. Checkered by the inevitable vicissitudes of war, its trials never disturbed the composure of the commander-in-chief, always calm, consistent and conscientious, never much elated by victory or depressed by defeat, never once by the utmost exigencies of war, betrayed into a breach of the constitution.[40]

Neither of these opinions is an unqualified panegyric. The implication of Ingersoll's appraisal might be that the United States was lucky to get off so lightly, or that Madison, sharing in its luck, slept more tranquilly than circumstances always warranted. But he and Brigham would agree that, for the United States, it is probably just as well that its commanders in chief have not "had the experience of Bonaparte"; and we may agree with them.

III

POLK

(1845–1848)

LEONARD D. WHITE

J AMES K. POLK was the second American president to wield power as commander in chief in wartime. James Madison during the War of 1812 had done little to reveal the actual authority that lay concealed in the title. Abraham Lincoln pushed the constitutional power of the commander in chief to its outer limits, but problems of this order did not arise in the War with Mexico. Polk gave the country its first demonstration of the *administrative* capacities of the presidency as a war agency. He proved that a president could run a war.

Polk became Chief Executive on March 4, 1845, after a long public career in his native state and in Congress. On May 11, 1846, Congress declared that a state of war with Mexico existed. The northern Mexican provinces were occupied as far south as Monterrey by October, 1846; Veracruz was taken in March, 1847; Mexico City fell in September, 1847; and ratifications of the treaty of peace were exchanged on May 30, 1848.

Polk therefore operated for about two years as commander in chief during war. . . .

Polk's activities during these years were profoundly affected by his concept of himself in the role of president. When he was about to set out for Washington in February, 1845, he let it be known that he intended to be *the president*. When war broke out he made it equally clear that he intended to be *the commander in chief*. He told his land office commissioner, James Shields, who was ambitious for military glory, that he hoped his friends in Congress would allow him to conduct the War with Mexico as he thought proper.[1] The president, Polk declared, was held responsible for the conduct of the war; he intended to be responsible, and he exercised that responsibility to the limit of his endurance.[2] He determined the general strategy of military and naval operations; he chose commanding officers; he gave personal attention to supply problems; he energized so far as he could the General Staff; he controlled the military and naval estimates; and he used the cabinet as a major coordinating agency for the conduct of the campaign. He told the Secretaries of War and Navy to give their personal attention to all matters, even of detail, and to advise him promptly of every important step that was to be taken. The president was the center on which all else depended; Hamilton's doctrine of the unity of the executive power was seldom more truly exemplified.

Among the principal civilians with whom Polk was in constant touch were the Secretaries of the War, Navy, and Treasury departments. William L. Marcy, Secretary of War, was a Brown University graduate who had studied law and engaged professionally in politics. He had held municipal and state offices in New York before going to the Senate in 1831, where he coined the famous phrase "to the victor belong the spoils." He resigned his seat to become governor of New York (1833–39). He was Polk's Secretary of War and Pierce's Secretary of State. He was a genial, honest politician with a lively sense of humor and a fondness for desultory reading.

George Bancroft, Polk's first Secretary of the Navy, was a Harvard man with graduate training in philosophy and religion in Berlin, an unsuccessful Unitarian clergyman, an unsuccessful schoolmaster, a highly successful Massachusetts machine politician, and a rising historian in 1845, when he took over the navy on his way to his first diplomatic mission in Great Britain. His successor, John Y. Mason, was a lawyer who had been active in Virginia politics, had served six years in Congress and about seven as a federal district judge before entering Tyler's cabinet and then Polk's. The Secretary of the Treasury, Robert J. Walker, a Mississippi lawyer best known as a land speculator and as an advocate of a tariff for revenue only, had served ten years in the Senate before taking his cabinet post.

On the military side, General Zachary Taylor was a farmer's son who began a forty years' career in the army in 1808 with a lieutenant's commission. Until the Mexican War his experience had been limited to fighting Indians before, during, and after the War of 1812. He had made an excellent record in such small-scale engagements. General Winfield Scott also joined the army before the War of 1812, and, although not a West Pointer, revealed a greater professional interest in the military art than most of his contemporaries. He became known later as a quarrelsome letter writer, much too greatly impressed with his own dignity and rights. General Thomas S. Jesup, the quartermaster general, had been one of Calhoun's able young men during the eight years of his administration of the War

Department when army management had been carried to such a high level.

President Polk took immediate responsibility for making the fundamental decision whether to wage a war on foreign territory with the regular army, or with the army supplemented by volunteers.[3] Here he made his principal mistakes. Instead of asking Congress for authority to recruit men to fill up existing regiments and add new regiments to the regular army, he requested authority to call for volunteers. He compounded this mistake by fixing the term of enlistment at twelve months *or* for the war, which was construed to give the volunteers an option to withdraw at the end of one year's service. So many took advantage of this option while General Scott's army was before Mexico City that military operations were halted for months.

In the broad field of over-all strategy Polk promptly took the lead. The general movements of the war were simple. The northern provinces of Mexico, south and west of Texas, were to be seized and held, and California was to be taken by sea and by land. If these movements failed to produce peace, an invasion of Mexico from Veracruz was to drive on to Mexico City. Geography suggested these grand outlines, and the cabinet concurred with Polk in settling upon them nearly a year before hostilities broke out.[4] The navy was to blockade most Mexican ports, and to transport men and supplies.

War once declared, Polk wasted no time in determining the precise course of the campaign. On the evening of May 14, 1846, Secretary of War William L. Marcy and General Winfield Scott came to the White House. "I gave it as my opinion that the first movement should be to march a competent force into the Northern Provinces," the President notified his advisers.

Marcy and Scott concurred.[5] Two days later the President presented a more detailed plan of operations to the cabinet. "My plan was to march an army of 2000 men on Santa Fé & near 4000 on Chihuahua . . . leaving Gen'l Scott to occupy the country on the lower Del Norte and in the interior."[6] In early June the expedition against California was agreed upon in cabinet, and an order to Colonel Philip Kearny read by Marcy. Polk rewrote it.[7] In July, Polk drafted instructions to Taylor in relation to the manner of conducting the war, depending on Colonel Benton for a part but himself preparing, as he said, the most important section. The instructions took the form of a letter from the Secretary of War to Taylor; Polk showed Marcy the text, and "the Secretary of War approved it."[8] In short, the President participated actively in every major decision regarding the military strategy of the war, initiated some of them, and at times presented a well-defined plan of operations. As will be seen later, he also directed a multitude of details.

A crucial aspect of military affairs is the choice of the high command. The President personally selected the commanding officers, so far as he had freedom of action, and tried unsuccessfully to maneuver both Taylor and Scott into a secondary position. Here he encountered some of his principal frustrations.

At the outbreak of war, Winfield Scott and Zachary Taylor were the senior general officers. Polk almost immediately lost confidence in Scott and eventually in Taylor. Some of the considerations that entered into the assignment of commanding generals may be illustrated by a view of the case of General Scott. Immediately after war broke out Scott was informed that he would be sent to Mexico with the volunteers "to reinforce Taylor"—and also by virtue of rank to supersede him in command. According to Scott, Democratic Congressmen went to the White House predicting that his anticipated success at the front would "prostrate the Democratic party in 1848." To prevent this, the House Democrats entered a bill to authorize the President to appoint two major generals and four brigadier generals, all presumably Democrats and designed to supersede Scott and other Whig generals. Scott saw the bill, at once "smelt a rat," and promptly told Marcy that he saw the trick. Believing, as he said, that he was a stronger man than any of his *"entrappers,"* he "flung, the next day, the 21st, a letter into the teeth of the poor Secretary (the mere tool in the hands of party)."[9]

In the course of the letter he declared that he did not desire to place himself in the most perilous of all positions: *"a fire upon my rear, from Washington, and the fire, in front, from the Mexicans."*[10] This was strong language for a military man to use in addressing a Secretary of War and, by implication, a President of the United States. This letter sufficiently demonstrated Scott's bad feelings. Polk concluded, "His bitter hostility towards the administration is such that I could not trust him. . . . Gen'l Scott's partisan feelings must not interfere with the public service if another suitable commanding officer can be had."[11] Much to Scott's dismay and surprise, he was ordered to remain in Washington.[12]

In due course of time Polk had to find a commander of the expedition against Veracruz. His dislike of Scott had not diminished and by this time he had also lost confidence in Taylor.[13] He turned to his cabinet for help, but all "were at a loss to designate who should be the chief in command."[14] Bitter necessity finally forced Polk to give the command to Scott.

The problem of selecting the field generals was complicated on account of the political connections of both Taylor and

Scott. Polk hoped to avoid winning the war with victorious Whig generals who might easily defeat a quarrelsome Democratic party in the 1848 election. But no general officer of the regular army was an avowed Democrat. Scott was a convinced Whig, and had been and was a receptive candidate for his party nomination. Taylor became a hopeful candidate during the course of the Mexican War.

Polk made an extraordinary maneuver to extricate himself from this difficulty by proposing to revive the rank of lieutenant general, last held by General Washington, with the intention of appointing to this office, as supreme commander, Senator Thomas H. Benton. Benton was willing, but the Senate was not. The scheme did Polk little credit. Major Elliott condemned it in a passage from his biography of Scott: "Nothing in Polk's clumsy direction of the war illustrates more graphically his utter ignorance of the history, the principles, and the necessities of warfare than this readiness to place in command of his armies the arrogant and self-confident civilian politician."[15] Senator Benton had held a militia commission, but his military experience was so inferior to his political availability that his senatorial colleagues put an end to this expedient. Much against his will Polk had to deal with two commanding generals he did not trust—feelings that came to be reciprocated on their part.

The President was active in selecting officers for lesser posts. He commissioned his former law partner, Gideon J. Pillow, as general, assigned him to Taylor, and used him as a confidential source of information. Polk himself proposed Patterson, Pillow, and Shields for the Tampico expedition.[16] He decided to appoint personally the officers of a newly authorized regiment of riflemen and, with Marcy, agreed that "a portion of the

officers should be Whigs." He spent hours examining the papers
and recommendations of applicants.[17] Later he spent more time
with Marcy in arranging the nominations of officers under the
Ten Regiment Bill. On this occasion he sought "in vain to turn
over the horde of applicants to the Secretary of War, that I
might have his Report upon their respective merits." For more
than a week he spent three or four hours a day hearing claims
for commissions. "I have pushed them off and fought them with
both hands like a man fighting fire, and endeavored to drive
them to the Secretary of War. . . . It has all been in vain."[18]
The President had brought all this on himself. Marcy wrote a
member of Congress who was trying to get a commission for a
constituent, "it is proper to say what I presume you are not
ignorant of, that the selections are not made by the War Department, but by the President himself."[19]

In 1847 Polk decided to appoint a few noncommissioned
officers who had distinguished themselves in battle to vacant
second lieutenancies. The army preferred West Point men, and
the adjutant general stubbornly delayed furnishing the list of
vacancies, a mild form of sabotage. Marcy could not get the
list. Polk sent for the adjutant general, who started to debate
the issue with him. Polk was much vexed and told the reluctant
adjutant general that he, Polk, was commander in chief, and
ordered him to produce the list. "I repeated to him," he wrote
in his diary, "that he must regard what I said as a military order
& that I would expect it to be promptly obeyed."[20]

Polk kept his hand on the field commanders as well. General
Scott detached Colonel William S. Harney from his regimental
command, an act which the President described in his diary as
arbitrary and tyrannical conduct. Polk ordered Harney to be
restored. Marcy, however, agreed with Scott and delayed writ-

ing to him. Polk learned of the postponement and told Marcy if he was unwilling to write the letter that he, the President, would. Marcy promptly yielded.[21]

Another major administrative problem in the conduct of war is supply and transportation. Polk had a shrewd common-sense grasp of the problems involved in maintaining an army in the field, and more capacity for forward planning than some of his staff officers. His diary contains many records of conferences with General Jesup, the quartermaster general, and other supply officers, and we may guess that the "details" he was constantly concerned with were primarily matters of supply. A few specific examples will illustrate his constant preoccupation with such arrangements, and with energizing subordinate military and naval officers.

Early in the course of the war, Polk asked Marcy to bring to the White House General Gibson, the commissary general of subsistence, and General Jesup. Polk had "a full interview" with both officers, telling them that he wished ample provision made for the army but no wasteful expenditure, and that he would hold each of them responsible for any failure. This was the first of many direct contacts between the President and the supply services during the war. Summer vacations took Marcy out of Washington, war or no war, and Polk then in effect became acting head of the department. Thus he recorded in his diary in September, 1847, "During the absence of the Secretary of War much of my time is occupied with the details of the War Department connected with the Mexican War. I saw the adj't Gen'l & the Quarter master Gen'l to-day & conferred with them, and gave directions in reference [to] many of these details."[22]

Procrastination was an evil that Polk was constantly fighting. The ship *Lexington* was scheduled to sail from New York with troops but sat in harbor. Polk learned of this and asked the Secretary of the Navy for an explanation. Bancroft cleared himself by stating he had sent orders by mail to the *Lexington's* commanding officer, who was in nearby Virginia, and simultaneous orders to New York that as soon as the troops were on board, the ship should sail with another officer, if necessary. No one knew where the negligent commander was. Polk ordered the ship to sail instantly, and the Secretary to court-martial any officer who had been guilty of unreasonable delay.[23]

A year later Polk was still having trouble in getting troops out of New York. A regiment under Colonel Stephenson was to proceed by sea to California. After repeated conversations with the Secretary of War, Polk learned that the delay was caused by lack of transports. He then sent for Jesup, who could give no satisfactory explanation beyond saying that orders had been issued to engage the vessels. Polk retorted that he thought there had been culpable delay, and ordered Jesup to see that the transports were procured.[24] Two weeks later Colonel Stephenson was still in Washington. Polk exploded; Stephenson gave some unsatisfactory explanations, and Polk told him that if further delay occurred, the negligent officers would be arrested and tried.[25]

The matter of army transport in Mexico was much on Polk's mind. In early autumn, 1846, he called in Jesup and asked why baggage wagons were being used by Taylor's army instead of mules. Jesup promptly gave "his decided opinion that baggage wagons should be dispensed with and mules employed. . . ." Polk then asked Jesup and Marcy, who was present, why mules had not already been provided. Jesup was evasive: "he had received no communication from Gen'l Taylor or the War Department on the subject. . . ." Marcy apparently was silent. The purchase of wagons went on just the same.[26]

Polk came back again to the issue of mules *vs.* wagons in the following spring, asking Marcy to come in with the acting quartermaster general, Colonel Stanton. The President roundly condemned the purchase and use of "miles of wagons" but declined to issue a positive order forbidding them. He then opened up on the purchase of 1,000 horses in Ohio to be transported to Mexico to mount the Third Dragoons, and the purchase of mules in the states. "I expressed the opinion strongly that this was great folly." Stanton could find no satisfactory explanation for failure to buy horses and mules in Mexico at one-fourth the price, except that he thought American specimens were larger and better. The President was "much vexed at the extravagance & stupidity of purchasing these animals in the U.S."[27]

Indeed, Polk was deeply dissatisfied with the lack of energy on the part of the military establishment. He found two reasons for failure to perform—superannuation and political unreliability. On the score of old age, well before the war he remarked that many of the army and navy officers had become so fond of their ease and comfort that it was necessary they should be taught their duty by enforcing rigid discipline.[28] Early in the war he told General Jesup that many of the officers of the regular army had become gentlemen of entirely too much leisure, "and that some of them required to have a coal of fire put on their backs to make them move promptly."[29] In the spring of 1847 he repeated these sentiments: "The truth is that the old army officers have become so in the habit of enjoying their ease, sitting in parlours and on carpeted floors, that most of them have no energy. . . ."[30] He had no easy way of getting rid of deadwood, since the army had no retirement system. The consequence was precisely the same as that which had undermined the army in the early years of the War of 1812; command by men in some cases far beyond their prime, bereft of energy and drive, and unable to stand the rigors of field campaigns.

The army tradition of 1846, at least as understood by Marcy, forbade a drastic solution of the problem by removal of officers at the head of the military bureaus. The Secretary of War disclaimed any personal responsibility for failures of supply. The law, he explained, had assigned the heads of the various military branches, meaning presumably by virtue of the seniority rule. "These could not be changed by me nor could I make them over. Instructions, admonitions &c. cannot give appropriate qualifications when nature has denied them."[31]

There was another limitation inherent in the situation. If it was out of the tradition to remove a quartermaster general, it was also difficult to appoint competent understudies for them. Many persons applied to both Marcy and Polk for military commissions, and some of them might have been useful in supply operations. Marcy explained his dilemma to his friend Wetmore: "I have to scold not a little at the Q.M. Department, & if I overrule them in the selection of subordinates they naturally say things would go better if you would give us the officers we ask for."[32] Civilian heads could go only so far.

On the score of political infidelity, Polk was equally dissatisfied. By September, 1846, he reached the conclusion that several of the officers in Marcy's immediate entourage were "politically opposed to the administration," an opinion shared by Marcy.[33] In 1847 Polk put down in his diary: "The Subordinate officers at the head of the different bureau[s] in the War Department are generally Federalists, and many of them are indifferent. . . . They take no sort of responsibility on themselves, and this renders it necessary that the Secretary of War & myself should look after them, even in the performance of the ordinary routine of details in their offices."[34]

Polk probably exaggerated the influence of politics on the bureau heads in the War Department. Their antecedents might have been "Federalist" and some of them might have been Whigs, but they were also professional soldiers. The supply services were faulty, but it is probable that the cause lay in the system and in poor judgment rather than in the deliberate intention of politically minded regular army officers to discredit the administration by risking loss of the war.

Congress accepted the recommendations coming from Polk and the Treasury for financing military operations. Indeed, after a warm battle in which the President had to exert all his influence, Congress agreed with Polk's bold proposal to reduce the tariff in 1846 when revenue needs were great and unpredictable.

The major precedent established by Polk in the field of finance was to reverse the historic practice by which the President had had no responsibility for the departmental estimates. This matter is dealt with at a later point.[35] For the first time the President insisted upon reviewing the estimates and controlling them. Polk was his own budget officer, and he acted with his customary vigor to overcome the resistance of the army officers against cuts in their figures.

The nature of Polk's fiscal preoccupations can be appreciated by events which came to his attention in the week from August 18, 1847, to August 25. On August 18 he learned that his plan to call out 6,000 more volunteers might be foreclosed for lack of available funds. This struck him with great astonishment. He sent for Treasury officers and cabinet members, and directed the quartermaster general, Jesup, to be ordered by telegraph back from New York. None of Jesup's clerks could explain the deficiency nor indeed could Jesup when he reported on the 21st.

On August 25 Jesup finally made a confidential report to Polk, the nature of which, as the President said, nearly made him sick. It appeared that on June 17 the chief clerk of the Treasury Department called on Jesup in company with Mr. Corcoran, of the banking house of Corcoran and Riggs, and asked Jesup to requisition $2,000,000 on quartermaster funds to be transferred to New Orleans. Jesup did not then need the money at New Orleans, but nevertheless he drew the requisition. Corcoran and Riggs became the transfer agents. On July 27, $400,000 had been paid over to the quartermaster in New Orleans, but at the end of August the bankers still held the balance. Jesup admitted that he understood the money was used by them for stock speculation.

Polk was greatly upset and condemned the whole transaction. He had no satisfactory explanation from Secretary of the Treasury Walker, nor indeed from any source. The whole episode confirmed his intention to watch every department to the limit of his capacity.[36]

One of the universal problems of administration is the proper coordination of various elements in a complex program. The problem is particularly acute in wartime, when military strategy, foreign relations, state and federal relations, internal politics, finance, contracts, transportation, and personal ambitions intermingle. Polk used the cabinet effectively as a major co-ordinating body. Indeed in his day, it was the only instrument of top coordination directly available to him, since no one had thought of the multiple agencies later invented for this purpose.

The cabinet considered every important aspect of the contest with Mexico, and some that were merely incidental. General strategy, basic orders to naval commanders and army generals, circulars of information to consuls abroad, selection of commanding officers, and commercial regulations in captured ports were among the general problems that Polk put to his cabinet colleagues. The decision to hold Taylor's forces at Monterrey and to strike the main blow at Mexico City through Veracruz came up for cabinet discussion and approval. It had obvious political as well as military implications and Polk put every member of the cabinet on record. The letter of instructions to Taylor "was fully considered paragraph by paragraph, and after undergoing various modifications was unanimously agreed to. It was a matter of so much importance that I was particular to take the opinion of each member of the Cabinet individually. . . . The subject was under consideration for more than two hours."[37]

The coordination of naval and military movements gave rise to one embarrassing moment for Secretary of the Navy John Y. Mason. He was discovered in cabinet session to be unaware of the date of the attack on Veracruz and had failed to order supporting naval vessels to the scene. Polk was greatly disturbed and said that he "had taken it for granted that they [i.e., Marcy in the War Department and Mason in the Navy] were constantly in conference with each other, and that each understood the movements & operations" of the other. Marcy lamely remarked that "he had supposed that the Secretary of the Navy knew all about it." The mortified Mason deserted the cabinet meeting to issue the necessary orders.[38]

The load of day-by-day business was, however, transacted not by the cabinet, but by Polk and Marcy, and to a lesser degree by Polk and Bancroft or Mason. The President became the coordinator in chief. It had been understood from the days of Washington that the president gave personal and immediate direction to the conduct of foreign affairs, but Treasury, War, and Navy had been left pretty much in the hands of their respective heads, and the Post Office Department had been unusually free from presidential attention. Now both War and Navy were forced into the position that the State Department had historically occupied.

In the case of the War Department, this consequence followed both from the vigor of Polk and the inadequacy of Secretary Marcy. Their relations are not unfairly illustrated by the repeated, and apparently customary, ritual in which Marcy brought dispatches to the White House, and, seated before the President, read them aloud to the commander in chief.[39] Marcy was not equal to his task, if Polk can be trusted. He was "overwhelmed with his labours and responsibilities," and so greatly oppressed with the duties of his office that Polk aided him by giving all the attention to them that his time would permit.[40] He seized the initiative in fact on many matters that Marcy might have been expected to handle in the first instance. Thus it was Polk and Benton who drafted Taylor's general instructions, not Marcy.[41] It was Polk who saw the prospects of obtaining revenue by raising the blockade on captured ports and Marcy who "concurred in this opinion."[42] It was Marcy who finally confessed his inability to control the quartermaster general's department and who asked Polk to call in its two principal officers.[43]

The Navy Department gave Polk much less concern. The two men who served at its head during the Mexican War were competent executives, and the Navy Department appeared much more in control of its affairs than the War Department. Its task was relatively simple.

Despite all the trouble that Polk encountered, despite all the shortcomings of organization, manpower, and system that are inevitable in any administrative structure, the army marched to the field, was supplied, fought a numerically superior enemy, won a series of victories, and conquered a peace. Taken in the large, this was a remarkable exploit by a commander in chief who had never donned a uniform, backed by a civilian cabinet composed of lawyer-politicians and a historian at the head of the Navy Department (Bancroft), and of whom only one (Marcy) had had the benefit even of elementary military lessons learned in a state militia. Their sense of over-all strategy was sound, and although Polk misdirected the expedition against Chihuahua[44] he was not only steadily thinking ahead of events, but was reaching decisions that were generally correct in view of the objects he set for the country.

Thoughtful persons who reflected upon the administrative lessons of the war as peace came in 1848 could have found some assurance in certain broad observations. It was clear the Congress could not run the war. Polk had denied the military aspirations of most Congressmen. He had taken the lead in war legislation and finance. He had governed the size and disposition of the armed forces. He had formulated the terms of peace.

At the same time Congress had a veto power which occasionally it used, notably in the refusal of its leaders even to consider replacing Taylor and Scott.

It had been demonstrated that a civilian commander in chief could—and did—function effectively as the single center for direction, authorization, coordination, and in lesser degree for control of a large military and naval effort. All lines concentrated in the White House, and the Chief Executive required every matter of consequence to be brought to him for approval. Thus was achieved a genuine unity of command that was not only unchallenged by either civil or military branches, but that succeeded in keeping in coordination the various movements in the field.

There were limits, nevertheless, to the personal capacity of even such a hard-working commander in chief as Polk. They included the universal limits of time and knowledge. Apart from the fact that presidents commanded no more hours in the day than clerks, it was also true that the commander in chief learned about many matters too late to enable him to have any influence. Polk frequently complained about the handicaps due to lack of information. The army apparently had almost no prior knowledge of Mexican terrain. The campaign against Veracruz was launched on the basis of sketch maps made in the White House by a former United States consul at that city whom Polk located in Boston.

There were limits also due to the capacity of the army to resist presidential suggestions, short of orders, for the conduct of the campaign. The classic case was that of the army mules. The commander in chief declined to take the responsibility of issuing a positive order on the subject,[45] and wagons continued to be used.

Another old lesson was confirmed by the Mexican War—that personal and political ambitions and considerations were not driven from the field by union to win a war with a foreign power. Polk was a Democrat, as well as commander in chief, and most of the top military posts at his disposal went to fellow partisans. Taylor and Scott, Wool, and others were Whigs, but as regular army officers the President could do nothing about them. The volunteer regiments, however, fought principally with Democratic officers.

Some administrative problems arose for which no answer was found. The monopoly of officer posts in the regular army, held by West Pointers, was not broken by Polk's single breach of the works. The disposal of superannuated army officers defied solution. The development of a *system* for army-navy coordination was not achieved. The failure to maintain an adequate medical corps was a constant drain on the effectiveness of the army. The means of energizing an organization like the regular army—an organization with a permanent corps of officers, with a marked professional solidarity, and with a rigid system of seniority—were not readily to be found.

While these and other administrative problems remained unsolved, one major administrative question had been answered. A president could also be a commander in chief. A president could run a war.

IV

LINCOLN

(1861–1865)

T. HARRY WILLIAMS

T HE CIVIL WAR was the first of the modern total wars, and the American democracy was almost totally unready to fight it. The United States had in 1861 almost no army, few good weapons, no officers trained in the higher art of war, and an inadequate and archaic system of command. Armies could be raised and weapons manufactured quickly, but it took time and battles to train generals. And it took time and blunders and bitter experiences to develop a modern command system. Not until 1864 did the generals and the system emerge.

In 1861 the general in chief of the army, which at the beginning of the war numbered about 16,000 men, was Winfield Scott. He was a veteran of two wars and the finest soldier in America. But he had been born in 1786, and he was physically incapable of commanding an army in the field. He could not ride, he could not walk more than a few steps without pain, and he had dropsy and vertigo.[1] The old General dreamed wistfully of taking the field. "If I could only mount a horse, I—," he would say sadly and pause, "but I am past that."[2] He was one of two officers in the army as the war started who had ever commanded troops in numbers large enough to be called an army. The other was John E. Wool, who was two years older than Scott. Wool had been a good soldier in his time, but he too showed the effects of age. He repeated things he had said a few minutes before, his hands shook, and he had to ask his aides if he had put his hat on straight.[3] Besides Scott and Wool, not an officer in the North had directed the evolutions of as large a unit as a brigade.[4] The largest single army that most of the younger officers had ever seen was Scott's force of 14,000 in the Mexican War.

There was not an officer in the first year of the war who was capable of efficiently administering and fighting a large army. Even Scott, had he been younger and stronger, would have had difficulty commanding any one of the big armies called into being by the government. All his experience had been with small forces, and he might not have been able to adjust his thinking to the organization of mass armies. The young officers who would be called to lead the new hosts lacked even his experience. Not only had they never handled troops in numbers, but they knew almost nothing about the history and theory of war or of strategy. They did not know the higher art of war, because there was no school in the country that taught it. West Point, which had educated the great majority of the officers, crammed its students full of knowledge of engineering, fortifications, and mathematics. Only a minor part of its curriculum was devoted to strategy, and its graduates learned little about how to lead and fight troops in the field. They were equally innocent of any knowledge of staff work—the administrative problems of operating an army or the formulation of war plans. Most of them never learned anything of it in the army, except for those few who could read French or who went abroad.[5] They spent most of their army careers fighting Indians or building forts, and there was not much of a staff organization in America for them to gain any experience with.

The staff of the army, such as it was, consisted of Scott and the heads of the important departments and bureaus in the military organization—the adjutant general, the quartermaster general, the chief of engineers, the chief of ordnance, and others. Some of these officers were men of ability and would do good work in the war. Their agencies were going concerns with years of experience behind them when hostilities started and needed only to be expanded to meet the larger needs of a larger army. None of the staff chiefs had made any plans for war, and none of them was accustomed to thinking in terms of supplying the needs of mass armies. Some of the departments, notably the quartermaster general's, made the shift from peace to war with efficiency; others never got completely adjusted. All of them were unready for war in 1861, and in that year and even later were not able to furnish field commanders with the technical information or advice or supplies which they were suddenly called on to provide. One of the most ironic examples of American military unreadiness was the spectacle of Northern —and Southern—generals fighting in their own country and not knowing where they were going or how to get there. Before the war the governments had collected no topographical information about neighboring countries or even about the United States, except for the West. No accurate military maps existed. General Henry W. Halleck was running a campaign in the Western theater in 1862 with maps he got from a bookstore.

With frenetic haste, the general set topographical officers and civilian experts to work making maps, but the resulting charts were generally incorrect. Benjamin H. Latrobe, the civil engineer, drew a map for a general going into western Virginia, but the best he could promise was that it would not *mislead* the expedition. General George B. McClellan had elaborate maps prepared for his Virginia campaign of 1862 and found to his dismay when he arrived on the scene that they were unreliable; "the roads are wrong . . . ," he wailed. Not until 1863 did the Army of the Potomac have an accurate map of northern Virginia, its theater of operations.[6] Poor staff work continued in some departments until the end of the war. As late as 1864 there was not an office in Washington that could tell a general organizing a campaign what railroads were under military control, what the condition of their equipment was, or how many men and supplies they could transport.[7]

In no section of the staff organization was there any person or division charged with the function of studying strategy or formulating war plans for even a theoretical war. The work of the staff was completely technical and routine. Scott, the general in chief, had done no thinking before the war about what strategy should be adopted if war came. He had busied himself chiefly with devising political schemes to avert civil conflict. When the shooting started, he had no strategic design in mind to subdue the South. No other officer had one. Nobody in the army had thought it was important to think of war in strategic terms.

At the head of the American military organization was the president, the commander in chief of all the armed forces of the nation. The man who was president when the war began had been a civilian all his life, had had no military experience except as a militia soldier in a pygmy Indian war, and in 1861 probably did not even know how to frame a military order. The president of the rival nation, the Confederate States, was a graduate of West Point; he had been in the regular army and had seen battle service in the Mexican War. Abraham Lincoln was a great war president; Jefferson Davis was a mediocre one. Nowhere in the history of war is there a better illustration of Clausewitz's dictum that an acquaintance with military affairs is not the principal qualification for a director of war but that "a remarkable, superior mind and strength of character" are better qualifications.[8]

With no knowledge of the theory of war, no experience in war, and no technical training, Lincoln, by the power of his mind, became a fine strategist. He was a better natural strategist than were most of the trained soldiers. He saw the big picture of the war from the start. The policy of the government was to restore the Union by force; the strategy perforce had to be offensive. Lincoln knew that numbers, material resources, and sea power were on his side, so he called for 400,000 troops and proclaimed a naval blockade of the Confederacy. These were bold and imaginative moves for a man dealing with military questions for the first time. He grasped immediately the advantage that numbers gave the North and urged his generals to keep up a constant pressure on the whole strategic line of the Confederacy until a weak spot was found—and a breakthrough could be made. And he soon realized, if he did not know it at the beginning, that the proper objective of his armies was the destruction of the Confederate armies and not the occupation of Southern territory. His strategic thinking was sound and for a rank amateur astonishingly good.[9]

During the first three years of the war, Lincoln performed

many of the functions that in a modern command system would be given to the chief of the general staff or to the joint chiefs of staff. He formulated policy, drew up strategic plans, and even devised and directed tactical movements. Judged by modern standards, he did some things that a civilian director of war should not do. Modern critics say that he "interfered" too much with military operations. He and his contemporaries did not think that he interfered improperly. In the American command system it was traditional for the civilian authority to direct strategy and tactics. The Continental Congress in the Revolution and the president and cabinet in the War of 1812 and the Mexican War had planned extensive and detailed campaigns. Lincoln was acting only as the civil authority had acted in every previous war. He was doing what he and most people thought the commander in chief ought to do in war.

Sometimes Lincoln made excellent plans and decisions; sometimes he made bad mistakes. Some of his mistakes resulted from his initial ignorance in 1861–62 of how to translate his strategic concepts into workable instructions for his generals. His first generals, especially McClellan, were equally ignorant of how to establish relations with the head of the government so that they could find out his ideas about strategy and counsel him. When Lincoln asked them for advice, he usually got *ipse dixit* opinions. McClellan, who succeeded Scott as general in chief, did not seem to know that he ought to offer guidance to his political chief.[10] If McClellan and other generals had known how to talk to Lincoln or had wanted to talk with him about the military situation, the President would have interfered in military affairs less than he sometimes did. On several occasions, he intervened because the generals had not frankly told him what they were going to do or had not explained their purposes to him in terms that he could understand. Sometimes Lincoln "interfered" without meaning to. He had the type of mind that delighted to frame a plan of military operations. He loved to work up a plan and spring it on a general. The mental exercise gave him pleasure, and he liked to get the reactions of soldiers to his schemes. He did not mean for the generals to adopt his designs, but they did not always understand this. What he intended as a presentation of his ideas or a suggestion to be considered sometimes came through to the military mind as an order from the commander in chief.[11]

Much of Lincoln's so-called interfering with the conduct of the war occurred in the first years of the conflict, when he believed, with some reason, that he was more capable of managing operations than were most of the generals. When the war started, he was inclined to defer to the judgments of trained soldiers. He soon came to doubt and even scorn the capabilities of the military mind. He asked of the generals decision, action, fighting, victory. They replied with indecision, inaction, delay, excuses. He became oppressed by the spectacle, so familiar in war, of generals who were superb in preparing for battle but who shrank from seeking its awful decision. "Tell him," he wrote in preparing instructions for one general, "to put it through—not to be writing or telegraphing back here, but put it through."[12] He wanted victories, but he got more letters than victories, letters from generals who wrote back that they could not put it through unless Lincoln provided them with more men and more guns . . . and still more.

One of the most important functions Commander in Chief Lincoln had to perform was choosing generals to manage the armies. He never had to worry that too few would apply for commissions. At the beginning of the war especially, he was showered with requests and demands for appointments from would-be generals and their political and military supporters: from officers who had spent weary years in the regular army in junior rank and now saw a chance to get their stars; from former officers who had resigned from the army to take lucrative civilian jobs and now wanted to return as generals; from politicians who thought military heroes would be popular after the war; from men who were ambitious, patriotic, able, mediocre, and incompetent. The rush for rank impressed, amused, and irritated the President. A popular jest of the war, one with a bitter undertone, was his reported remark about a brigadier general who got himself captured along with some horses and mules: "I don't care so much for brigadiers; I can make them. But horses and mules cost money."[13]

Lincoln handed out many commissions at the start of the war for reasons that were completely political but completely sound in a military sense. He used the military patronage to unite discordant groups in support of the war and to keep down divisions in the North. Creating and maintaining national unity was a necessary and vital phase of war-making in 1861, and Lincoln performed brilliantly with his appointments. He had to satisfy his own Republicans, who thought he gave too many commissions to Democrats, and he had to soothe the Democrats, who thought he was letting Republicans run the war.[14] He dispensed commissions to ambitious political chieftains with large personal followings, especially if they were Democrats, like Nathaniel P. Banks, John A. McClernand, and Ben Butler. These selections saddled the army with some prize incompetents in high places, but they were good investments in national cohesion.[15] Some of Lincoln's appointments went to men who were leaders of important nationality groups like the German-

Americans. Lincoln realized the importance of enlisting the Germans in support of the war, but he was amused by their eagerness to get their prominent men on the list of generals. Once a staff officer heard a conversation between the President and Secretary of War Edwin M. Stanton about some appointments of brigadier generals. Lincoln said he agreed with most of Stanton's recommendations, but, continued the President, "there has got to be something done unquestionably in the interest of the Dutch, and to that end I want Schimmelfennig appointed." Lincoln uttered the name with great enjoyment. Stanton said there were German officers who were better recommended. "No matter about that," said Lincoln; "his name will make up for any difference there may be." It had to be Schimmelfennig, and he went off repeating the name.[16]

With Schimmelfennig, Lincoln was getting a saving laugh out of a serious situation. He was escaping momentarily from the grimness of war in the same way he did when he told one of his stories to a pompous senator or read Artemus Ward in a cabinet meeting. Selecting generals was a galling, dull business, and he seized every chance he had to get some fun out of it. He liked to have attractive wives of officers besiege him for promotions for their husbands. In the Lincoln Papers is a list he made in 1861 of officers he wanted to remember when he made appointments. After the name of Lieutenant Slemmer is the notation: "His pretty wife says a Major, or first Captain."[17] Of another wife who wanted him to make her husband a brigadier general, he wrote: "She is a saucy woman and I am afraid she will keep tormenting me until I may have to do it."[18]

In dealing with the applicants for appointments and promotions, Lincoln demonstrated his most skilled techniques in managing men and situations. Once the Pennsylvania Congressional delegation came buzzing angrily at Lincoln to get a promotion for the state's son, General Samuel P. Heintzelman. They extolled him, said he was a fine general, a good man. Seizing on the last claim, the President agreed that Heintzelman certainly was a good man; in fact he was "a good egg," and therefore he would keep. "You must trust me," he said, "to see that the General has justice done him." There was a pause, and then one of the delegation said: "We have trusted you a long time on this." "Gentlemen, you must do so longer," said Lincoln, and bowed them out.[19]

Lincoln probably enjoyed his exchange with the Pennsylvanians. But sometimes he got terribly angry when people criticized his military appointments. Once General Carl Schurz, the ebullient and incompetent German-American officer, wrote Lincoln that the administration was failing politically because the war was failing and that Lincoln was to blame for it all because he had entrusted the important commands to men whose hearts were not in the war. By men without hearts, Schurz meant Democrats. With a dramatic reference to his brave boys dying in an aimless war, he concluded: "I do not know whether you have ever seen a battlefield. I assure you, Mr. President, it is a terrible sight."[20] Lincoln liked Schurz, but he was angered by the General's letter. And he had no intention of letting Schurz patronize him. In a cutting reply, one of the best of his war letters, he read Schurz a lecture on how to pick generals. Who is to decide who shall be generals? he asked. "If I must discard my own judgment and take yours, I must also take that of others; and by the time I should reject all I should be advised to reject, I should have none left, Republicans or others—not even yourself. For be assured, my dear sir, there are men who . . . think you are performing your part as poorly as you think I am performing mine." Republican and Democratic generals had been about equally successful, continued Lincoln, naming some officers from each party who had performed well. Then came the crusher: "I will not perform the ungrateful task of comparing failures."[21] Anybody else but Schurz would have been demolished. He kept on writing letters.

Lincoln never discarded his judgment to others in choosing generals. But he was willing to discard his judgment of what was good strategy and take the opinion of any general whom he considered to be able. He was willing to yield the power to direct strategic operations to any general who could demonstrate that he was competent to frame and execute strategy. Lincoln sensed that there was something wrong in the command system. Somewhere, he thought, there ought to be a division of function between him and the military. But where should the line be drawn? And who was the general to whom he could confide the power to control? Lincoln was to go through some bitter and agonizing experiences before he got the answers to these questions. In the process, he and the army and the nation were to learn a lot about command. By 1864 the United States would have a modern command system. Lincoln did not know it in 1861, but he was going to make a large and permanent contribution to the organization of the American military system.

V

McKINLEY

(1898)

ERNEST R. MAY

LINCOLN'S WAR MACHINE had been torn apart as soon as it had served its purpose. Veterans who had gone down the Mississippi Valley, through Georgia or to Appomattox, went home, to march again only in torchlight parades of the Republican party. The minuscule regular army busied itself on the narrowing borders of the Sioux and Apache empires, while sergeants, lieutenants, captains, and colonels grew old as sergeants, lieutenants, captains, and colonels. By 1898, when an army was needed again, the nation had little more ready military strength than in 1861. All that remained of Lincoln's legacy was the lesson the Civil War taught or reaffirmed—that victory lay with big battalions under resolute leadership.

The navy had had a different history. A curious impulse to compete with other sea powers had come over congressmen in the 1880's, and eight heavily armored big-gun ships had been built. Very few people had a clear notion what these battleships and cruisers were to do. Some expected them to serve as coast-watchers; others thought of them as escorts for merchant vessels; still others looked to their sailing out against the massed warships of some yet unsuspected enemy. Confusion existed not only among amateurs but also among the bureau chiefs who shared control over the fleet. While the army of 1898 seemed a dilapidated machine, the navy bore some resemblance to a large, intricate, and well-oiled toy.

The president who was to control these engines was, however, the most soldierly ever to be a wartime commander in chief. William McKinley had served with the Ohio volunteers through all the Civil War, been commissioned at nineteen, and twice cited for gallantry under fire. Subsequently he had been universally known as "the Major." Though at fifty-five he ran to fat and the muscles in his Roman face sagged, he carried himself with parade-ground stiffness, and his dark shadowed eyes, stiff-set mouth, and cleft chin left him with an air of command.

When war with Spain opened in April, 1898, McKinley immediately made the White House a command post. Strategy councils with the Secretaries of War and the Navy, the Commanding General of the Army, and the Naval War Board took place in a second-floor study. In a smaller room, where large wall maps were flagged with colored pins, there were twenty-five private telephone lines to connect the President with branches of the War and Navy departments. No previous commander in chief had had either such personal background or such equipment for command.

The war that McKinley was to direct, however, was not one which reawakened the zeal of the major of Ohio volunteers. In

1895 a revolt against Spanish rule had broken out in Cuba, and partisans of the rebels had gradually stirred up enthusiasm in the United States. McKinley's predecessor, Grover Cleveland, had stubbornly resisted agitation for intervention. His cautious policy had been applauded by businessmen from both parties who feared that war might upset the country's gradual recovery from the depression of 1893. McKinley identified himself with the business community: he would readily have subscribed to Coolidge's dictum, "The business of America is business"; and he set himself to prevent war. But accumulated passions, touched off by the sinking of the *Maine* in Havana harbor, proved too powerful. Trying to hold back a bellicose Congress and public, McKinley found that his picture was being hissed in theaters and his effigy burned in village and town demonstrations. When editors and party leaders warned him that the Republican party was in danger and that if the administration failed to lead, the result might be a wave of demagoguery that could end in revolution, McKinley reluctantly abandoned diplomacy and led the country to war.[1]

As a result, despite his experience of soldiering and the elaborate apparatus in the White House, the President had only hazy notions of what kind of war he wanted to fight. The *casus belli* lay, in effect, in Spain's refusal to grant independence to Cuba. But Congress had not voted recognition of the Cuban insurgent government. Though the two houses had passed a resolution saying that the United States should not annex the island, many felt war would not be justified unless it brought some return in new territory. Among these were businessmen and business spokesmen who had originally opposed war and who were among McKinley's most important supporters. To the President it cannot have been at all clear whether he was to seek revenge for the *Maine,* liberate Cuba, or conquer new land for the United States.

At the outset McKinley met this issue simply by approving whatever the War and Navy departments proposed. As far back as September, 1897, he had been told by Assistant Secretary of the Navy Theodore Roosevelt that in case of war the navy would blockade Cuba, dispatch a flying squadron to the Spanish coasts, and attack the Spanish Asiatic squadron based on Manila. When war seemed certain, the Secretary of the Navy asked permission to carry out the first and last of these schemes. McKinley made him wait until hostilities were actually at hand but then issued an official proclamation that the coasts of Cuba would be blockaded. He also authorized orders to Admiral George Dewey, commander of the American squadron at Hong Kong, "Proceed at once to Philippine Islands. Commence operations at once, particularly against the Spanish fleet. . . . Use utmost endeavors."[2]

The President also approved the apparent plans of the army. The possibility of war had been commented on frequently by Secretary of War Russell A. Alger, a choleric, sickly lumber magnate who was manager of the Republican machine in Michigan and who had been a major general of cavalry during the Civil War. Alger had spoken of a large expedition to Cuba. The President had held him in check so long as war was not formally declared. Indeed, Alger later testified that McKinley forbade him to spend money for any purpose except coast defense. But as soon as hostilities commenced, the President not only indicated that the Secretary could do as he wished but also called for 125,000 volunteers in order to give Alger the men he needed.[3] McKinley seemed disposed to let the navy and army fight Spain where and how they chose.

Nor did it trouble him that the armed forces won their first victory ten thousand miles from Cuba, in a place which the President later said he had to search out on his office globe. Admiral Dewey attacked the ancient Spanish squadron huddled in Manila Bay, destroyed it completely, and notified Washington laconically that he could be master of the city if sent 5,000 troops for support.[4]

Had McKinley reflected upon this request, he might have realized that it involved grave issues of policy. Once American forces controlled any part of the Philippine archipelago, he would face the issue, not of whether to ask Spain for some or all of the islands, but of whether or not to give them back to her. By agreeing to reinforce Dewey, the President would make annexation almost inevitable. He later remarked ruefully, according to one of his friends, "If old Dewey had just sailed away when he smashed that Spanish fleet, what a lot of trouble he would have saved us." But apparently he authorized an expeditionary force without a second thought.[5] For the time being, McKinley acted as a rubber-stamp commander in chief.

Then suddenly he changed. He learned to his dismay that Alger had no adequate plan for a large-scale landing in Cuba. Nelson A. Miles, the strutting but experienced Commanding General of the Army, came to see him. Commenting on the Secretary of War's order for an expedition of 70,000 to land near Havana, Miles pointed out that the Spaniards had 125,000 troops there, well supplied with ammunition, equipped with 100 field guns, and manning 125 strong emplacements. He observed that even if the American volunteers were fully trained and equipped, which they were not, they did not have enough ammunition for one major battle, let alone a long campaign, and an adequate supply could not be manufactured inside two months. From an angry Secretary of the Navy the President also learned that Alger had foreborne to make arrangements for convoying an expedition.[6] McKinley realized all at once that he could not simply leave matters to the armed services.

Miles's information presented him, moreover, with a dilemma. On the one hand it was evident that the public wanted triumphs. Within days after the outbreak of war newspapers had begun asking why the army was not fighting alongside the brave Cubans. Though Dewey's victory had temporarily silenced criticism, it was sure to revive if weeks or months went by with no further successes. On the other hand, as Miles warned, an ill-planned operation could end in disaster. In either case, the President might find himself in precisely the situation he had hoped to escape by going to war—facing a political revolt against conservative Republican leadership.

As he meditated this terrible choice, an inspiration seemed to come to him. American newspapers were copying English press reports on affairs in Spain, and these dispatches said that the Spanish government had been badly shaken by the defeat at Manila. Though there had been periodic rebellions in the Philippines, the colony had been far less troublesome than Cuba, and it was now far richer. What would be the result, McKinley evidently asked himself, if the United States should appear to threaten conquest of the islands? According to the ambassador who had represented him in Madrid, the Spaniards thought Cuba as good as lost. Would they not agree to abandon it and make peace in order to hold their Asian colony?

Seeking to avoid a campaign in Cuba, McKinley took this hope as basis for new tactics. Instead of large-scale landings in Cuba, there was to be nothing more than a reconnaissance in

force intended to hearten the insurgents and make small head-
lines at home. A substantial part of the regular army, accompanied by the fittest units of state militia, would strike
instead for the Philippines. Though McKinley had given off-
hand approval to Dewey's request for reinforcements, final
orders had not been drawn up. Miles and Wesley Merritt, the
general designated to command the expedition, had fallen to
quarreling about its composition, both officers insisting that it
should number three times the 5,000 men Dewey had requested. Warned in the meantime of the possible political
implications of taking Manila, the President might have can-
celed the whole project. Instead he gave Merritt 20,000 men
and instructions to accomplish "the twofold purpose of com-
pleting the reduction of the Spanish power in that quarter and
of giving order and security to the islands while in the possession of the United States."[7]

Through a discreet, efficient secretary, George B. Cortelyou,
the President fed information to the press. From the middle of
May onward, newspaper correspondents told in exaggerated
detail of the mighty force sailing toward Manila. Foreign
diplomats interviewing the Secretary or Assistant Secretary of
State meanwhile found talk drifting gently to the topic of
Spain's need for an early peace. The same theme crept into
dispatches from the Washington correspondents of London
newspapers.[8] The President obviously hoped that it would be
possible to win the Cuban war by pressure on the Philippine
Islands.

For a few days at the end of May, it seemed as if this venture
might succeed. John Hay, the American ambassador in London,
cabled that a member of the British government had approached him informally and unofficially, asking how the

99

United States would react if Spain offered to withdraw from Cuba. Since McKinley had been discussing possible terms of peace with his cabinet ever since the interview with General Miles, the Secretary of State could fire back a detailed reply, saying that the President would be glad to make peace on such a basis, provided only that Spain also ceded Puerto Rico and a coaling station in the Philippine Islands. These extra conditions were presumably conceived as minimum satisfaction for members of the public who felt no war should be fought without profit. No indemnity was to be asked; the United States was to assume payment of its own claims in Cuba; and the Philippine archipelago was to be abandoned to what even the anti-imperialist *Springfield Republican* termed "a dominion hated, crushed, and unregenerate."[9] If Spain quickly agreed, McKinley would not have to chance untried troops against the defenses and fevers of Cuba.

But just as his tactics seemed near success, McKinley abandoned them. Hay reported the British government willing to communicate America's "liberal" terms to Madrid, but the Secretary of State directed him to abandon the project. "The President cannot make proposals for peace," he cabled.[10]

The reasons for this new and equally sudden change of front are obscure. In a private letter to Hay, the Secretary of State explained that the Philippine insurgents had become a factor to be considered. Consular reports belatedly coming in from the Far East indicated that Dewey might have negotiated some *de facto* alliance with the rebels; their leader, Emilio Aguinaldo, had called for a republic under American protectorate. McKinley may have concluded that he would risk a breach of trust if he simply abandoned the Filipinos in the interest of an immediate peace with Spain.[11]

He would not have felt so punctilious, probably, had he not been heartened by fresh and more optimistic reports from the armed services. The Spanish battle fleet, long a source of worry, had finally been located and pinned down in Santiago harbor. Admiral William T. Sampson, commanding the American squadron in the Caribbean, reported not only that the Spaniards could be overwhelmed at sea but also that a force of 10,000 could easily take Santiago and its environs.[12] Coupled with mounting tallies of supplies and ammunition and somewhat overenthusiastic accounts of the readiness of volunteer units, Sampson's advice may have given the President more courage for a descent on Cuba.

In all likelihood, however, McKinley was influenced most of all by what went on at home. The notion that the Philippine Islands had become America's and ought to remain so had spread far and wide. Veteran imperialists like Henry Cabot Lodge had needed only hours to discern where the finger of destiny pointed. Chauncey Depew, a railroad magnate, warned the New York Republican Club, "a strong feeling is spreading over the whole land in favor of colonial expansion. The people are infatuated with the idea." An anti-imperialist Baptist minister in Chicago wrote of a developing "popular craze" for annexations.[13] The ferment seemed to spread among some of the very groups and classes that had earlier called for intervention in Cuba, and McKinley may have sensed that it could be as dangerous to forsake the Philippines as to risk a campaign in Cuba.

Whatever the case, the President suddenly reverted to the original scheme of a large-scale expedition. The planned reconnaissance in force was to have been under the command of General William R. Shafter, a gruff and extravagantly fat veteran of innumerable staff assignments. Owing primarily to the navy's preoccupations, the task unit had never been moved from Tampa. In the meantime supplies and troops had rapidly accumulated there, and on June 7 the President himself directed Shafter to take such forces as he could transport and move at once on Santiago.[14]

This directive was not carried out to the letter. The navy thought mistakenly that a Spanish warship was loose off the Florida coast. The chase for it, coupled with delay in arranging for a convoy, made postponement inevitable. The loading of transports was complicated by, among other things, the free enterprise of officers like Colonel Theodore Roosevelt who seized space and supplies not assigned to their units. A week after the order for immediate sailing, the telegraph officer in the White House was wiring Tampa impatiently, "Has expedition started? Answer quickly for the President." And it was evening on June 22 before McKinley received word that American soldiers had set foot in Cuba.[15]

Despite his twenty-five telephone lines, the President had little choice thereafter but to leave events to his generals and admirals. For political reasons, he had attempted to give priority to the Philippine theater. So numerous were the forces he had assigned to Merritt, however, that several months' delay was predicted before they could all move across the Pacific. With Spain's Atlantic fleet bottled up, there were no longer conceivable dangers to America's coast. There was no place left for American troops to fight except in Cuba, and Shafter's landing had committed the President to send there every man and gun that could be used.

McKinley did remain mindful that he was commander in chief. According to Charles G. Dawes, the young Comptroller of the Treasury and one of the President's ardent admirers, "His strong hand was always on the helm of the War Department." When issues rose between the army and navy commanders in Cuba, he mediated. After the great sea battle of July 3, when the whole Spanish squadron sailed out and was destroyed, Shafter insisted that Sampson should steam into Santiago Bay and cannonade the fortifications that blocked his advance by land. Sampson took the position that the army should invest Santiago so that his men could first sweep the channel mouth of mines. When appealed to, the President ruled delphically, "General Shafter and Admiral Sampson should confer at once. . . . After the fullest exchange of views they should determine the time and manner of attack."[16]

McKinley did not actually give an order to Shafter until the Santiago campaign was nearly at an end. When the general began to telegraph pessimistically that his lines were stretched thin, that he might have to retreat, and that he himself was ill, the President directed Miles to go in person to Cuba. He did not place Miles in command, but he told him to "give such orders as might be required for the welfare and success of the army." While Miles was en route, McKinley learned that Shafter would hold his ground but wished to negotiate for the surrender of the city. It was then that the President sent an instruction to the general: "you will accept nothing but an unconditional surrender."[17]

Eventually McKinley did agree to conditions. Both Shafter and Miles warned him that fever cases were mounting and that evacuation of the jungles east of Santiago might become necessary for reasons of health. The President anxiously discussed this news with his cabinet. In the end he agreed that the Spanish troops could be sent back to Spain and even accompanied by their arms, and on this basis terms were made. Santiago and all of eastern Cuba were surrendered on July 14.[18]

But the war was not over. The commander in chief now faced the question of what to do next. Though the obvious course seemed either to march Shafter's troops west or else land other forces in the neighborhood of Havana, there was much to be said against further operations in Cuba. The rainy season had come, making bogs of the clearings and rivers of the roads. Fever had spread so widely that the sick had to be moved back to Florida by the shipload. A fresh campaign could well be costly, long, and barren of noteworthy victories. It might even stretch out and influence the November Congressional elections.

McKinley decided that he would exert pressure on Spain elsewhere. Miles had all along advocated the taking of Puerto Rico, and the President authorized him to take forces from Shafter's command and land on that theretofore peaceful island. More dramatically, McKinley decided to threaten Spain in her home waters. At the outset of the war, rumors of possible expeditions against the Canary Islands or the Spanish coasts had produced menacing editorials in the European press. That and the need to meet Spain's Atlantic fleet with superior force had induced the navy to put aside any such scheme, but it was revived even before the naval battle at Santiago. A small raiding squadron was formed from among Sampson's ships, and the Secretary of the Navy announced that it would sail for European waters. After the destruction of the Spanish fleet, when even right-wing German newspapers swung around and began to praise the American navy, this publicity grew louder. On July 12, the day that Santiago's surrender became virtually certain, orders went to Sampson to prepare all his armored vessels for movement to the Mediterranean. Knowing that Spain's cabinet was rocking and that her treasury was empty, the President obviously meant to make her yearn for peace.[19]

As it turned out, his preparations were needless. The Spanish cabinet had already agreed that Spain would have to come to terms as soon as the generals in Cuba consented. After the surrender of Santiago, the Captain General in Havana notified Madrid that he desired an armistice, and the Spanish Foreign Ministry began telegraphing Paris, asking the French government to approach the United States in Spain's behalf. The French minister in Washington brought this news to the President during the last week in July. Though the terms of an armistice proved hard to arrange, largely because McKinley insisted on leaving the Philippine question for later negotiation, the war effectively ended early in August.[20]

McKinley's duties as commander in chief were to last beyond the armistice. Judging Cuba at least temporarily unfit for self-rule, he installed a military governor who remained in control until 1902. In the Philippines he found Aguinaldo's forces ready to fight against American annexation, and through the remainder of his presidency he was countersigning orders dealing with the so-called Philippine insurrection. But McKinley managed to detach himself from these unpleasant happenings much as he also succeeded in dissociating himself from the "bully beef" scandals that swept over Alger and the War Department. In the latter case, he appointed investigating commissioners and left it to them to do nothing; in the former, he named generals and left it to them to do whatever needed doing. After August, 1898, McKinley made little use of his powers as commander in chief.

It is hard to appraise his four months of real service, but no harder than to judge any other aspect of his career. McKinley was an extraordinarily secretive man whose public utterances were oracular and whose private writings hardly exist. People who knew him well had vastly different opinions of him. Dawes, later nicknamed "Hell and Maria" and fully earning a reputation for tactlessness and toughness, kept a diary. During the crisis that led to the war, he wrote: "In the greatness of McKinley the safety of the situation lies. . . . When his mind is made up he is inflexible and immovable. . . . The Commander in Chief of the Army and Navy is cool and calm but in earnest. . . . He is making a magnificent fight for peace." In a famous comment of a similar date, Theodore Roosevelt said McKinley had "no more backbone than a chocolate eclair."[21] McKinley concealed his character to such an extent that neither of these divergent opinions can be contradicted.

Certainly, McKinley did not manage military affairs as well as either Polk or Lincoln. He kept Alger long after realizing that he was unreliable and probably incompetent. To command in the jungles of Cuba, he named Shafter, who weighed three hundred pounds and who had to be lifted onto a burro. The only clear qualifications possessed by either Shafter or Merritt were that, unlike Miles, both were too old and had lived too isolated lives to cherish political ambitions. Though McKinley had little to do with appointments in the navy, he refrained from intervening between Sampson and Commodore Schley, with the result that their dispute over relative credit for the Santiago victory became a *cause célèbre* after the war. If McKinley showed any genius as commander in chief, it was in the inventiveness with which he tried to avoid a campaign in Cuba, and even that has to be discovered by inference.

Nevertheless, McKinley had exercised supreme command in a war that deserves to be known better than mockingly as "the splendid little war." It was, after all, America's first limited offensive war. Despite the passions that existed, McKinley never contemplated a direct attack on Spain or any effort to reform or regenerate the Spanish nation. He rejected from the outset the possibility of making the war a crusade to revenge the *Maine,* and from beginning to finish his aim was to stop the war whenever the public could be satisfied.

But even more remarkable was the fact that its external purposes were altogether secondary. The conquest of the Philippine Islands came almost as an accident. The termination of Spanish rule in Cuba could plainly have been secured with a simple blockade. The real objects of the Philippine expedition and the Santiago campaign were internal rather than external. McKinley's aim was to check, subdue, or master an irrational movement in domestic opinion. The real enemy to him was not the Spaniard but the Democrat, and the true measure of his strategy came, not at Manila Bay or off Santiago or on San Juan hill, but in November, 1898, when the electorate gave his party majorities in both the House and Senate and in November, 1900, when he was re-elected by nearly 900,000 votes.

VI

WILSON

(1917–1918)

ERNEST R. MAY

W HEN WOODROW WILSON wrote criticizing the etching that represented him in military uniform, he not only commented that the framers of the Constitution had meant the president to be a civilian, he also asserted, "the armed forces of the country must be the instruments of the authority by which policy [is] determined. . . . I do not think this is a mere formal scruple on my part. I believe it goes to the root of things."

In this letter Wilson showed that he held a peculiar notion of the office of commander in chief. He did not think of himself, in Hamilton's *Federalist* phrase, as the "first General and admiral of the Confederacy." On the contrary, viewing the armed forces as something separate from, almost alien to, civil authority, he tried not to mix himself in their affairs. He believed that the president should control but not command.

His attitude came in part from experience. Sixty years old in

1917, he had grown up in Georgia during the Civil War. Lee was a boyhood hero, and two of his uncles had been Confederate generals, but when looking back he remembered only the horror—the wounded hospitalized in his father's church, the gaunt, bedraggled Union prisoners kept in the churchyard. He recalled the struggle, as he wrote in the *Atlantic Monthly* in January, 1901, as "a dark chapter of history." As an active, popular professor of political science at Princeton, he must have had to comment on the brief Spanish war, but what he said or thought is lost. And in his writings, *Congressional Government, The State,* and even *Division and Reunion, 1829–1889,* a volume that covered the Civil War, he mentioned military affairs only in passing and as if he shrank from discussing them.

As president he preserved this aloofness. The armed forces had developed a planning bureaucracy in hope of not repeating the blunders and improvisations of 1898. The navy had a General Board, the army a General Staff, and the two services a Joint Board of the Army and Navy. In 1913, when Japan seemed to threaten war over maltreatment of Japanese in California, Wilson obtained advice from these bodies. The Joint Board recommended certain fleet movements to safeguard the Philippines. The President discussed these proposals with his cabinet but then politely turned them down. He said to the Secretary of the Navy, "The Joint Board has of course presented the military aspect of the situation as it sees it and it may be right, but we are considering this matter with another light, on the diplomatic side, and must determine the policy." When the Board protested and asked that the decision be reconsidered, Wilson's long jaw tautened. He spoke icily to the Navy Secretary: "When a policy has been settled by the Administration and when it is communicated to the Joint Board, they have no right to be trying to force a different course and I wish you would say to them that if this should occur again, there will be no General or Joint Boards. They will be abolished."[1]

Nevertheless, Wilson's conception of "policy" had a hidden corollary. It implied that there was some duty or function, however inferior, belonging exclusively to men in uniform. He was rigid in forbidding military interference with policy. Even when involvement in the great European war had become distinctly possible, he could not read in a newspaper that the army was planning possible campaigns against Germany without feeling outraged. He ordered such activities stopped.[2] But he thought it equally clear that if military men should not involve themselves in policy, neither should policy-makers meddle in military affairs. When he decided to use force against Mexico in 1914, he let the navy make its plans and carry them out until he changed his policy and elected to negotiate a settlement. Similarly, in 1916, when he authorized pursuit and punishment of Pancho Villa's raiders, he left it to the army to decide what should be done. He later felt that he might have been mistaken in not ordering the punitive expedition back before it penetrated three hundred miles into Mexico, but he was not even sure of that, and he did not interfere until he had again changed his policy and decided to make peace.[3] Even before April, 1917, when the United States declared war on Germany, Wilson had given evidence that he would apply a new and distinctive definition of the command-in-chief.

At the very beginning of the war, he selected one general and gave him as much power as possible. He named John J. Pershing to captain the American Expeditionary Force, and he did not make Pershing responsible to the chief of staff or any other officer in Washington. Indeed, when a new chief of staff was to be chosen early in 1918, Wilson picked an officer from the A.E.F. staff whom Pershing recommended. It is true that Pershing did not receive authority to decide where American forces should fight. Wilson did not believe that the United States had any choice. As the Secretary of War stated to a Congressional committee in 1918, "It was not a thing for us to decide where our theater of war should be. The theater of war was France. . . . It was not for us to decide whether we would have the maneuvering of large bodies of troops in the open. There lay the antagonists on opposite sides of 'no man's land' in the trenches at a death-grapple with one another."[4] But the directive given Pershing empowered him to decide when, where, and how troops were to be used in France: "in general you are vested with all necessary authority to carry on the war vigorously . . . and toward a victorious conclusion." The Secretary of War told him that his only orders were "one to go to France and the other to come home, but that in the meantime his authority in France would be supreme."[5]

Wilson did not find it so easy to delegate his responsibility as commander in chief of the navy. The Navy Department was better organized, more faction-ridden, and hence less flexible than the War Department. Though Admiral William S. Sims, the Commander of United States Naval Forces Operating in European Waters, was determined, combative, and articulate, he was subordinate to two officers in Washington, neither of whom felt disposed to give him a free hand. Admiral Henry T. Mayo jealously guarded his authority as Commander in Chief of the Fleet; Admiral William S. Benson, the Chief of Naval Operations, regarded Sims as an upstart, an Anglophile, even an intellectual. Neither the irrepressible Franklin D. Roosevelt, who was Assistant Secretary, nor the mild, affable, somewhat wooly-minded Secretary, Josephus Daniels, would or could resolve disputes within the hive over which they presided. Since Sims represented the United States in Allied naval councils, he could in any case circumvent his superiors and have his recommendations pressed by the British Prime Minister or the American ambassador in London, both of whom communicated directly with the President. As long as Wilson's naval forces were divided between overlapping commands, Sims' in London and the Navy Department's in Washington, differences between the two had to be resolved by the commander in chief.

Wilson had to decide between alternate methods of combatting the German submarine threat. He could not doubt that the issue was critical. Both Sims and Ambassador Walter Hines Page reported from London that the rate of sinkings jeopardized Britain's ability to continue the war. But Sims called for convoying merchantmen with all available naval craft, while experts in the Navy Department criticized convoys as inefficient, and Benson insisted that some ships should be kept at hand to protect the coasts and the Caribbean against raids. One bureau in the Department suggested that the United States might take the offensive, lay barrages of mines in the Channel and North Sea, and thus prevent submarines from coming out into the Atlantic. Detailed memoranda, defending each of these various views, found their way to the President's desk.

Wilson felt irritated not only because his naval advisers disagreed but also because no one of them offered a compelling and decidedly preferable alternative. If convoys had so much merit as Sims said, Wilson could not understand why the British Admiralty had failed to employ them. Neither, however, could he sympathize with the caution and conservatism of Admiral Benson. He was attracted by the notion of mine barrages, and he thought at least fitfully of actually taking on responsibility as "first . . . admiral of the Confederacy" and imposing some strategy of his own. Speaking to the officers of the battleship *Pennsylvania* in August, 1917, he remarked, "We are hunting hornets all over the farm and letting the nest alone." He also said musingly, "Nobody ever before conducted a war like this and therefore nobody can pretend to be a professional in a war like this. . . . We have got to throw tradition to the wind."[6]

He did not, however, give in to this vagrant impulse. Instead he adhered to an opposite view which he had voiced earlier in a different context when saying, "I feel that I have no choice . . . but to follow experts in a war of experts." Sims advised that the mine-barrage scheme was "wholly impracticable" and insisted eloquently on convoys as the only answer to the U-boat. Since Benson and officers in the Navy Department criticized this dictum without offering other positive alternatives, Wilson eventually satisfied himself that Sims' was the bold, original, and dashing course. He cabled personally to the admiral, "I do not see how the necessary military supplies and supplies of food and fuel oil are to be delivered at British ports in any other way than under convoy." Though he did not direct that all fighting ships be employed in this service, he did make it plain to Benson, Mayo, Roosevelt, and Daniels that he thought no mission more important than moving troops and supplies across the Atlantic. He even ruled in favor of suspending capital ship construction in order to allow more building of escort vessels.[7]

Wilson not only decided in favor of concentrating on the war against the U-boat, he also decided in favor of Sims as against

Benson, Mayo, or the Navy Department. Officers in Washington had to fret away at minor chores while the admiral in London directed the major naval operations of the war. Wilson did not split Sims's command, and so long as Sims did not differ with the Allied Naval Council there were no real issues to be brought before the commander in chief. As with the army, so with the navy; the President divested himself of his uniform and delegated command to one officer.

Inevitably, however, this simple transfer of responsibility failed to work. Though Sims's cordial relations with the Allies meant that no major naval questions came back for Wilson's decision, the clash of armies on the western front brought up issues which could not be crammed into separate boxes labelled "policy" and "command." These issues could be settled, if at all, only by the highest authority, the president and commander in chief.

During the first months of America's participation in the war, Pershing could make nearly all the decisions. He fixed the Expeditionary Force's goal—a million men in France by May, 1918. He and his staff decided what portion of the western front should become America's responsibility, examining the question, as a staff paper stated, "not only from the standpoint of strategy but including political considerations." Wilson did not feel it necessary to talk with the Chief of Staff or discuss military questions with the Secretary of War. He did not even study the war maps posted in the cabinet room of the White House.[8]

In the autumn of 1917 this situation changed. There arose a demand for reconsideration of the whole pattern of command and warfare on the western front. For three years soldiers in separate British and French sectors had battered bloodily and uselessly against the enemy's lines, sometimes paying hideous prices for the gain or loss of a few acres of ground. Feelings ranging from despair to frustrated rage coursed through the trenches and crept into assemblies, councils, and cabinets. David Lloyd George, the volatile, imaginative Welshman who had become Prime Minister of Britain at the end of 1916, began to ask if the strategy of frontal assault was wise, if it would not be possible to strike the enemy in what one of his distinguished successors would have called the "soft underbelly." He contended that, at the very least, it was imperative to integrate the resources and plans of the various Allies, and his questions could not be answered by Pershing, if only because they were raised by a head of government.

Wilson did not know what reply to make. When considering the convoy issue, he had become convinced that Allied strategists, at least those of the British and French admiralties, lacked imagination and courage. He was moved, even horrified, by the seeming futility of the trench war. Yet he hesitated to embroil himself in disputes among the European Allies or to cross the line he had drawn between his responsibility and that of Pershing. He discussed these doubts with his closest friend and adviser, Colonel Edward M. House, and House subsequently noted in his diary, "The President thought he could not go much further toward meeting Lloyd George's wishes than to express a feeling that something different should be done in the conduct of the war than had been done."[9]

Wilson was eventually persuaded to take a hand. A long personal letter came to him from Lloyd George, making a powerful case against existing strategy and command arrangements, cautioning that decisions by the Allies would seriously affect American forces in France, hinting that the President's fresh and vigorous voice might prove controlling, and concluding with a buttery appeal to Wilson's vanity, an expression of appreciation for speeches that were "a profound and masterly exposition of the Allied cause" and that had "given to the bruised and battered peoples of Europe fresh courage to endure and fresh hope that with all their sufferings they are helping to bring into being a world in which freedom and democracy will be secure."[10] At once exhorted, warned, tempted, and flattered, Wilson decided that in the new inter-Allied conference for which Lloyd George was calling he woud be represented.

And he would not be represented by Pershing. The conferees were to be the heads of the Allied governments and their chiefs of staff. Though Wilson could not attend himself, he asked House to go. The Colonel was not a military man; his commission and title had been given him by a Governor of Texas whom he had helped to elect. He was, however, an experienced negotiator who had earlier acted for Wilson in trying to arrange a compromise peace and who already knew most of the Allied leaders. He would sit as the President's alter ego, and with him would be the retiring Chief of Staff of the Army, General Tasker H. Bliss. The two would represent Wilson not only as president but also as commander in chief.

The conferees assembled in the midst of disaster. Lenin, Trotsky, and the Bolsheviks had become masters of the Petrograd Soviet. Within days they were to seize the government and appeal to the Central Powers for terms. Almost simultaneously, a German and Austrian force struck the Italian line around Caporetto in northeastern Italy, killing, wounding, or capturing 600,000 men. Lloyd George and the French Premier, Paul Painlevé, hastily patched together a plan for unifying control of Allied forces. There was to be a Supreme War Council composed of heads of governments, meeting irregularly; there was also to be a Permanent Committee of Military Advisers sitting continuously in Paris. House cabled that the Italian Premier accepted this scheme and that all three Allied governments believed it "imperative that we should be represented in it because of the moral effect that it will have here." House recommended that the United States join the military committee but not commit itself to continuous participation in the civilian Council, and Wilson quickly accepted his advice. After conferring with the Secretary of War, he ordered that Bliss remain in Europe.[11] As a result, there were thereafter two generals instead of one acting for the commander in chief.

Owing largely to Bliss's modesty and tact, this arrangement did not mean that Wilson immediately had to resume his military functions. Fearing that any disagreements between himself and Pershing would be exploited by the Allies, Bliss took the position that it was his duty to back up the A.E.F. commander. The few differences that did arise were composed in face-to-face meetings and not referred to Washington. The fact of having two generals in the same theater, holding overlapping jobs, did not in itself compel the President to make military decisions.

What did force Wilson to act as commander in chief was the overlap between Pershing's authority and that of the new international body which the conference had created. Inevitably the issue of how Pershing's forces should be used came before the Permanent Military Representatives. The American Expeditionary Force plan called for the build-up in France of an American army co-equal with the British and French armies. But the creation of this force was not simply a matter of moving soldiers to Europe. The independent army required artillery and transport, medical and other services; port facilities for it had to be built and manned; so did rail lines and roads from the French coast to the front. The army's rate of growth depended on transport, the creation of barracks and other facilities in the United States, and on the training of troops, line officers, and especially staff officers. The result was that the A.E.F. had companies, battalions, regiments, brigades, and divisions long before it had the equipment or command structure to make use of them. British and French forces meanwhile dwindled in numbers and quality. Britain was calling up youths of eighteen and men of forty and still finding insufficient replacements. As soon as numbers of American soldiers arrived, the Allied governments naturally began to suggest that they be put into the line temporarily in British or French service.

Before the creation of the Supreme War Council, Wilson had been able to dodge these demands. When the British and French premiers appealed to him directly, he did nothing but advise Pershing of their representations. "The President," Pershing was told, ". . . desires you to have full authority to use the forces at your command as you deem wise." Even when the Allies suggested that American troops at least be camped near the junction of the British and French sectors in order to be available to either in case of emergency, the general was given no directive. "This suggestion," he was informed, "is not pressed beyond whatever merit it has in your judgment, the President's sole purpose being to acquaint you with the representations made here and to authorize you to act with entire freedom in making the best disposition and use of your forces possible to accomplish the main purposes in view."[12] When Pershing ruled against any amalgamation, Wilson did not question him.

After the creation of the Supreme War Council, however,

Wilson had to reconsider the problem. French President Raymond Poincaré proposed that the location and use of idle American forces be debated by the Permanent Military Representatives. Wilson had endorsed the creation of this committee. Indeed, he had cabled, "we not only accede to the plan for a single war council but insist on it."[13] Faced with Poincaré's request, he could only agree. He replied, "The judgment of the Council . . . will, I need hardly assure you, be conclusively influential with the Government of the United States. Our only desire is to do the best thing that can be done with our armed forces, and we are willing to commit ourselves to the general counsel of those with whom we have the honor to cooperate in this great enterprise of liberty."[14]

Even so, Wilson was not obliged immediately to override any decision of Pershing's. In the first place, Bliss prevented the committee from coming to a head-on clash with the American general. In the second place, though Pershing was an autocrat, he was a prudent autocrat. A visitor to his headquarters noted, "John Pershing, like Abraham Lincoln, recognizes no superior on the face of the earth."[15] But he had scrambled his way to four-star rank partly by anticipating the desires of those who made out his promotion recommendations, and he was shrewd enough to realize that Wilson was commander in chief and could act if he were forced to. Pershing endeavored to reach a compromise with the Allies.

Despite reservations and suspicions, shared in higher degree by his staff, he agreed that American units might train with French commands. When massed German forces struck in the Somme region in March, 1918, and threatened to slice through at the point where the British and French sectors joined, Pershing went even farther. He offered his troops for any emergency service requested by the Allies. He entered no protest when the Supreme War Council resolved that the United States should concentrate on bringing over infantry and machine-gun units. He thus agreed not only to let American troops serve under Allied commands but also to defer the formation of an integral, independent American army.

Since these decisions prevented open conflict between Pershing and the Permanent Military Representatives, Wilson was not called upon to resolve disputes between commanders. He did have reservations about the wisdom of amalgamation. As he explained to Sir William Wiseman, he feared criticism at home if it seemed that America could not supply officers for her own men. He knew, moreover, that his own Secretary of War and General Staff were rigidly insistent on a separate army. Nevertheless, as he also said to Wiseman, he would risk almost any criticism in order to back Pershing's judgment.[16] Not only did he endorse the general's arrangements with the French and the Supreme War Council resolution, but he also approved understandings between Pershing and the British.

In order to get his forces to Europe faster, the general had agreed that if six American divisions were brought over in British transports, they could serve temporarily with the British army. During the crisis brought on by the German offensive, he further agreed that Britain could have the use of any American regiments or battalions she brought over in April, May, or June. With some reluctance the President consented to all these arrangements, commenting merely that the Allies should understand there was no "commitment from which the United States Government is not free to depart when exigencies no longer require it."[17] Owing to Pershing's compromises with the Allies, the existence of a rudimentary dual command did not compel

Wilson to make military decisions. It merely forced him to review those of the commander to whom he had delegated his powers.

Once inter-Allied coordination gave way to real unified command, the President was obliged to abandon his policy of simply backing up Pershing. At the time of the Supreme War Council's creation, Wilson had felt that the Allies should perhaps go farther. Bliss, Secretary of War Baker, and even Pershing came to feel this more and more strongly. Bliss recommended "unified control, even unified command in the last resort," and urged the President to demand it.[18] Though Wilson did not do so, he allowed Bliss and others increasing freedom to press it on their own. When the smashing German offensive in the spring of 1918 shook Allied generals and politicians and stampeded them into naming a supreme commander for the western front, Wilson quickly gave his approval. As a result, though Pershing still held the President's commission, so now did another general, the new supreme commander, Ferdinand Foch. The inter-Allied agreement signed at Beauvais on April 3, 1918, stipulated that each national commander should have the right of appeal to his government, and differences between Foch and Pershing could be resolved only by Wilson.[19] The effect of the new arrangement was to put before the President some of the very issues he had originally set off as business for the military and not for the policy maker.

One such issue was the tortured problem of amalgamation, for Foch at once protested that the agreement between Pershing and the British limited his ability to use all Allied forces according to his own estimate of sector requirements. He and Georges Clemenceau, the tough, crusty septuagenarian who had recently become French Premier, demanded that the

Anglo-American agreement be abrogated and that American troops be available for service in French as well as British formations. Pershing sought a new compromise, proposing that, insofar as consistent with the rapid creation of an independent American army, the first six divisions brought over by the British serve under British command while the rest be available for disposition as Foch saw fit. Reporting to Washington that the issue had aroused "rather warm discussion" in the Supreme War Council, Pershing offered assurance that under his plan, the "question is now settled definitely."[20]

In fact, however, neither Foch nor the French and British governments found Pershing's formula satisfactory. The general described it as the basis for an understanding which produced "good feeling and satisfaction all around," and Wilson applauded it. "I agree with you," he wrote Secretary of War Baker, "in thinking the agreement entirely satisfactory and as having been arrived at by just the right sort of conference in the right way."[21] But Wilson soon learned through diplomatic channels of the real sentiments of Foch and the Allies, and he must have felt grievously disturbed. He sympathized with Pershing on this particular issue; he trusted him; he had relied upon him to shoulder responsibility for military decisions. On the other hand, he had endorsed the principle of unity of command and approved the nomination of Foch. If he refused to support the supreme commander against his own general, he would be doing precisely what he condemned the Allies for doing—letting national jealousies and separate interests take precedence over common progress toward victory. Wilson faced an issue of command which only he, as commander in chief, could resolve.

The President resolved his dilemma by making a wholesale

transfer of authority to Foch. He authorized the Secretary of War to notify Pershing tactfully that Foch would renew discussion of the troop-use question, "and the President hopes you will approach any such interviews as sympathetically as possible."[22] Wilson could not without offense have made it clearer that the power of command had been shifted to the French Marshal. Perhaps to make assurance doubly sure, he shortly downgraded Pershing. Peyton C. March, the general who had been brought from A.E.F. headquarters, was allowed to publish an order announcing that he, as chief of staff, held "rank and precedence" over all other officers in the army.[23] Pershing was thus told that he was subject to orders from the General Staff, and Wilson, through the General Staff, told him to obey Foch.

After this shift the President was once again free. Pershing could have battled Foch, but he was prudent enough not to do so. Though he kept as much independence as possible, he did not take issue with the French general until the very last days of fighting, and the war was over before Foch ever had to appeal again to Wilson. The delegation of authority from the President to the generalissimo was almost as extensive as the earlier delegation to Pershing. Bliss observed that his government always asked, "Have you consulted General Foch? Does he agree with you? Does he ask our assistance in gaining approval of this measure?" When it was proposed that a small Allied force should be landed at Murmansk, Wilson saw little military justification for the move and viewed it as politically dubious. So did the majority of his advisers in Washington, including March and the General Staff. Yet when Foch expressed approval, Wilson readily accepted his judgment.[24]

Though Wilson could escape most responsibilities by shifting authority from Pershing to Foch, he could not entirely avoid the issue that Lloyd George had raised, the question of whether the Allies should seek some theater other than France. The Caporetto disaster had forestalled debate in 1917. The outcome of the Russian Revolution, the beginning of peace negotiations between the Bolsheviks and the Germans, reopened it. Generals and politicians on both sides of the Channel cast about for some means of re-creating a second front, of somehow preventing the enemy from concentrating all his power in the west. The French General Staff became entranced with the notion of landings in Siberia. Such a move, they reasoned, would block the transfer of materiel and tie down German troops in Russia. The project won quick support in England from those who despaired of triumph in the trenches and also from those whose motto was that the French were always right. Japan's offer to provide the necessary forces swept away the possible argument that troops were not available for diversion. Foch recommended the project, and the French and British cabinets approved and put the proposition to Wilson.[25]

Wilson could not simply follow Foch's judgment in this case. He had not endorsed the landing at Murmansk until assured that Russian authorities would welcome it. Though he had little sympathy for the Bolsheviks, he feared that landings in Siberia might be regarded as a hostile invasion not only by them but also by the Russian people. He suspected the Allies of wanting to use forces in Siberia to shore up one or another of the reactionary counter-revolutionary movements. Having recently spatted with the Japanese over their encroachments on Chinese sovereignty, he also had some doubts about letting them loose on Russian territory. For these political reasons, he questioned the wisdom of Foch's proposal. His General Staff also opposed it, but on the ground that it would require a diversion of American troops and American shipping. The President was thus put in the position not simply of deciding whether to override Foch on an issue of policy but whether, in effect, to support his own military people against the generalissimo.

Wilson eventually gave in, agreeing to a small Allied expedition which would include an American contingent. He was influenced by reports of Bolshevik collaboration with the Germans. He was also affected by evidence of the intensity of Allied feeling. House, who had originally opposed the project, warned him that continued intransigence might wreck inter-Allied unity. Perhaps fearing that Japan might act alone, he concluded that the prudent course was to cooperate with her and thus possibly restrain her. But one factor in his thinking, however minor, must have been recognition that if he vetoed one of Foch's projects, he would risk being drawn into debate on military issues. He might have to act as commander in chief, and he did not want to do so.

After having agreed to the Siberian expedition, he could revert to the position he had taken earlier. Bliss warned him that various diversionary operations were likely to be proposed: some Englishmen would suggest a more intensive effort in Macedonia; others would propose action in the Middle East, the reinforcement of partisan groups in Armenia and the Caucasus, or the augmentation of forces at Archangel and Murmansk. Wilson moved to forestall appeals to the White House. He addressed a long *aide mémoire* to the Supreme War Council, explaining that the United States could not, "so long as the military situation on the western front remains critical, consent to break or slacken the force of its present efforts by diverting any part of its military forces to other points or objectives. . . . At the same time the Government of the United States wishes to say with the utmost cordiality and good will that none of the conclusions here stated is meant to wear the least color of criticism of what the other governments associated against Germany may think it wise to undertake. It wishes in no way to embarrass them in their choice of policy."[26]

The President's position seemed that of a "westerner," as those favoring concentration on the western front were called. His General Staff was entirely of this persuasion; so was Pershing; so, on the whole, was Foch. But Wilson's stand differed from theirs and from that of other "westerners" in that he did not insist on the concentration of all Allied strength in France. He not only entered no objection to the development of other theaters by the Allies; he almost invited it. His own position was simply that the United States would concentrate her forces in France and that he did not want to be bothered by questions of theater priority. Wilson was to some extent relying on and backing up the judgment of his professional military chiefs, but he was also deliberately evading the necessity for making military decisions.

During the whole year and a half that the United States was at war, Wilson endeavored to avoid acting as commander in chief. Though his attitude grew in part from lack of interest in and ignorance of military affairs, there were other and probably more important reasons for it. Unlike his predecessors, Wilson had to fight a coalition war. Unlike his successors, Roosevelt and Truman, he was not in a position to control his allies. The United States was not expected to have an army in Europe equal to the French and British armies until 1919. Though America's potential influence was not to be measured entirely in terms of relative troop strength, Wilson's advisers would not say until late summer, 1918, that the voice of the United States could control an inter-Allied council on strategy. Earlier, the President could reasonably have feared that, while his personal intervention in a military debate might prove effective, the result might well be subsequent demands from the Allies for concessions to their views. By abstaining from interference with the generals in France, by pushing off responsibility, Wilson minimized American involvement in and commitment to the alliance.

And this deliberate object was constantly in Wilson's mind. While the United States was still neutral, he had made it clear, in his peace note and in his "Peace without Victory" address, that his aims and aspirations were not the same as those of the Allies. After the declaration of war, he refused the title of ally; he insisted that America was merely an associated power. In 1917, he wrote House, "England and France *have not the same views with regard to peace that we have by any means*. When the war is over we can force them to our way of thinking, because by that time they will, among other things, be financially in our hands; but we cannot force them now."[27]

Unlike Polk, McKinley, and Truman later, Wilson was not seeking the conquest or liberation of any given territory. He did not care particularly what real estate came into Allied possession. Unlike Lincoln and Franklin Roosevelt, he was not even seeking the destruction of his enemy's power. Though he invoked "force to the utmost, force without stint or limit," he refused to wage anything like total war. He wrote, for example, "I desire no sort of participation by the Air Service of the United States in a plan . . . which has as its object promiscuous bombing upon industry, commerce, or populations in enemy countries disassociated from obvious military needs to be served by such action."[28] When the Germans suggested armistice negotiations, he agreed despite strong evidence that both the Allies and the American public wanted the war continued until complete victory had been achieved.[29] From the first day of the war to the last, all that Wilson sought was a peace that could be secured by a League of Nations, a peace that would make the world safe for democracy.

He refused to act as commander in chief because to do so would have jeopardized this aim. Any attempt to steer Allied strategy would almost certainly have led to political complications. Wilson felt strongly that "indefinite trench warfare" should not go on. In a memorandum probably drafted in November, 1917, he asked himself, "Is the Mediterranean impracticable?"[30] But had he ever advocated a stronger effort in Italy, the Balkans, or Russia, he would undoubtedly have been asked to accept formulas for the postwar distribution of conquered territory. Had he, consistent with his "western" *aide mémoire* of 1918, asked for greater concentration in France or urged abandonment of the campaigns in Macedonia and the Middle East, he would have been obliged to consider Allied proposals that he guarantee their postwar interests in these regions. By allowing such questions to be dealt with almost entirely by generals possessing his delegated powers, he evaded requests for such political commitments. In the meantime, as he foresaw, the potential influence of the United States grew. When the armistice was negotiated, he could and did demand acceptance of his principles, his conditions for peace, not only by the enemy but by the Allies as well. He evaded duty as commander in chief in order to do his larger duty as president of the United States.

VII

F. D. R.

(1941–1945)

WILLIAM R. EMERSON

To claim the powers of American commander in chief is one thing; to wield them is another. Constitutionally and administratively the office is merely a title, and different presidents have interpreted it and used it in different ways, dependent upon their personalities and their circumstances. No war president, however, has construed his powers more broadly or wielded them more vigorously than Franklin Roosevelt during World War II.

In the growing world crisis of the late 1930's, he asserted these powers early. In July, 1939, conscious of the approach of war and jealous as always of his authority, Roosevelt, invoking a rarely used presidential power, issued a Military Order which transferred the Joint Army-Navy Board, the Joint Army-Navy Munitions Board, and several other military procurement agencies from the service departments into the newly-established Executive Office of the President.[1] The army Chief of Staff and the Chief of Naval Operations, who, with certain of their advisers, made up the Joint Board, were to work under the "direction and supervision" of the commander in chief, as they continued later to do when reconstituted as the Joint Chiefs of Staff. At the same time the Munitions Board and other procurement agencies were also placed under the direct control of the President, acting in this instance through the Assistant Secretary of War, Louis Johnson. Just as the Joint Board became in 1939 the President's principal agent in the field of strategy, the Assistant Secretary of War, working through the Joint Munitions Board, became the deputy for home-front mobilization, to a certain degree independent of his own superior, the Secretary of War. The teeming war emergency agencies which later inherited and amplified the powers of the Joint Munitions Board were in their turn to enjoy the same close relationship with the President.[2]

The immediate results of this new arrangement were modest but significant. The principal war agencies in both the strategic and the production fields were clearly established as presidential, not departmental, agencies. At the same time the Joint Board, while preserving its old form and organization, altered its nature. Before 1939 it had functioned primarily as an interdepartmental consultative agency, advisory to the service secretaries and concerned in large part with adjudicating disagreements over matters of joint interest to the War and Navy departments. The Military Order of 1939 had the effect of raising the Joint Board above the departmental level. By placing the chiefs in a special relationship to the President, it made them in some way independent of their immediate civilian superiors. In their new circumstances, the chiefs extended the range and scope of their interests. Increasingly after 1939 the

Joint Board, under the control of the President, concerned itself with questions of national rather than service strategy. In pre-war studies it produced basic plans that were to have great influence later.[3]

By this little-noticed Military Order of 1939, Franklin Roosevelt laid the institutional foundations of his powers as commander in chief. The new arrangements were not a model of administrative symmetry. Like so many of Roosevelt's arrangements, they were, in Secretary Stimson's words, "inherently disorderly." In particular the service secretaries were placed in an anomalous position; they retained control over, and responsibility for, their departments but *not* their military chieftains, who, with their advisers, operated directly beneath the President. If the service secretaries were indeed the principal agents of civilian control over the military, it would seem that in strategic matters the chiefs, as Admiral Leahy was to remark at the end of the war, were "under no civilian control whatever," apart, of course, from that exercised by the President himself.

Both before and after our entry into war, the secretaries were little consulted in strategic questions, and during the war they were never included on the regular distribution lists for Joint Chiefs of Staff papers despite the fact that the Joint Chiefs continually dealt with questions for which the secretaries were legally responsible.

Similarly the new organization had the unfortunate effect of stultifying attempts at co-ordination *between* departments. Under the new dispensation, the Standing Liaison Committee of the War, Navy, and State departments, set up in 1938 at Secretary Hull's instance to co-ordinate foreign and military policies, lost much of its importance. As the prewar crisis deepened, the Joint Board, under Roosevelt's supervision, stepped up its planning activities and, in effect, shouldered aside the SLC. Though the latter agency did not altogether cease to function, its improvised and somewhat informal efforts had little effect on events and policies.[4]

Meanwhile, basic military procurement and production planning, although placed under authority of the Assistant Secretary of War, was carried out—separately—within the departments. Both before and during the war, decisions in this sphere in effect were initiated within the departments, not by the Joint Chiefs as such, and were decided in the Executive Office of the President. In its origins, this arrangement appears to have been a Rooseveltian device to "get around" his isolationist Secretary of War, Harry Woodring. Its results were lasting, for it had the effect, unforeseen in 1939 and perhaps never clearly appreciated during World War II, of divorcing production from strategy—or, at any rate, from joint strategy.[5]

All this was somewhat ramshackle, though very characteristic of Roosevelt's administrative penchant. "Roosevelt's normal way of organizing a department," one authority has observed, "was to split it right down the middle."[6] Within his cabinet and within his administration generally, he permitted and encouraged a duplication of effort, an overlapping of authorities, and a development of personal antagonisms amounting in some cases almost to civil wars. Whatever his motives, the effect was to increase, and at the same time often to disguise, his own authority. The Military Order of 1939 had, on the whole, that effect. As concerned foreign policy, strategy, and military procurement, it left Roosevelt the sole co-ordinating link between the various subordinate agencies in these fields. Co-ordination as a consequence was not very effective.

Despite these flaws, the new arrangements were not without merit. For one thing, they provided that personal relationship so congenial to Roosevelt's temperament and his administrative methods. They greatly magnified the power and independence of the military chiefs. Finally, and not least important, through its very dispersion of subordinate authority, the Military Order of 1939 gave the President powers of decision in the military field which were real and not merely apparent, for in many areas of military concern, he, the Commander in Chief, alone *could* decide.

In this respect, the Military Order of 1939 set the pattern for American civil-military relations in World War II. Jealous of his powers and deeply sensitive to the swirling political tides within Washington and the country, Roosevelt was ever unwilling to share his authority. He meant to exercise to the full his powers as commander in chief.

From the very beginning of the American rearmament program, the President had shown that his independence and self-confidence were no less marked in strategic than in other matters. In November, 1938, Roosevelt, alarmed by the Munich crisis, summoned his principal military advisers to a White House conference on rearmament.

At this conference the President as usual did most of the talking. His objectives were broad and startling: production of 10,000 military aircraft by 1940, establishment of plant capacity for producing 10,000 planes annually—and nothing less! This "program" clashed with considered military opinion on rearmament. The impetus for it came from diplomatic rather than military considerations. Roosevelt knew that an immediate attack on the United States was unlikely. Conscious, too, of the deep isolationism that still gripped the country, he knew that

American armed forces could not be committed to rescue victims of aggression. Realistically, therefore, his duty was not to arm his own country but to alert Hitler to America's tremendous resources and to help rearm the British and French in case the German Chancellor failed to heed this warning. As General Henry H. Arnold later recalled, the President did not seem to want an American air force at all, feeling that new barracks in Wyoming "would not scare Hitler"; what he wanted was "airplanes—now—and lots of them."[7]

Whatever the President's aims, he was persistent. He brushed aside General Staff requests for a balanced military force and ignored General Marshall's sharp warning that his plans were "contrary to the considered judgment" of his military advisers. The presidential decision was accepted, under protest. General Marshall and the War Department staff sought from 1938 to meliorate the effects of the President's desire to concentrate exclusively on aircraft production and in the end managed to win considerable concessions. But if Roosevelt gave ground to his professional advisers, his own view of rearmament needs prevailed from the start. The vital impulse came from the President. As the official historian of the Chief of Staff's office has noted,

> . . . this Presidential proposal must be regarded as far transcending—in its importance as an impulse to actual acquisition of weapons—the recommendations of the War Department officials, civilian and military, which antedated the November 1938 meeting. . . . The summaries of Army needs . . . were placed in the President's hands, and ultimately they would prove useful. But they do not appear to have had any immediate result.[8]

These events of November, 1938, set a long-persisting pattern

in the President's relations with the military. Like many of his
interventions in military affairs, Roosevelt's interest in airplanes
appeared somewhat off-hand; General Marshall's biographer
says that Marshall, deeply angered, felt the President was
"acting irresponsibly" and had "surrendered to a momentary
whim."[9] In such matters—as was most notably the case in
Roosevelt's casual announcement of the unconditional surrender formula at Casablanca—the President's manner often
disguised his purposes. Rightly or wrongly, he was convinced
that aircraft held the key to the diplomatic situation in Europe
and the depth of his belief was shown by his willingness in
1939 and 1940 to buck isolationist sentiment on this point
almost alone.

"Planes—now—and lots of them" remained his constant
theme. He repeated it in his 1939 budget address and sought
consistently in the last months of European peace and later,
during the period of "phony war," to make American aircraft
production facilities available to England and France. The
crisis of 1940 merely strengthened his conviction. On May 16,
1940, amid the Allied disasters in Flanders, Roosevelt in a
characteristic gesture called for an annual aircraft production
of 50,000, a figure which he had arrived at on his own calcula-
tion and—apparently—without consultation of, or advance
notice to, the Secretary of War or responsible officers in the
War Department.

These officers remained critical. The President's new proposal
was received with some skepticism in a War Department
already overburdened with what one officer ruefully called
"the mass production of programs."[10] As was almost always the
case, military planners were able to trim the President's estimates, and they even succeeded in winning his approval for

limited increases in ground forces and their munitions and equipment. But in 1940, as in 1938, Roosevelt paid little regard to those who advised building balanced forces. His primary, if not his sole, concern was maximum production of aircraft.

The President's policies and predilections in this sphere are open to serious criticism. Great efforts—and even greater publicity—were devoted to American rearmament. Looking back at the period in afterlight, it is doubtful if these efforts during the years 1938–1940 contributed in any considerable degree to military strength; as one student of American war production has observed, "to hindsight, the story of the things left undone during the lost year of 1939–1940 is unbelievable."[11]

But, rightly or wrongly, military strength was not Roosevelt's sole—or even his major—aim at the time. From the beginning of the rearmament program, Roosevelt sought not rearmament but the appearance of rearmament. He was concerned with the "show-window," not the "stockroom." If this military policy was ambiguous, so, too, were the situations which the President faced in the prewar period, for beneath American rearmament and the gradual veer of American policy away from isolationism lay a major question which was never finally answered until the day of Pearl Harbor. Was American rearmament a *preparation for,* or an *alternative to,* war? Lesser figures on the crowded national scene had their own very various views in the matter. Roosevelt to the bitter end was never willing completely to abandon the latter alternative.

It lay behind his decision to provide "all aid short of war" to Britain, China, and Russia. It lay behind his orders to move the Pacific Fleet to the distant base at Pearl Harbor, a show of strength designed to deter Japanese aggression but strongly protested by the fleet commander, Admiral Richardson. It lay,

JAMES MADISON
BY ASHER B. DURAND

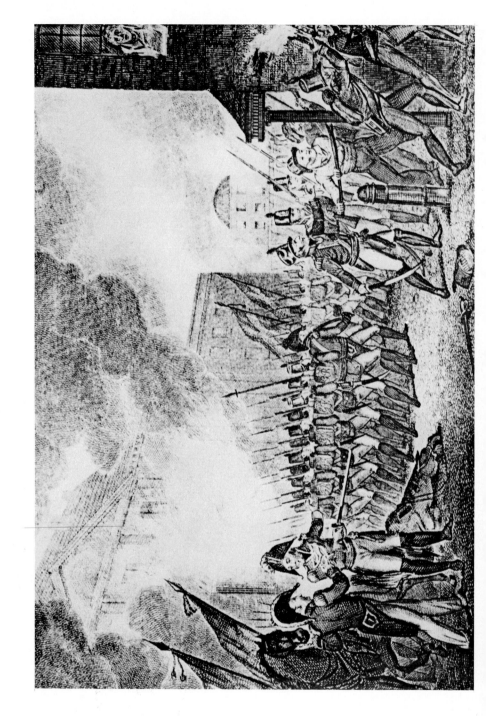

JAMES K. POLK
BY MATHEW B. BRADY

4. ABRAHAM LINCOLN

5. LINCOLN AT ANTIETAM

6.   MCKINLEY AT CAMP WIKOFF

FOCH AND PERSHING AT GENERAL HQS., AEF

8.   WOODROW WILSON

9. FRANKLIN D. ROOSEVELT EN ROUTE TO CASABLANCA

Air Force Photograph

1. NAGASAKI UNDER ATOMIC BOMB ATTACK

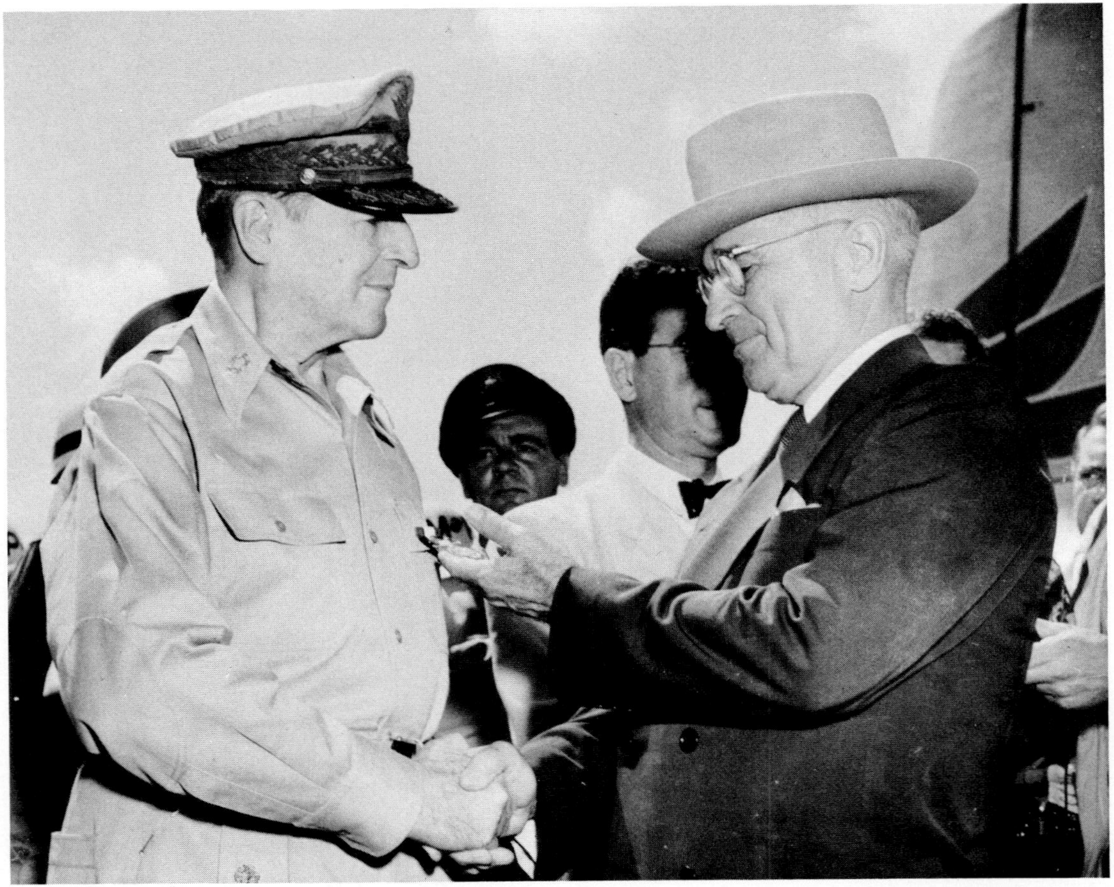

International News Photos

"We've Been Using More Of A Roundish One"

From "The Herblock Book" (Beacon Press, 1952)

HERBLOCK CARTOON, MARCH 1951

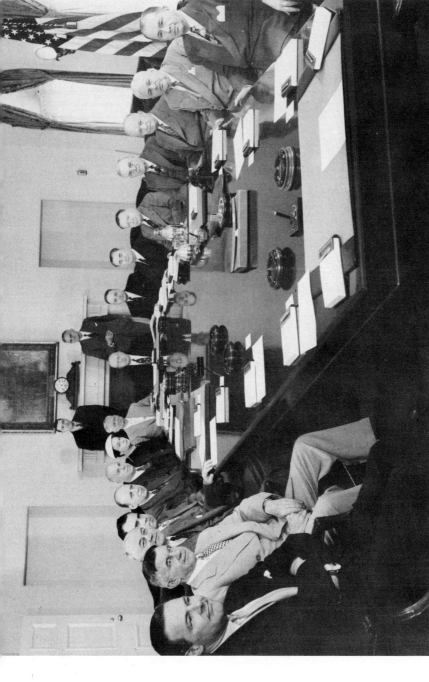

15. FIRST EISENHOWER CABINET

Official U. S. Navy Photogra

16.   POLARIS LAUNCHING, JULY 20, 1960

too, behind the President's insistence on high production goals rather than balanced military forces. On the eve of Pearl Harbor the army, under prodding by the President, was reluctantly planning to deactivate eighteen National Guard divisions in the interest of conserving material and manpower needed in the factories.[12] Such a weakening of American ground strength at a time when the Far Eastern crisis moved toward disaster seems incredible in retrospect. But the fact remains that the actions of the President, as commander in chief, were coherent with and properly subordinate to the major lines of his diplomacy. From the Munich crisis onward, Roosevelt pursued a diplomacy of deterrence in which military appearances, including aid to allies, were no less important, in many respects were more important, than military realities.

The fact that Roosevelt exercised his military powers independently of, and on occasion in flat disagreement with, his chiefs of staff is all the more worthy of emphasis because in the later stages of World War II Roosevelt followed very closely the strategic counsels of his joint chiefs; Sir Winston Churchill, indeed, speaks of the President on one occasion as having been "oppressed by the prejudices of his military advisers."[13] This is an impression widely shared and Roosevelt himself contributed to that impression unconsciously, perhaps on some occasions quite consciously. In a 1943 discussion with an itinerant British general, for instance, he remarked, "As you know I rely entirely on my constitutional technical advisers, particularly in military matters, which, I gather, is not the case in some other countries."[14] This is not altogether borne out by the facts of prewar days. In many instances Roosevelt followed the advice of his chiefs. In many others, the military were able to mitigate or even vitiate strategic and production proposals of the President. But whenever the military advice of his chiefs clearly diverged from his own notions, Roosevelt did not hesitate to ignore or override them.

He took his powers as commander in chief literally and on occasion used them high-handedly. In 1940, for example, an air force planner presented detailed figures and charts to show that aid to Great Britain was undermining American air rearmament. The President cut him off with a breezy "Don't let me see that chart again!"[15] In the deepening crisis of 1940–1941 and the slow American drift toward war, the basic military decisions were largely taken upon presidential rather than military opinions, and the views of the Commander in Chief and his military advisers were increasingly divergent.

In 1940 and afterward the planners of the Joint Board, as their RAINBOW war plans crystallized and their strategic views grew clearer, consistently advised concentration on building up powerful *American* defense forces designed to protect our interests in the western hemisphere. Elsewhere, particularly in the Far East, they urged gaining time through diplomacy. At each crucial stage on the road to war, they put forward plans and memoranda embodying this advice. At each stage, the President, while agreeing in principle with these strategies, neglected to follow them.

It was a constantly repeated pattern. In June, 1940, Roosevelt overrode the advice of the Joint Board and decided to extend full military assistance to Great Britain.[16] Committed to this course against their initial judgment, the military chiefs in the following months had perforce to accept the fact that American rearmament would be considerably slowed down by the weight of British needs. They sought therefore to limit commitments elsewhere, namely in the Pacific area.

Military advice on this score was exigent. The Pacific Fleet commander, Admiral Richardson, came to Washington in autumn, 1940, to plead that the fleet be moved back to San Diego from Pearl Harbor. At about the same time, the Army War Plans Division, surveying the deteriorating situation in the Far East, warned that a crisis there would find that "we are not now prepared and will not be prepared for several years to come."[17] The army Chief of Staff, General Marshall, and the Chief of Naval Operations, Admiral Stark, concurred, and from these considerations emerged a firm and carefully argued Navy Department proposal to concentrate forces in the Atlantic, the famous plan "D" (or DOG in naval parlance) memorandum of November 12, 1940. Plan DOG in turn became one of the bases of a joint army-navy proposal of late 1940, based upon the RAINBOW 5 war plan, for "a rapid increase of army and navy strength and abstention from steps which would provoke attack by any other powers."[18] These advices were put forward as the formal American strategic position in the subsequent conference in Washington with British military authorities (code-named the ABC conference), and were urged as such upon the President.

But the President's thoughts were still governed by diplomatic and political considerations. He neither approved nor disapproved the Joint Board's proposals.[19] Over protests, he insisted that American aircraft production be shared 50–50 with the British, retarding thereby the build-up of American air strength. American convoys in the western Atlantic led to demands for army garrisons, which seriously overstrained the army's limited capabilities. In May, 1941, Lend-Lease aid was extended to China. In July, 1941, in a climactic act, the President imposed an oil embargo on Japan and, on the same day, nominated

General MacArthur to command all army forces in the Far East and called the Philippine army into American service. Though War Department plans had previously assumed the Philippines to be indefensible, from August onward troops and supplies in increasing tide flowed into that distant outpost to build up a powerful deterrent force against the Japanese. The Joint Board had advised strongly against the embargo and, although the circumstances remain somewhat obscure, the President himself appears to have decided on the appointment of General Mac-Arthur without consulting the War Department and, indeed, with little advance notice to it.[20] Roosevelt believed that the Japanese were bent on attacking British and Dutch possessions in Asia and that the best chance of forestalling war lay in a display of American resolution and strength.

Gambling to preserve peace, the President disregarded or overrode the warnings and recommendations of his military chiefs. By late 1941, events had brought about the very situation which Roosevelt's military advisers had sought within the limits of their power and persuasion to avoid: a diplomatic crisis which portended war on two fronts and a serious dispersion of American military forces. Conscious of weaknesses—a navy only partly ready for war and an army which, as one observer put it, was "to a large extent closed for alterations"— the Joint Board at each stage opposed new commitments. At each stage, Roosevelt, influenced by other and weightier considerations, accepted other counsels. To the very end of 1941, the Joint Board systematically opposed any steps which might provoke Japan. "War between the United States and Japan should be avoided while building up the defensive forces in the Far East," a Joint Board estimate warned on November 5, 1941, "[and] no ultimatum should be delivered to Japan."[21] Though

Roosevelt accepted this estimate, Secretary Hull's Ten Point Program—in effect an ultimatum to the Japanese—was devised without formal consultation of either the military chieftains or the civilian service secretaries.[22] In the hurrying crisis, the Joint Board's counsels and warnings were largely ignored.

Roosevelt's gamble failed. The Japanese were not deterred. They chose to accept war, and on December 7 struck the American fleet and base at Pearl Harbor. Germany joined in declaring war, and the United States found itself in the very predicament that Roosevelt's military chiefs had feared. War on two broad fronts came suddenly and disastrously upon an America only partially prepared and everywhere overextended militarily.

In assessing Roosevelt's performance as commander in chief, however, the historian must distinguish cause from effect. The Joint Board's wisdom appeared to be proved by events but, as the chiefs themselves would have been the first to admit, the President had to fit military advice into a larger picture. It may be that Roosevelt failed to do this with sufficient system. Secretary Stimson complained in his diary in 1940 about "the President's haphazard way of hopping about from one Department to another to do another Department's work. . . . I doubt whether we shall be able to hold him to any very systematic relations because that is rather entirely antithetic to his nature and temperament."[23] Again in 1941, Stimson complained, "He has no system. He goes haphazard and he scatters responsibility among a lot of uncoordinated men and consequently things are never done. . . . He has flashes of genius but when it comes to working out a hard problem in a short time and with the aid of expert advisers, he just doesn't quite connect and it doesn't work."[24] At about the same time, General Marshall voiced the same feelings—they were in fact Harry Hopkins' feelings—in a conference with his staff:

We are frittering away material without tangible results, . . . the influence and accomplishments of the State Department have been unfortunate . . . and the President must be protected against the importunities of those who are not fully aware of the seriousness of the present situation. . . . [We must] . . . begin the education of the President as to the true strategic situation—this coming after a period of being influenced by the State Department.[25]

But Roosevelt was also accused by the State Department of disregarding its advice, and the same complaint was voiced by members of Congress, representatives of outside pressure groups, and statesmen and soldiers in London and Chungking. The President, and the President alone, bore responsibility for reconciling the divergent demands of diplomacy, strategy, and domestic opinion. In retrospect Roosevelt may seem to have performed poorly as prewar commander in chief. The light of restrospect is clear and harsh, but it may distort.

The point here, however, is that Roosevelt made the grand strategic decisions of the prewar period on his own initiative as president and commander in chief, and in many instances he made those decisions without consulting his military chiefs.

It is important to be clear on this point, for it forms part of the necessary background for understanding Roosevelt's wartime relations with his staff. During the prewar period, the main outlines of American policy and strategy were set by the Commander in Chief, assured of his own powers, confident of his judgment, and, in certain large matters, oblivious to the advices of his military chieftains. As the official historian of the office of the army Chief of Staff has observed in a survey of the prewar period,

. . . Roosevelt was the real and not merely a nominal Commander-in-Chief of the armed forces. Every President has possessed the constitutional authority which that title indicates, but few Presidents have shared Mr. Roosevelt's readiness to exercise it in fact and in detail and with such determination. . . . Nobody, reading the record, can doubt that the determining influence in the making of military policy in these prewar days was that of the President as Commander-in-Chief, as is the constitutional design. . . . Right or wrong, with professional approval or without it, the decisions *were* made at the presidential level and . . . in these and other instances the dutiful behavior of the Chief of Staff was determined by his civilian superior as precisely as orders from the Chief of Staff in their turn determined the dutiful behavior of his subordinates.[26]

I

War brought changes in the relationships of commander in chief and the military services. In late 1941 and early 1942, amid wide disasters, the problems of the prewar period, wherein political and diplomatic advices weighed more heavily than military advice, gave way to the harsher problems of battle front and coalition. Strategic initiative passed into enemy hands and the vast Japanese amphibious conquests in the Pacific theaters in early 1942 overthrew the very basis of prewar American and allied strategy.

On this gloomy scene the key figures on the American side were theater commanders like MacArthur, Nimitz, and Stilwell, presiding with wide discretionary powers over operational commands and dealing as best they might with enemy thrusts. While subordinates, they nevertheless held powerful influence in molding strategy in the early days of defeat as later in the years of victory.

Above them there grew up a rudimentary military high command. In Washington, the War and Navy departments were drastically reorganized in the aftermath of Pearl Harbor. By early 1942 they had in effect become command posts from which the chiefs, General Marshall and Admiral King, directed —or in those early defeats, reacted to—the ebb and flow of a world-wide battle. At the same time, the requirement of cooperation with the British brought about the transformation of the old Joint Army-Navy Board into the new Joint Chiefs of Staff, General Arnold, the Army Air Forces commander, being raised to membership so that the American staff might fit the British model. And from this early strategic collaboration grew the Combined Chiefs of Staff, which from the time of the conference code-named ARCADIA (Washington, December, 1941) functioned as the supreme Allied military authority.

War, then, brought a great elaboration of American military structure and these organizational changes in their turn subtly altered the relationships between the President and his military chieftains. In 1942, and afterward in increasing measure, Roosevelt dealt with men who were his personal military advisers, as before the war, but who at the same time were supreme commanders of their services in a global war. Beneath them, in War and Navy departments which increasingly took on the character of operational military staffs, lay another level of military authority—the planning staffs. They had great importance. At the planners' level the far-ranging details of global war were sifted and ordered amid masses of paper work; here the directives of higher authority were given precise and substantive military meaning. In theory the planners served as advisers to their chiefs, performing the vital but subordinate duties of staff officers. Actually the staffs, working more closely than their chiefs with the details of war, often took the initiative and produced basic strategic conceptions such as the BOLERO plan of 1942 (an invasion build-up in Britain). As in all organizations, pressures flowed in both directions, up as well as down. And although it would be easy to exaggerate the staffs' influence on the larger war decisions, it must be remarked that the military chiefs to a great extent saw the war through the eyes of their planners. The staffs' role, then, was as much an active as a passive one; their work was often conclusive in small issues and always influential in large ones.[27]

With the coming of war, the Commander in Chief found himself at the apex of a vast structure of military command. In theory the machinery was under his control and supervision. In fact the immensity of the war panorama as well as the burden of Roosevelt's other concerns as President meant that his control could be only partial and somewhat indirect in its working. The relative independence of the theater commanders, the central position and influence of the planning staffs, the wide powers and public respect enjoyed by his chiefs of staff— all these factors placed real limits on the Commander in Chief's independence of action which had not existed during the pre-war period. His role had become highly institutionalized.

In some spheres, it is true, Roosevelt's role remained a personal and intimate one; this was the case in his relations with the British Prime Minister and with his top military advisers. In other and broader spheres the authority of the commander in chief was mediated through a machinery of command vast and impersonal in its workings, a machinery which was not easily subjected to the influence of a single individual and which tended to run on its own momentum. Throughout World War II, the Joint Chiefs and their planners enjoyed a considerable autonomy, far greater than the energetic British Prime Minister permitted his military commanders. In the sphere of war production, for example, over-all requirements after the outbreak of war were established by the separate services with little apparent control or interference by the Commander in Chief (in contrast to his prewar inclinations!) or even by the Joint Chiefs in their collective capacity. There was indeed very little attempt in World War II to co-ordinate production and strategy from the top.

Similarly, Roosevelt did little to affect American strategy in the Pacific theaters of war, although his concern for the postwar politics of that area was stronger by far than his interest in postwar Europe. He intervened, it is true, in the controversies over command and strategy in the China theater and he overrode the Joint Chiefs' recommendation for an offensive in Burma and the Bay of Bengal in 1943. But, deep though his interest was in the naval war in the Pacific, Roosevelt exercised little if any direct influence on the development of strategy in that theater. After the defensive victories of 1942, Pacific strategy emerged as a result of successive accommodations between the views of General MacArthur and the army staff and those of Admiral Nimitz and the navy staff, without interventions from above. Roosevelt's principal interest in the Pacific war was to limit the demands which it made upon the European theaters of war, not to direct its course.

Unlike Churchill, finally, Roosevelt never meddled in operational planning or in the duties of theater commanders. No less than Churchill, the President was fascinated by the events of war and gave close attention to daily reports from the fighting fronts. He had a considerable though amateur flair for strategy. With some few exceptions, however, he was content to work through the established military channels and to leave the details to others. Over a very wide range of military issues the Joint Chiefs and their staffs, free from presidential interference, settled the daily business of war and were dominant in their own spheres.

But if war altered and somewhat lessened the authority of the commander in chief, it did not overthrow it or Roosevelt's willingness to exercise that authority. It is true that in the later stages of the war, after the first Quebec conference and after the Cairo-Teheran conferences, Roosevelt, while retaining to a certain extent his role as mediator between British and American strategic views, concurred generally with the military counsels of his chiefs and supported them with considerable tenacity against the strategic arguments of the British chiefs and their eloquent Prime Minister. After mid-1943, Anglo-American strategy increasingly took on the massive character which had been so long urged by the American chiefs and particularly by General Marshall and the army staff, and with the Normandy invasion the war effort in Europe moved inexorably toward the goal of total victory over Germany, as American army planners had foreseen it from the time of the Victory Plan of 1941.

During this period American strategy, as one student has remarked, "emerged from the White House much as it had emerged from the Pentagon."[28] The Commander in Chief's role in this appears, and to a very large extent was, a passive one. It is indeed from this closing period of the war that the presently prevailing image comes of Roosevelt as a commander in chief concerned only to win the war as quickly and as completely as possible, attentive to and largely reliant upon the strategic advices of his military men and reluctant to disagree with them on technical matters. For instance, Robert Sherwood in his authoritative *Roosevelt and Hopkins* has argued that Roosevelt overruled the opinions of his chiefs on only two occasions during the entire war—in July, 1942, on the North African invasion and in December, 1943, on the question of a projected operation in Burma and the Bay of Bengal.[29] Accepting this, Professor Huntington in his study of the American high command in World War II has concluded:

Too much harmony is just as much a symptom of bad organization as too much conflict. On the face of it, something is wrong with a system in which, during the course of a four-year major war, the political Chief Executive only twice overrules his professional military advisers. This can only mean that one of them was neglecting his proper function and duplicating the work of the other.[30]

This is in many ways a misleading picture. Roosevelt's relations with his wartime chiefs, it is true, never took on the dramatic and forensic tones of Churchill's relations with *his* chiefs. Beneath the surface, however, there were serious stresses and strains on the relations of commander in chief and the military, stresses and strains which the unanimity of opinion during the closing phases of the war has somewhat obscured. In the earlier stages of the war, throughout 1942 and midway into 1943, Roosevelt's role and actions as commander in chief were much closer to the pattern of his actions in the prewar days than to those of 1944 and 1945. Until the first Quebec conference, it is no exaggeration to say that the prewar pattern prevailed, that the basic decisions which molded strategy were made by the Commander in Chief himself, against the advice of his own chiefs and in concert with Churchill and the British chiefs.

There were various reasons for this. The American chiefs could not always agree on priorities during the beginning phases of the war; King with his eyes on the needs of the Pacific naval war, Arnold with his attention focused on the requirements of the air battle, and Marshall, ever sensitive to the demands for great land forces in Europe, found it difficult to present an agreed case to the President. Moreover, British and American strategic views diverged widely in 1942 and early 1943, the American staff from the beginning arguing for a cross-Channel invasion and the British emphasizing the need for operations in the Mediterranean. Most important of all, the enemy everywhere held the strategic initiative during the early period of the war. In the Pacific theaters, in the Indian Ocean, in Russia, and in the Mediterranean, strategic decision was made the more difficult for Allied war planners by virtue of the hard fact that they had for the most part to respond to enemy initiatives rather than to plan their own.

In these circumstances, Roosevelt in 1942 found it impossible to back his Joint Chiefs. And in the absence of agreement among the chiefs, he became subject, in Maurice Matloff's words, to "the gravitational pull" of other arguments, notably those of Churchill and the British chiefs.[31] At no time during the course of the American war effort did political direction and military advice drift so far apart as during 1942. The result was a display of presidential independence in military affairs which repeated, under war conditions, the story of the prewar period.

The events surrounding the Allied decision to invade North Africa are perhaps the most revealing in this connection. The background of this story is well known. War Department planners, worried over the demands of the Pacific war and the dispersion of American forces over the world, pushed hard for agreement with the British on a cross-Channel invasion in 1943 —the BOLERO—ROUND-UP concept (the planned landing in France). In spring, 1942, the British authorities tentatively accepted the "Marshall Plan," as they called BOLERO— ROUND-UP, but with reservations. This agreement, never wholehearted, was overthrown by the events of the summer of 1942—the Japanese thrusts in the Indian Ocean and the Solomons, Rommel's defeat of the British Eighth Army and his *coup de main* at Tobruk, the shakiness of the Churchill government before a rising English public and political opinion, and, not least important, the slowness of American war production and preparations to hit their stride.[32]

Through all of this, the American chiefs stuck grimly to their views and even contemplated switching American forces to the Pacific in the event of continued British disagreement.[33] In a scene of crisis and of rising Anglo-American acrimony, Roosevelt in July, 1942, intervened, powerfully and even ruthlessly, to assert his powers as commander in chief. He ruled out any diversion of forces to the Pacific, saying that it was like "taking up your dishes and going away," and he dispatched Marshall and Hopkins to London to seek an agreed strategy with the British. Moreover, he revised beyond recognition the original War Department draft instructions to the Hopkins-Marshall mission, and the final draft in effect closed the issue in favor of British strategic conceptions, and, as Herbert Feis has observed, in an "imperative tone such as he seldom employed."[34] Not least revealing, he signed these instructions, "Franklin D. Roosevelt, Commander-in-Chief." Finally, on the same day that the Combined Chiefs reached "conditional decision" on TORCH (the landing in North Africa) in London, Roosevelt in Washington informed his aides that he was making the decision *unconditional* and this decision he reinforced in September, 1942, in the face of some War Department shuffling.

The crisis in the American high command over TORCH was significant in several respects. Politics is a vital part of strategy, and Roosevelt, as his position required, was of course far more sensitive to the political aspects of the TORCH decision than his chiefs were or should have been. In 1942 the political aspect was vital and it proved decisive in Roosevelt's judgment. The chiefs had for some time been aware that a North African invasion had attractions for Roosevelt; it was, in Secretary Stimson's words, his "great secret baby." This important fact, however, was apparently given little weight in their deliberations.[35] That failure undermined their position. Looking back on the TORCH decision in after years, General Marshall recalled that he learned a great lesson from it: "in wartime the politicians have to do *something* important every year."[36] TORCH held together the Anglo-American coalition during this difficult period of "bringing defeat underfoot," and this fact far outweighed in importance the operational and logistical considerations on which the War Department's plans had so largely rested. In recognizing and acting upon this fact, the Commander in Chief fulfilled his constitutional responsibilities.

Beyond this is the strategic significance of the TORCH decision. In war as in logic, the greater includes the less. The fundamental American strategic concept—to concentrate first against Germany—was sound and was so proved by the issue of the war. In the controversy over TORCH the Commander in Chief intervened forcefully to preserve that basic strategy at a time when his Joint Chiefs, indignant over what they considered British inconstancy, seemed ready to abandon it and to redeploy their forces against Japan. It is of course impossible to say whether such a redeployment could have been effected under the conditions of 1942 and, if it had been possible, what its distant consequences might have been. But if the considerations which had led to concentration against Germany were sound in January, 1942, they were sounder still in July, 1942—the summer of Dieppe, of Tobruk and Alamein, and of Stalingrad. It may well be thought that in intervening to save the Germany-first concept in 1942 Roosevelt showed a sounder strategic judgment than did his chiefs.[37]

At about the same time as these disputes went on over TORCH Admiral William Leahy appeared at the White House. Conscious, perhaps, before the event of the approaching crisis in his relations with Marshall and King, Roosevelt, on the recommendation of Marshall himself, had in July, 1942, nominated Leahy his personal Chief of Staff. It was an appointment for which no precedent existed and for the remainder of the war Leahy's powers were never precisely set down in chit or charter; in a press conference shortly after Leahy's appointment Roosevelt contented himself with describing him as "a sort of leg man."

Despite the ambiguity of his position, Leahy functioned thereafter as liaison officer between the President and the Joint Chiefs, a task the performance of which was facilitated by his service seniority and by an old and warm friendship with Roosevelt dating back to World War I days. The resulting liaison between the President and the Pentagon was not perfect and never approached the high standards of the elaborate British war cabinet machinery; until the end of the war the

American chiefs often learned of presidential decisions only by way of the British secretariat in London and the British Joint Staff Mission resident in Washington.[38] But as a consequence of Leahy's position and personality, never again were the views of the White House and the Pentagon permitted to drift so far apart. Roosevelt, it is true, met with his chiefs only at intervals—General Marshall once told the harassed and envious Alan Brooke that he often did not see the President for a month or six weeks—but Admiral Leahy saw him daily and, as Leahy has recorded, passed on to the chiefs "the basic thinking of the President on all war plans and strategy . . . [and] in turn brought back from the Joint Chiefs a consensus of their thinking." His role is difficult to document but it was an important one.[39]

The events surrounding TORCH, then, and the appointment of Leahy disclosed once and for all the limits on the very real wartime autonomy enjoyed by the Joint Chiefs and their military staffs. Roosevelt, unlike Churchill, was not inclined to meddle with his military men or to dispute matters with them. Indeed, in his relations with them as in his relations with his political associates, Roosevelt loathed and shunned controversy as systematically as the great Englishman sought it. But as the intervention in TORCH planning had shown, Roosevelt was a commander in chief who held views of his own and felt no compulsion to accept and rely solely on the technical advice of his chiefs. Churchill, Hopkins, and Leahy perhaps had as much influence as they, and the President's mind roamed the world scene as actively and perhaps as eccentrically as did Churchill's, discerning strategic alternatives not revealed, mercifully in many cases, to the sharper professional gaze of his advisers. The chiefs, on their part, appear to have drawn their own conclusions from these events, for TORCH was a demonstration of the Commander in Chief's powers which was not repeated during the war. Henceforth disagreements between Roosevelt and the Joint Chiefs were rare, the one indisputable instance being over BUCCANEER operations at the Cairo conference. But this "harmony" is susceptible of more than one interpretation. Despite his intervention in TORCH planning, Roosevelt, in his relations with his military advisers as in political life, preferred the role of mediator to that of protagonist. And he knew how to decide issues by ignoring them, understanding that in war even more than in peacetime politics, indecision decides by default.

The result was a war leadership indirect in its methods and most difficult to document but one to which the Joint Chiefs had perforce to accommodate themselves. The ideas and projects of his great colleague Churchill were loudly and eloquently advanced, vigorously pushed, exhaustively documented. Roosevelt's motives and intentions during the war, except on rare occasions, were difficult for his chiefs to penetrate; he seldom discussed these matters with them, seeming to prefer that they attempt to read his mind, accepting or rejecting the results of this process for reasons which he never made altogether clear to them. As an old political associate of the President's—the Bronx leader Edward Flynn—observed, "Roosevelt would adopt ideas only if he agreed with them. If he disagreed, he simply did nothing." TORCH was the one great exception to this rule during World War II.

II

TORCH, then, exhibited once again and even improved upon the established prewar pattern of President Roosevelt's relations with his chiefs. From the earliest time—from Plan DOG at least—the Joint Chiefs had attempted to persuade Roosevelt to commit himself to a strategic rationale in the developing crisis. Their efforts were unsuccessful. He had, it would appear, accepted and made his own their basic idea of concentration in Europe, as the planners found to their discomfiture in July, 1942. But in other, repeated efforts they had failed. Roosevelt, politician that he was, always declined to commit himself too far in advance of the event; hypotheses and "iffy questions" had little appeal to him. Thus Plan DOG, the ABC-1 memoranda (the British-American conversations in early 1941), the army's "Victory Program" of 1941, and finally the BOLERO plan were considered, neither accepted nor rejected, and ultimately ignored. It is impossible to say whether or not Roosevelt either deeply understood these plans or agreed with the strategic analyses on which they were based. His own strategic judgment was in many ways quick but it was rarely explicit. It is however clear that he was unwilling, under the circumstances obtaining in the early stages of the war, to support the plans of his chiefs against the British. During this period the American and British chiefs debated strategy; the President and the Prime Minister decided it.

In 1943 Roosevelt, for so long independent of his chiefs in the strategic sphere, turned at last to support of their conceptions against those of the British. The change was not immediate. Allied involvement in extended Mediterranean operations after the launching of TORCH deranged the War Department's plans for an early and decisive concentration of forces for attack on northwestern Europe, and in late 1942 the BOLERO concept was swamped by clamorous demands on Allied resources for the Pacific, for anti-submarine warfare, and for an air offensive in Europe. In these circumstances, the Joint Chiefs and their planners were unable to reach satisfactory agreement among themselves on strategic priorities. After their preparatory discussions for the Casablanca conference General Marshall had to report to the President that there were considerable differences of opinion among the planners and some differences between the chiefs although they tended to regard a cross-Channel invasion as more suitable for 1943 than an extension of operations in the Mediterranean. Roosevelt warned that "at the conference the British will have a plan and stick to it." Despite this warning, the Joint Chiefs were unable to concert their views, and there was as a result no American "position" at Casablanca.[40]

At no time during the war was the need for unanimity among the Joint Chiefs more dramatically illustrated. His preconference suggestion that the Joint Chiefs seek a compromise position between the BOLERO concept and British Mediterranean projects having been ignored, Roosevelt did not feel bound to support the chiefs at Casablanca and he hardly discussed with them the "unconditional surrender" formula which he announced there. The American planners as a consequence were in disarray. The result was complete victory for British strategic conceptions. "Our ideas had prevailed almost throughout," wrote an exultant British general in his diary after the conference.[41] Equally terse was the reaction of the chief American army planner, General Albert Wedemeyer: "We came, we listened and we were conquered."[42] The war in early 1943 proceeded along the Mediterranean bias TORCH had given it. The arguments of General Marshall and the army staff had been unavailing, and, in many ways, the Casablanca conference was a low point in the cooperation between the President and his military advisers.

Such disagreements, after Casablanca, became exceptions to the rule. Roosevelt, it is true, overruled his chiefs at the Cairo conferences on the proposed Burma and Bay of Bengal operations (BUCCANEER) and in the summer of 1944 he made his weight felt—although to what effect is still not altogether clear —in the controversy over whether Formosa or the Philippines should be the next objective in the Pacific.[43] But the low point at Casablanca was also the turning point. In the later conferences of the war, Roosevelt came in ever-growing measure to accept and sponsor the strategic views of the American staff and, when support was required, proved willing to support them in their arguments against Churchill and the British chiefs.

In this the President's role was perhaps made easier by an increased willingness on the part of the Joint Chiefs to meet their British colleagues half-way. Aware after Casablanca that invasion of northwestern Europe must in any event be postponed until 1944, the American chiefs were willing during 1943 to compromise their position on campaigns in the Mediterranean although they never gave up their view that strategically such campaigns caused a diversion of Allied resources. In return for their concessions they sought a firm British commitment to the BOLERO concept and at length won such a commitment. It was not an easy victory, for the British to the very end were reluctant to hazard a cross-Channel invasion, but the American chiefs' hands were strengthened in controversy by Roosevelt's sudden and rather surprising adherence to their strategic conceptions in the months after Casablanca. At the conference code-named TRIDENT (Washington, May, 1943) Roosevelt for the first time pressed on Churchill the merits of BOLERO, and at the first Quebec conference (July, 1943), in Secretary Stimson's exultant words, "The President went the whole hog on the subject of ROUNDHAMMER [another name for BO-LERO, the planned landing in France]. He was more clear and definite than I have ever seen him since we have been in this war and he took the policy that the American staff have been fighting for fully."[44]

Once tardily converted to BOLERO, Roosevelt remained its advocate and, as a logical consequence, opposed—although never intransigently—British schemes for widening the war in the Mediterranean theater. His tenacity was impressive. A British proposal in October, 1943, to seize Rhodes, Cos, and Leros was rejected by Roosevelt on the ground that it might divert forces from operations in Italy or from the projected cross-Channel assault—eight months before the event! At the Cairo-Teheran conferences, the President was no less zealous than the American chiefs in protecting the BOLERO concept, now entitled OVERLORD, from the threat of diversions in the Mediterranean, and he was even more zealous than they in protecting it and the Mediterranean theater from the threatened diversion of a Burma campaign, overruling the Joint Chiefs on this point. Meeting Secretary Stimson on his return from Cairo, Roosevelt observed, "I have thus brought OVERLORD back to you safe and sound on the ways for accomplishment."[45]

After a delay of more than a year the Allied war effort turned in 1943 into the channels which the American staff had marked out from the beginning. And the President's support for their European strategy, belatedly given, was never thereafter with-drawn. The new concurrence between President and Joint

Chiefs in the months after the TRIDENT conference did not "shut down" the Mediterranean theater of war, much as some American planners would have liked to do that. American insistence on OVERLORD did not indeed prevent some concessions on the part of the Joint Chiefs to British-backed projects in that theater in late 1943 and 1944. Assured after Teheran that OVERLORD would be carried out and strengthened by their newly-won presidential support, the American Joint Chiefs proved willing, with some protest, to delay their OVERLORD shipping schedules to accommodate the shipping needs for the Anzio landing and to provide some much-regretted American reinforcements for the Italian theater. Other less weighty concessions were made to the British. All in all, the American staffs displayed more flexibility in their dealings with their British allies in the later stages of the war than had earlier been the case, and Allied amity prospered.

On the major points, however, the American chiefs were firm in defending their established strategic conceptions, and in 1944 and 1945 they enjoyed almost without exception the support of their Commander in Chief. Roosevelt backed them in the controversy over the southern France invasion; he supported their refusal to reinforce and widen the Italian theater in August, 1944; and he backed them and their principal subordinate, General Eisenhower, in controversies over the European command structure.

On the major issue emerging at the close of the war—the question of dealing with growing Russian aggressiveness—the views of Roosevelt and the Joint Chiefs were identical. It is difficult, as always, to say how far the President's unreadiness, even under provocation, to deal harshly with Stalin in 1944 and 1945 reflected the *advice* of the chiefs. But their advice, solicited by Secretary Hull as early as May, 1944, coincided with Roosevelt's own inclinations in the matter, though it was of course based on quite different considerations, and there was on this great question an effective unanimity of opinion.[46] It is very doubtful if the "deadly hiatus" in the spring of 1945 between the authority of the dying Roosevelt and the authority of his successor, Truman, so much regretted by Churchill, had great influence on the movement of events in Europe during early 1945. If one may judge from the relations of Roosevelt and his chiefs through late 1943 and 1944, the President, had he lived, would probably have backed his military staff in the discussion with the British over the questions of Prague, Berlin, and a showdown with the Russians no less sturdily than President Truman was to do. Roosevelt may have made mistakes in his dealings with the Russians, and Stalin's rudeness and suspiciousness in 1945 grieved and angered him. But he was ever reluctant to admit mistakes, and it was late in the game.[47]

How can we explain this reversal in the Commander in Chief's role during the latter period of the war? It is never easy for the historian to establish motives, and Roosevelt, as so many of his associates have recorded, concealed his motives more deeply than most men. The chiefs themselves, dealing intimately with Roosevelt during the war years, never fully comprehended the train of reasoning which led him to accept and support their strategic views after TRIDENT and the first Quebec conference.

It is difficult to decide on the historical record. More reliant in the early days on the counsels of Harry Hopkins than on the advice of his military chiefs, Roosevelt in 1943 seemingly developed greater confidence in the judgment of his chiefs than he had had in 1942 and more particularly in the prewar period.

It is possible, too, that as the war wore on he developed a greater confidence in their subordination as well.

If Roosevelt found little reason to overrule his chiefs in the latter phases of the war, this is in some part attributable to the fact that the chiefs, after their experiences over TORCH and Casablanca, were perhaps more sensitive to the President's leanings and strategic tendencies than they had been in 1942. And the liaison between them and the White House grew closer. As one student of the Joint Chiefs, Captain Tracy B. Kittredge, has observed,

It may be true that the President formally overruled them on very few occasions but this was only because informal discussions of the President with Leahy, Marshall, King and Arnold usually led them to know in advance the President's views. They no doubt frequently recognized the advantages of accepting the President's suggestions with their own interpretations, rather than of risking an overruling by presenting formally proposals they knew would not be accepted.[48]

The growing mutual confidence was influenced, after the Allied victories in Tunis and Guadalcanal and the defeat of the submarine campaign in 1943, by another important factor—the change in the shape of the war. With the sea lanes secured and North Africa and Guadalcanal conquered, the defensive phase of the war came to an end in all the theaters.

From the beginning, Roosevelt, like the chiefs, had wished to defeat Germany decisively and as quickly as possible. Unlike them, however, he gave first priority in 1942 to maintaining and solidifying the Anglo-American coalition which the controversies over BOLERO and TORCH had placed under great strain. In the later stages of the war the strategic situation changed as Allied forces moved to the offensive. At the same time Roosevelt's gaze shifted from the Anglo-American coalition to the broader question of American relations with Russia and the complementary question of America's role in postwar Europe. The political considerations seen by the President and the logistical and strategic considerations seen by the chiefs paralleled one another, in 1943 and afterwards. The consequence was a close concurrence of political and military views in the American high command during the last two years of the war, perhaps the most important factor in bringing Roosevelt's views closer to those of his military advisers.

This is a factor worthy of examination. From the beginning of the war, the President's cardinal aim in the European theater was to avoid American embroilment in the tangled and melancholy political affairs of Central and Eastern Europe. As Herbert Feis has well said,

The President wanted to keep clear of responsibility for the future pattern of relationships within Central and Eastern Europe, since he feared that it might lead to a call to keep American troops in Europe permanently. . . . he continued [throughout the war] to restrain official interest in Eastern and Central European matters except as they might affect sentiment in the United States. He was determined to have a lot to say . . . about the settlements in the Pacific. But, since he thought it was nearly impossible to find happy solutions for many European problems, he wanted to remain as clear of them as he could, except for those involving Germany.[49]

It was a cornerstone of Roosevelt's policy, settled in his own mind from an early date, that the American people would be unwilling and the American government therefore unable to provide occupation troops in Europe for any lengthy period after the end of the war, that such occupation troops as we might provide would be limited to Germany alone, and that American strategy therefore should avoid situations which might make American occupation troops necessary for an indefinite period.

This policy arose not only from the President's natural concern over the great portending burdens of the Japanese war, but also from his disinclination, based upon his reading of American public opinion, to ensnare American troops and American interests in the troublous affairs of Europe—a Europe with, as he put it in one of his prewar speeches, its "ancient hatreds, turbulent frontiers, the 'legacy of old forgotten, far-off things and battles long ago' . . . [and] its new-born fanaticisms."

As concerned the complex political affairs of postwar Europe, Roosevelt like the great majority of his countrymen was still in part an isolationist. As he put it in a letter to Stettinius in February, 1944,

I do not want the United States to have the post-war burden of reconstituting France, Italy and the Balkans. This is not our natural task at a distance of 3500 miles or more. It is definitely a British task in which the British are far more vitally interested than we are. From the point of view of the United States, our principal object is not to take part in the internal problems of Southern Europe but is rather to take part in eliminating Germany at a possible and even probable cost of a third World War.[50]

Quite apart from the prefigured burdens of the Pacific war, American war policy in Europe throughout was haunted by the specter of a recurrent isolationism in the postwar period. Fear that Russian intransigence would alienate American public

opinion was perhaps as strong a motive for Roosevelt's concessions to Stalin as his desire to increase the Soviet's sense of
security. His sense of the fragility of the American will to
intervene in European affairs colored Roosevelt's public depic-
tion of American war aims, and it underlay the urgency with
which he sought to establish the United Nations Organization
during the war, before isolationist sentiment had an opportunity to reassert itself.

These fears and prepossessions greatly influenced his approach to questions of European strategy. He had led the
American people through the crisis of 1940–1941 and into a
world war. But even this master of the moods and impulses of
American public opinion doubted his ability to lead his countrymen further into world affairs and to persuade them to take up
the cares and responsibilities of the peace. At the Teheran
conference, for instance, Roosevelt, who had proposed that the
wartime Big Four serve as guardians of the new peace, informed Stalin that in event of any postwar European crisis the
United States would limit her intervention to planes and ships
but that no American ground troops could be sent.[51] He was
reluctant even to permit *any* American forces to remain on
occupation duty in Europe after the war.

At the Yalta conference he placed a limit of two years on
occupation forces and in earlier discussions with his staff he
had indicated that an occupation of only one year would be
preferable. In November, 1943, in preparatory conferences with
the Joint Chiefs before the Cairo-Teheran meetings he had
said that the United States could accept no responsibilities for
furnishing occupation troops outside Germany proper and
warned, "we should not get roped into accepting any European
sphere of influence."[52] As a consequence he refused at first to

provide American occupation forces for Austria and was won away from this stand only in December, 1944, on the strong representations of Winant. Similarly he wished, in defiance of military logic, to place the postwar American zone of occupation in northwestern Germany, as far as possible from Central European affairs, an ambition which in view of the position of the British armies on the American left flank during the campaign in Germany would have necessitated an impossibly difficult shifting and shuttling of British and American troops in the postwar period.[53] Once the war ended, Roosevelt felt, American forces must withdraw from Europe, and campaigns in Europe should be planned and fought in such a way as to facilitate their early disengagement. In his opinion, American military intervention in World War II did not imply clear postwar responsibilities in Europe, and in any event American opinion would not accept such responsibilities. This was a political decision from which Roosevelt never moved; it was strongly held and it was influential.

This distaste for even a temporary American involvement in postwar European politics was a powerful factor in the approval he gave to the BOLERO-OVERLORD concept. It formed the basis of his European policy. More important for our purpose, this policy, based upon the President's judgment of the likely temper of postwar public opinion in the United States—a remarkably accurate judgment, it might be added—complemented the plans of American military planners for a short and decisive campaign in Europe. Though the political motive was founded on considerations quite distinct from those underlying BOLERO-OVERLORD, the one reinforced and buttressed the other. The disagreements between the President and his staff during the earlier stages of the war arose less over strategic conceptions than over questions of timing. In the later stages of the war, this source of disagreement between Roosevelt and his military chieftains was removed. If political reasons had counselled in 1942 that American force be diverted into the Mediterranean basin to support, directly, the faltering effort of our British ally and, indirectly, the Russians in their summer of disaster, political reasons in the changed circumstances of 1943 argued no less strongly that, for the reasons we have seen, those Mediterranean efforts should not be extended into the Balkans or South-Central Europe: Roosevelt for reasons of his own was no less chary of involvement in Yugoslavia and Central Europe than the Joint Chiefs. In this judgment, again for reasons of his own, he found himself in agreement with the strategic and logistical arguments of his military advisers and willing therefore to support them. In the later stages of the European war, then, American policy and American strategy flowed along in a merging stream, the result less of an identity than of a congruity of motives. And in the high tides of victory in 1944 and 1945, the President was, after his own fashion, no less stalwart in opposing the strategic views of the British and in backing his own military staffs than he had been independent in his exercise of the powers of commander in chief during the earlier stages of World War II.

III

The time has not yet come for the historian to pass full judgment on Franklin Roosevelt's role as the American commander in chief. The events of the war are still too recent and relatively too poorly documented for that. Only with the passage of much time and the completion of much work will the historian undertake this task with anything other than diffidence. Even so, enough is known to permit some tentative and general conclusions.

First and most important, the prevailing harmony of view between Roosevelt and his military chieftains in the later stages of World War II has left an impression of his war leadership which is at variance with the facts. As in so many things connected with Roosevelt, appearances differ from the realities. His casual manner of dealing with great issues and his ingrained methods of dealing with—and surviving!—his subordinates more than once misled observers unacquainted with the man. This was markedly the case in Roosevelt's exercise of his military powers. Students of the war, by concentrating their attention too closely upon its closing stages, have presented a picture of a commander in chief concerned only to win the war in the military sense as quickly and as cheaply as possible and too responsive therefore to purely military advices, ignoring those long-range political aspects which make up so large a part of war. Thus one student of American civil-military relations in World War II, Professor Samuel P. Huntington, stated that "so far as the major decisions of policy and strategy were concerned, the military ran the war." And as another critic of Roosevelt's policies, the military analyst Hanson Baldwin, has observed, "We forgot that politico-military is a compound word."[54]

Now, "politico-military" affairs are complicated and tangled. And "major decisions," too, are difficult to isolate from minor decisions, the more so if they are made, as so many of Roosevelt's decisions were made, by default rather than by dramatic actions. But if Roosevelt's war leadership is viewed as a whole and proper stress laid on its early and middle phases, somewhat different conclusions emerge.

Roosevelt took seriously his powers as commander in chief. None of our war presidents has grasped those powers more firmly. But their use and their influence were not always obvious, and Roosevelt was far more sparing of them than was Churchill in the exercise of his powers as Prime Minister and Minister of Defense. In most instances, when his military subordinates presented agreed recommendations, Roosevelt tended to follow them provided they did not conflict with his political purposes as they did, for example, during the period of prewar rearmament. When his military chieftains could not agree among themselves, as at the Casablanca conference, the President merely followed his own course, for at no time was he solely dependent on their counsels; unanimity among the Joint Chiefs was a rule which events, not Roosevelt himself, imposed.

Where high political affairs—especially those bearing upon the coalition—came in question, Roosevelt's intervention could be decisive and powerful. His chiefs, it is true, had great freedom and great authority. But if Roosevelt's relations with his military subordinates were more even in tenor than Churchill's with his chiefs, Roosevelt's ascendancy was no less real and his control, indirect but persuasive, over the major decisions of the war no less marked. As the presidential Chief of Staff, Admiral Leahy, has recalled in his reminiscences of the war,

There were two men at the top who really fought out and finally agreed on the major moves that led to victory. They were Franklin Roosevelt and Winston Churchill. They really ran the war. Of course, they had to have some people like us to help them, but we were just artisans building definite patterns of strategy from the rough blueprints handed us by our respective Commanders-in-Chief.[55]

At the same time a study of Roosevelt's wartime role does
little to diminish the basic ambiguity in the commander in
chief's powers and it is difficult, in World War II as in earlier
American wars, to trace clearly the line separating the actions
of the president from the actions of the commander in chief.
This is the more the case because Roosevelt, with some
important exceptions, exercised the commander in chief's
powers as indirectly and with as much adroitness as he exercised his other powers. In the field of strategy, as had been his
wont in domestic politics, his preferred role was that of mediator, drifting between the conflicting pressures and the divergent
views which global war produced and attempting to reconcile
differing opinions rather than attempting, as Churchill did, to
impose his own strategic conceptions. Disdaining argument
with subordinates, reluctant, as the politician generally is, to
undertake long-range commitments, Roosevelt employed his
powers as commander in chief in their true but negative function, as the shield and buckler of his presidential powers and his
presidential policies.

A study of his wartime role suggests that his interventions in
the *hows* and *wheres* and *whens* of strategy arose principally
from a desire to protect and advance his political objectives. In
the period before Pearl Harbor his aim was to deter the aggressors by a display of American rearmament and of military support for the Allies. In the defensive phase of the war his
primary aim was to hold the coalition together under the
enemy's hammer blows. In the days of victory he sought to
limit America's postwar responsibilities in Europe and to transfer American power as quickly and completely as possible to
the war against Japan and, in the last part of the war, that

motive led Roosevelt's strategic views, such as they were, to coincide fully for the first time since 1938 with those of his military chieftains.

Throughout, the political motive was uppermost in his mind. And it was a dominating political motive which was by and large negative in character. Critics of his war policies have given this fact too little consideration. Roosevelt's great war colleagues, Churchill and Stalin, were both moved by positive motives arising from their desire to strengthen, in war, the postwar military position of their empires. From beginning to end, Roosevelt's motives were very largely negative ones—to prevent war if possible by a show of American strength and resoluteness; to limit the spread of the war after 1939 by deterring the Japanese in the Pacific and aiding the Allies in Europe; and, finally, to fight the war after 1941 in such fashion as to weld together the wartime coalition for the purposes of peace while committing the American people as little as possible to the perplexities of postwar European politics.

Animated by these powerful though negative motives, Roosevelt was far more sensitive than is generally realized to the political aspects of the war; he performed truly the function of the American commander in chief, which is to bind together the varied political and military strands which make up war, keeping each in its proper relation to the whole. If criticism must fall upon his war presidency it probably should fall upon the soundness and realism of his political motives rather than upon his military actions. For in 1945, after a war which was on the whole soundly conceived and prosecuted, Roosevelt's—and American—hopes foundered upon the paradox of fighting a war of total victory for political purposes essentially conservative and negative in character. In 1939–1941 Roosevelt cautiously but bravely led forth the American nation from isolationism. As melancholy postwar events were to show, he failed in fact to replace isolationism with a true and coherent alternative policy. He seemed indeed to have doubted the ability and willingness of the American people to shoulder new, weighty, and, as the event has shown, unavoidable responsibilities. The great defect of his policies arose from the fact that he hoped, in the changed world of 1945, to pursue a course of action which would preserve the benefits while avoiding the disadvantages of isolation.

Throughout World War II his actions as commander in chief were consistent with these goals of policy. Events since then have plainly shown that they were inadequate and unrealistic. But what was generally considered to be adequate and realistic *at the time* is another thing. The poet warns that

> What's done we ofttimes may compute
> But know not what's prevented.

More so than appears in the afterlight of victory, World War II was for the Allies a war of narrowly averted disasters, of harsh choices, and of somewhat disheartening possibilities— truly "an option of difficulties," in General Wolfe's words. Historians of the future, sitting in judgment on Franklin Roosevelt's war presidency, may perhaps conclude that what was prevented was more important than what was done and that his leadership of the coalition, given the conditions under which it was exercised, was sounder than his statesmanship.

VIII

TRUMAN

(1945–1953)

WILBER W. HOARE, Jr.

Harry S. Truman has been commander in chief in two wars. This in itself is a distinction, since none of our other presidents has been so honored by fortune. Yet, because the human mind focuses on the man who lays the cornerstone and ignores the one who places the finial, Truman's part in World War II is obscured in the shadow of Roosevelt, and his war leadership is generally linked only to the Korean War.

It is true that when Truman succeeded to the presidency on April 12, 1945, he felt bound by the decisions and commitments of the four years past, and by his own lack of knowledge, to continue the war policies of Roosevelt. Vice-President for only eighty-two days, during most of which Roosevelt was away from Washington, he had but the barest of initiations into the current business of the executive. According to his memoirs, he had learned little by his attendance at the cabinet meetings, where he found few subjects of real importance discussed before the whole group. What he knew of the strategic direction of the war he had learned chiefly through his service in the Senate, especially as chairman of the Special Committee to Investigate the National Defense Program. His information, therefore, was necessarily limited, since the Truman Committee had concerned itself with the only part of the total war that was within easy reach of Congress while the battle was still on: the mobilization and procurement program. So important a secret as that of the Manhattan Project's war-stopping work on the atomic bomb had not been shared by Roosevelt with his vice-president.[1]

It is also true that by April, 1945, the "prize we sought" was almost won, that the United States had sailed too far on a set course for any turning into uncharted waters. The defeat of Germany was visible on the horizon, actually nearer than it seemed. Beyond that the fall of Japan could be seen as inevitable. But political and military decisions vital to the future of the country and the world still remained to be made. Such questions as the timing of, and the price to be paid for, the defeat of Japan, the occupation of the enemy nations, and the use of the atomic weapon had to be settled by the new commander in chief. And if the ghost of F. D. R. stood at Truman's elbow in Potsdam, at least no dead hand drafted the order that sent the atomic bomb to Hiroshima.

Thus, to regard Truman's five-month tour as commander in chief during the greater war as merely an apprenticeship for his Korean "assignment" is to ignore the fact that he acted as a full-fledged master of the guild from the day he took the oath of office. Never one to back away from responsibility, he went to work with the determination of a man trained to command. Problems set before him were disposed of with clarity and firmness. He was, of course, forced to rely heavily on the advice, and especially the knowledge, of Roosevelt's military chiefs and cabinet officers. But insofar as it was possible for him, by intensive study and winnowing discussions with his advisers, he made every top-level decision his own. In the rare instances when he had to approve an action wholly on the advice of another, he nevertheless made it understood that he took complete responsibility for it. The military doctrine of command responsibility, according to which the commander is accountable for all actions of his organization, he held applicable to the presidency. Because of this, and because of his decisiveness and frankness, he had no difficulty in winning and keeping the respect of those military leaders who worked closely with him.

If Truman held to the war policies of his predecessor and retained the latter's military leaders and advisers, he nevertheless changed the methods of leadership and administrative direction to suit his own more rational and prosaic temperament. In one passage of his memoirs, he characterizes Roosevelt as "a man of vision and ideas," who admitted that he was no administrator and who preferred to delegate administrative responsibility to others.[2] In another place, he states that Roosevelt bore too much of the burden of the direction of the war alone, doing himself many things that he should have left to his cabinet.[3] The apparent contradiction between these two statements lay not in Truman's observations but in the frequent inconsistency of Roosevelt's methods, which permitted great freedom of decision and action to some officials and advisers while severely restricting that of others, and which made a cabinet officer powerful in his own domain at one period and reduced him to near-impotence at another. Truman's system of administration, on the other hand, was generally consistent—consistent within itself and consistent with the organization of government as he inherited it and as he later modified it.

This, indeed, is the basic difference between the two commanders in chief. Roosevelt exercised his leadership by directing the tremendous power of his personality and intellect toward solving by himself whatever problem was most critical at the moment, acting, at times, as his own Secretary of State, his own ambassador, or his own chief of staff. Truman, although constrained to some extent to follow the path of personal diplomacy blazed by Roosevelt, worked with and through the established executive agencies whenever he could. The personal influence of Roosevelt surged over the banks of the presidency to cover the nation and the world. The personal influence of Harry Truman was felt chiefly by his staff and cabinet and generally was imparted to the outside world through official channels. Whereas Roosevelt personified ideas and magnetized others into a realization of them, Truman sought to make sound decisions based on traditional and "common-sense" ideals and to see that they were carried out by men charged by law with that responsibility. In fact, Truman tried to run the executive branch much in accordance with school textbooks on government.

Given his bent for operating with and within established structures of government, Truman as Commander in Chief in the Korean conflict is to be understood largely in the edifice of defense that was built between the wars. Long concerned with military affairs, the President had come to the White House a convinced advocate of service unification. The August 26, 1944, issue of *Colliers* had carried an article written by Truman, then still a senator, in which he called for integration of the army and navy under the secretary of a single department, with a unified general staff controlling tactics and strategy without the necessity for compromises among the chiefs of independent services. In most of his public and official statements on unification from that time until the passage of the National Security Act of 1947, he seemed to lay a greater emphasis on eliminating waste in procurement, ending duplication of effort and matériel, and integrating strategic plans with the military budget, than on efficient action in war. Two facts account for this. First, his experience on the Truman Committee enabled him to speak at length and with authority on matters of procurement and mobilization. Second, the postwar atmosphere made savings in money and matériel particularly attractive to the public and the Congress. But, as shown by the defense structure called for in his *Colliers* article and in his message to Congress of December 19, 1945, effectiveness in the direction of combat forces was his primary aim.

The organization of the Department of Defense that emerged in the National Security Act of 1947[4] was at most a diluted version of the single department with a general staff proposed by Senator Truman in 1944. Interservice disagreement and congressional jealousies and reservations made it a compromise between the vested interests of the past and the felt necessities of the future. Except for the fact that it introduced the Secretary of Defense as the coordinating authority over three coordinate services, the new organization for the most part confirmed and institutionalized the command structures and practices developed during World War II. But, strengthened by the National Security Act amendments of 1949, it provided a machinery of command that, if not adequate in all respects, at least required no *ad hoc* revision during the three years of the Korean War.

On the eve of the conflict, the military command structure at the disposal of the Commander in Chief comprised three essential elements: the Secretary of Defense, the Joint Chiefs of Staff, and the commanders of unified and specified commands. The Secretary of Defense was "the principal assistant to the President in all matters relating to the Department of Defense" and under the direction of the President exercised "direction, authority, and control" over his department. Since the amendments of 1949 had reduced the service secretaries to heads of "military departments," with almost no direct influence on strategy or command, he was the military establishment's sole representative in the cabinet.[5]

Responsible for preparing plans and providing strategic direction of the military forces were the Joint Chiefs of Staff, who were designated by law as the principal military advisers to the President, the National Security Council, and the Secretary of Defense.[6] Not the law but a directive by the Secretary of Defense, approved by the President, gave the Joint Chiefs "general direction of all combat operations."[7] Basically the same organization that it was in World War II, the Joint Staff of slightly more than two hundred officers from all services and a sizable secretariat drafted and implemented the decisions of the JCS, but more as the servants than the masters of the three services. In contrast to World War II, when Admiral Leahy had represented the President in presiding over their meetings, the JCS now had a chairman, who presided, provided the agenda, and represented them before the President, the National Security Council, and the Secretary of Defense.[8]

Representing the Joint Chiefs in the field were commanders of unified commands, composed of the forces of two or more services, and specified commands, comprising the forces of only one service with a broad and continuing mission, such as the Strategic Air Command. Such commands were established by the Joint Chiefs of Staff and their commanders were responsible to them, and through them to the Secretary of Defense and the President. Although not recognized by law, the World War II practice whereby the Joint Chiefs of Staff designated one of their members their "executive agent" for general administration and operational control of a unified command had been formalized as one of the results of the Key West conference in 1948.[9]

If the command structure of the Korean War was thus not essentially different from that developed during the greater war that preceded it, certain not unimportant changes had taken place, partly because of the alterations in the structure itself and partly because of evolution in practice. The creation of a single Secretary of Defense had strengthened civilian control within the military establishment. He was in a much more powerful position vis-à-vis the Joint Chiefs of Staff than were the former Secretaries of War and the Navy. Even though the Joint Chiefs were still the "principal military advisers to the President" the Secretary now stood at least in the doorway when they approached the Commander in Chief, if not, as was almost always the case under Truman, behind the President's desk. The replacement of the Chief of Staff to the President by the Chairman of the Joint Chiefs of Staff further strengthened the Secretary, removing the most inviting channel through which he could be bypassed, whether from above or below. And if the Secretary could not alter or short-stop communications from the Joint Chiefs of Staff to the President and the National Security Council, he at least saw them and could communicate his own views, when he forwarded them.

Within the organization of the Joint Chiefs of Staff itself, the introduction of the office of chairman operated to remove the chiefs of the services from the presence of the commander in chief. Though by law without "vote" or power to command, the chairman spoke for them before the President and the National Security Council. The World War II comedy showing a Chief of Naval Operations seeking a favorable decision from the President, only to find that the latter had already said yes to the army Chief of Staff, would not be played to an audience in the 1950's. The scope of the service chief's individual influence had been reduced in order to enlarge that of the JCS as a corporate body—again, the type of institutional development that Truman favored and that suited his method of working, giving him a tighter control at the top of the pyramid.

Other changes had been wrought by eight years of joint operations. Despite the fact that the JCS could not avoid differences over the basic question of roles and missions, the "joint" spirit had begun to take hold, especially within the Joint Staff. Here, as in other joint agencies, loyalty to the "unit" and the "mission" tended to wilt the sharper thorns of service rivalry. Officers who had had experience with joint operations in the Pacific, Europe, and Africa worked with a staff machinery considerably refined from the rather hasty improvisations of 1942. By the time of the invasion of South Korea in June, 1950, the Joint Chiefs of Staff and their organization were ready to direct smoothly a "joint" war, however much difficulty they might have with a joint peace.

They were also ready, as never before, to wage a war in accordance with complex and shifting political aims. The National Security Act of 1947 had been a double marriage license. Not only had it put the military services under the same roof, but it joined the State and Defense departments—political and military policy—in the National Security Council. Prior to World War II contacts between the State Department and the military had amounted to little more than flirtation; politico-military decisions sprang almost exclusively from the head of the President. In 1944, however, the immense problems that arose in both fields with the impending defeat of the Axis demanded extensive cooperation, and a trial marriage, the State-War-Navy Coordinating Committee (later the State-Army-Navy-Air Force Coordinating Committee, or SANACC), was instituted, to be superseded by the more formal National Security Council.[10]

At the beginning of the Korean War the NSC was comprised of the President, Vice-President, Secretaries of State and of Defense, and the Chairman of the National Securities Resources Board. Although he had statutory authority to appoint heads of other executive departments to the group, Truman chose not to do so. He did, however, approve the attendance at meetings of officials who, though not members, were concerned with policies being discussed. The Chairman of the Joint Chiefs of Staff, or in his absence one of the service chiefs, always accompanied the Secretary of Defense to the weekly sessions, where he could explain and defend the views of the JCS, even against the opposition of the Secretary.[11]

This was the structure of the presidency and the command-in-chief on June 24, 1950, when President Truman at his home in Independence, Missouri, received an electrifying telephone call. "Mr. President," said the voice of the Secretary of State, "I have very serious news. The North Koreans have invaded South Korea."

As soon as enough information came to him to prove the

attack a real invasion rather than a mere border raid, the President directed the Secretary of State to summon the Secretary of Defense, the service secretaries, and the chiefs of staff, and he himself sped back to Washington by private plane. As he flew, he relates in his memoirs, he thought of Manchuria, Ethiopia, and Austria. "I remembered how each time that the democracies failed to act it had encouraged the aggressors to keep going ahead. . . . I felt certain that if South Korea was allowed to fall Communist leaders would be emboldened to override nations closer to our own shores. . . . If this was allowed to go unchallenged it would mean a third world war."

Since the White House was under repair, the President's quarters were temporarily in Blair House, an early nineteenth-century town house on the opposite side of Pennsylvania Avenue, and it was there that he met his advisers on the evening of June 25.

Why, since the NSC was ostensibly erected to amalgamate political aims with military capabilities, was not the decision to enter hostilities in Korea made by that agency rather than in extemporaneous gatherings of State and Defense officials? The answer to this question lies partly in the fact that the practices of the Council, established in a time of relatively little stress and used only for matters of broad general policy, were too ponderous. Normal procedure required the establishment of departmental positions in at least the State and Defense departments, the melding of these positions, if possible, by the NSC staff, the submission of considered comments and recommendations by the Joint Chiefs of Staff, discussion in the NSC itself, and finally, action by the President on the recommendations of the Council. Obviously, decisions made by this process would require days, if not weeks. Then, too, Truman regarded the NSC as an advisory rather than a decision-making body. Its recommendations, though important, were not essential to the direction of government. His decisions were.[12]

In calling together at Blair House on the nights of June 25 and 26, 1950, the Secretaries of State and Defense and of the military departments, the Joint Chiefs of Staff, and several high State Department officials, the President was, for all practical purposes, consulting the NSC, but telescoping its deliberations. True, the Vice-President and the Chairman of the NSRB were absent, neither being immediately available, but their advice was not required. The Secretary of State was present to propose a course of action—one which had already been talked over and agreed to by officials of State and Defense. The Joint Chiefs of Staff orally outlined for the Commander in Chief the military costs and implications. After hearing the views of each of those present, Mr. Truman approved the recommended action and gave instructions for its implementation.[13] Thus all the elements of an NSC action were employed except the form. However much Truman preferred to adhere to conventional and legal structures of government, he could forego form when occasion demanded, and he did so when deciding to support the South Korean republic.

Whether in acting without the consent of Congress he also foresook form for speed is not entirely clear. In all likelihood, Truman and his advisers considered that the measures taken were within the prerogatives of the commander in chief. There is no evidence at hand to indicate that the question was even discussed at Blair House. Nor, apparently, did Truman make any attempt to justify his action when he met with Congressional leaders on June 27, although he did stress the point that it was the United Nations that was acting.[14] In Congress, Senators Taft, Kem, and Wherry challenged the decision as a usurpation of Congressional authority, but approval of the principle of defending South Korea was so general that the question of Constitutional principle remained moot.

Did the United States, during the last week of June, 1950, stumble into war through a series of decisions not all of which were well thought out or sufficiently discussed? This has been the conclusion of some observers, who hold that the nation was not finally committed to the defense of South Korea until the President sanctioned the use of American ground forces. But the impression left with the reader of his memoirs is that Truman himself considered the deliberations of the first Blair House conference to be decisive. Apparently he was already resolved, on June 25, to do whatever was necessary to save South Korea, and he felt that his resolution had the unanimous support of his diplomatic and military counsellors. Once this decision had been made, the progressive commitment of forces and the enlargement of their scope of action was only a reflection of increasingly clear intelligence reports from the battlefield.

As soon as it became obvious that something more than logistical support was needed by Syngman Rhee's army, United States air and naval forces were launched against targets in Korea south of the 38th parallel. Continued advances by Communist troops brought American planes and ships against military targets north of the parallel. When General MacArthur reported, after a personal survey of the field, that only American foot soldiers could halt the invaders, Truman did not hesitate. At five o'clock in the morning on June 30, he authorized by telephone the dispatch of one regimental combat team, and only a few hours later he gave MacArthur full authority to use the ground forces of the Far East Command.[15] Thus the involvement of the United States in the Korean War was the result of a single politico-military decision. While it was still possible, for a brief time after the first Blair House meeting, to stop short or to reverse the decision, orders resulting from the second meeting brought the United States beyond the point of no return. After that, defeat of South Korea would mean defeat of the United States—unacceptable even though only naval and air forces were involved.

Once the "week of decisions" was past, what might be termed the organization of the commander in chief settled down to working as it was intended to work. Strategic direction of operations was centered in the Joint Chiefs of Staff, who labored together with little evidence of the interservice jealousy often visible during World War II. The testimony at the MacArthur hearings in May and June, 1951, indicates that up to that time, at least, few if any split papers on Korean War matters had been sent up for the Secretary of Defense or the President to resolve.

Compared to its operation in the previous war, the functioning of the JCS decision-making machinery was unspectacular. Nearly a decade of development in routine contributed to the orderly consideration of problems—which, since the conflict was limited in nature, seldom attained the proportions or urgency of the numerous larger problems of World War II. Whether originating in the Far East, the United Nations Command, the NSC, the State Department, or one of the services, problems referred to the JCS typically were considered by one of the groups of the Joint Staff, which drafted a paper for decision by the Joint Chiefs of Staff. If their decision resulted in a directive to "Commander in Chief, Far East," it was first sent to the Secretary of Defense for approval. Since President Truman had ordered that all except the most routine directives to the theater should be seen by him before being dispatched, it would then be carried to the White House either by the Secretary of Defense or by General Omar N. Bradley, Chairman of the Joint Chiefs of Staff. After receiving his assent, the more important directives were sent as messages in the name of the JCS, the less important dispatched by the Army staff.[16] Only on a few occasions, when they felt that a voice of the highest authority was needed to lead or to restrain, to congratulate or to relieve, did the President or the Secretary of Defense address the theater commander directly.

During the early days of the war, the JCS were in daily contact with the President through their Chairman, who was at the White House every morning. Later, when the situation on the battlefield was not so precarious, his visits were reduced to three in a week. The thorough briefings that General Bradley gave the President took the place of the map-room briefings received by Roosevelt.[17] But more than that, they kept the Commander in Chief abreast of the thinking and actions of the JCS. And, scarcely less important, the frequent conversations between the two kept the JCS constantly informed of what was in the mind of the President. Uncertainty concerning White House position had often plagued the JCS of World War II. The chiefs who served under Truman were seldom, if ever, in doubt on this score.

The institution of the United Nations Command, authorized by the United Nations Security Council resolution of July 7, 1950, had no effect on the operating methods of the Joint Chiefs of Staff or on their relationship to the Commander in Chief. Under the terms of the resolution, the United States government acted as executive agent for the United Nations. It had full powers in the realm of strategy, and cleared its decisions and plans with no UN agency. The biweekly report required by the resolution from the United Nations Command was only a type of after-action report on the course of the battle, and rarely, if at all, did it contain information not already heard by the public in the buzzing of the swarm of reporters in Tokyo.

Except in name, the United Nations Command was scarcely more than the United States Far East Command, augmented by South Korean troops and smaller contingents from other members of the United Nations. Since he was already the executive agent of the Joint Chiefs of Staff for the Far East Command, General J. Lawton Collins, Chief of Staff of the Army, naturally acted as executive agent for the United Nations Command. Thus the organization of command under which the United Nations fought its war in Korea was wholly that of the United States, which had been developed under Truman out of the experience of World War II. The liaison officers maintained by some of our allies in the headquarters in Tokyo had no voice in the direction of strategy; General MacArthur was responsible only to the Joint Chiefs of Staff and the government in Washington. No direct channel of communication was ever permitted to develop between his headquarters and the United Nations.[18]

No commander in chief in American history has been more fortunate in the officers of his high command, especially at the beginning of a war, than was Truman in his Joint Chiefs of Staff in 1950. All had served prominently in the second rank during World War II and required no training at high command. All combined high professional qualifications with modesty, capacity for teamwork, and devotion to the principle of civilian supremacy in the making of policy. All were committed to the success of unification; both General Collins and the Chief of Naval Operations, Admiral Forrest P. Sherman, had been among the architects of the National Security Act of 1947.[19] If none of them became outstanding strategists like Marshall and King, it was largely because "war by committee" had developed to the point where individualism was not demanded or even encouraged. The limited nature of the war in Korea, the merging of political and military strategy, and the ever-tight control of the President over decisions, combined to deny them the comparatively broad freedom of action enjoyed by the first Joint Chiefs of Staff. The only one among them, who, by virtue of prestige and position, might have bid for dominance was the mild-mannered, fatherly General Bradley. He, however, never sought to impose his own opinions on the service chiefs other than by persuasion, and represented their views faithfully to the President and the Secretary of Defense.

With one exception, Truman was equally fortunate in his Secretaries of Defense. Under more normal circumstances, Louis Johnson would certainly have proved an adequate, if not a good, Secretary. That the Korean invasion found the United States with its military trousers at half mast was not primarily his fault. To Truman himself belongs the chief responsibility for the poor state of defense preparation in 1950, for he had relaxed his leadership to follow the desires of Congress and the public in restricting military budgets. Nevertheless, the popular identification of Johnson with the low level of the armed forces reduced his usefulness. Whether or not it was a factor leading to his all-but-forced resignation is not clear. In his testimony at the MacArthur hearings, Johnson asserted that he did not know why he was "out," and Truman has not made his reasons public. Of the speculations current at the time, the most plausible is that Johnson was released because he did not work well with Truman's first officer of government, Secretary of State Dean Acheson. Reports of disagreements and outright quarrels between the two were numerous. Although Johnson consistently denied the existence of any schism with the State Department, he had put an end to the "Indian-level" cooperation between the Pentagon and the diplomats across the Potomac that had persisted after the demise of SANACC.[20] In a war where military policy had to be linked at every point with foreign policy, lack of coordination between State and Defense below the level of the NSC was intolerable. General Marshall, who replaced Secretary Johnson in September, 1950, did not wait long before ordering the resumption of informal consultations with State Department personnel and instituting regular weekly meetings between State officials and the Joint Chiefs of Staff.[21]

A former Moltke who had studied Bismarck's trade, General Marshall was ideally suited to head the Defense Department in a limited war. The almost universal confidence accorded him, especially in Congress, enabled him to accomplish quietly his primary task, to prevent a runaway mobilization while presiding over the orderly build-up of the military forces to "long-haul" levels. His friendship with Dean Acheson, who had served under him when he was Secretary of State, insured the coordination of the military hand and the political arm. His prestige as a military leader and wartime chief of staff, as well as the fact that he was the oldest-ranking five-star general, gave him an authority in speaking to MacArthur beyond that possible to a Secretary with a different background. By no means least important, Marshall had the trust and respect of the

President more than any other military figure, more perhaps than any high official. Much could be left to his judgment that Truman might have been unwilling to permit to another, giving the hard-working President more time for other matters.

When Marshall returned to the Pentagon, he brought with him as Deputy Secretary of Defense the man to whom he bequeathed his own office a year later, Mr. Robert A. Lovett. Like James Forrestal an investment banker, Lovett had served as wartime Assistant Secretary of War for Air and had been Marshall's Undersecretary of State. By the time he succeeded Marshall as Secretary of Defense in 1951, he was trained to the job as few cabinet officers have been. His appointment was not only a nonpolitical appointment (he was a Republican) but also a professional one. And professionalism in Defense affairs was what Truman and the situation demanded.

Marshall's tour of duty as Secretary of Defense saw the consummation of the marriage of foreign policy and armed force. Up to that time, although the National Security Council had provided something more than a ceremonial bed for two rather frigid partners, the informality of a successful marriage had been lacking. Under Marshall, restricting channels of communication were dissolved. Proposed military actions involving political considerations were discussed informally with officials of the State Department and cleared with Secretary Acheson before submission to the President. Conversely, diplomatic projects having military connotations were carried to the JCS. Since as a rule only those measures affecting broad and basic policies went to the NSC, this type of cooperation went beyond what was contemplated in the National Security Act of 1947.[22] But without it, the NSC would have had to descend to a lower level of policy consideration for which it was not organized.

Although by September, 1950, Truman had a staff that functioned almost as an integral part of his own mind and will, he never for a moment abandoned the tiller to anyone, neither to Acheson nor to Marshall, nor, especially, to the military chiefs. As he saw it, only the President could make the important decisions. The actions of the Secretary of Defense and of the JCS all fell into one of two categories—advice to the commander in chief or implementation of his directives. Orders to the theater commander he viewed as his orders, and he expected them to be obeyed as such. When General Mark Clark, in his book, *From the Danube to the Yalu,* stated that he had not been surprised at the relief of General MacArthur because of the latter's dispute with the JCS,[23] he was thinking in terms of a bygone war. In 1951, any disagreement with established policy or strategy was a disagreement with the President.

This was a fact that MacArthur, too, did not fully comprehend, just as he failed to understand many of the changes of the postwar years. Though one of the greatest soldiers of the first half of the twentieth century, the beginning of the second half found him a politico-military anachronism. His world was the world of the second great war and the Japanese occupation. To the advances of unification he gave only perfunctory recognition. His staff was not a joint staff but a one-service army staff, dominated by officers who had been with him for years. His theater command he regarded not as a unified command, the creation and agent of the JCS, but as the powerful independent command of World War II. The necessity for the complete subjection of theater to world strategy, for the intertwining of foreign and military policy, he claimed to understand, but his understanding of the changes in world power relationships bore only a surface resemblance to that of the leaders in

Washington and Europe. The apparent success of his leadership in Korea, during the first hundred and fifty days of the war, was owing to the fact that outwardly, at least, the conflict was comprehensible in World War II terms. Only in those terms could the Chinese intervention, all of a piece with the North Korean invasion, be called a "new war." His sense of frustration and rage at being denied an unequivocal victory were not those of a man who understood the reasons for denial and opposed them, but of one who did not understand at all.

The Chinese intervention came at a moment when Mac-Arthur felt himself on the verge of one of the triumphs of his career, one that he would have to share with no one as he had had to share the laurels of World War II with Eisenhower. It would have crowned a campaign begun against heavy odds and marked by a flanking maneuver worthy of the young Napoleon.

The North Korean army that had crossed the 38th parallel on June 25, 1950, had been well trained, well organized, and well armed. It had shattered the lightly-armed South Korean formations, capturing Seoul, the capital, within five days. Only by throwing in three U.S. army divisions from Japan, and a marine brigade from the United States, was MacArthur able to hold an arc of hills and rivers north and west of the port of Pusan.

Then, after five weeks of vicious fighting on the "perimeter," MacArthur, with the approval of the President and the JCS, made his move. Withdrawing the marines from Pusan, and combining with them the last army division in Japan, he sent them crashing into the west coast port of Inchon on September 15. His forces quickly secured nearby Seoul and cut the main lines of communications between the Communist troops and their homeland bases. At about the same time the United

Nations divisions around Pusan broke out of the perimeter and clawed their way northward, chasing the North Koreans back across their frontier.

Early in October, United Nations forces, in two columns, crossed into North Korea and pursued the broken enemy toward the Manchurian border. On the 20th the tide of advance reached the Communist capital of Pyongyang, rolling over it with scarcely a pause. By the end of the month, however, enemy resistance had begun to stiffen, and the capture of the first Chinese prisoners had emphasized the ever-present possibility of massive intervention from across the Yalu River.

Operations during the first two weeks of November revealed the presence in Korea of large numbers of Chinese soldiers. Their intervention, MacArthur reported, increased the enemy's capability three hundred per cent, and caused him to redeploy his forces for large-scale coordinated action. But the end of the second week found the United Nations formations again only lightly resisted, and on November 24 MacArthur launched an enveloping attack that he hoped would push through to the Yalu and end the war.

His hopes ended in bitter disappointment. His attack was met by an overwhelming Chinese thrust that forced U.N. units back in hasty, and not always organized, retreat. In the weeks that followed MacArthur gave up the ground he had won in North Korea and fell back south of the parallel. Seoul again passed to the Communists in January as his forces withdrew to defensive positions south of the Han River. Here, however, the Communist offensive lost its momentum and the Eighth Army under General Ridgway began at the end of the month a series of operations that was to take the United Nations flag again to the parallel by Easter.

On November 28, four days after he had launched his "end the war" offensive, MacArthur had proclaimed that the U.N. forces "face an entirely new war." Following his announcement he bombarded Washington with recommendations for action against the new aggressor, among them a blockade of the Chinese coast, destruction of Chinese bases, and the employment of Chinese Nationalist forces. But the President was not willing to acknowledge that MacArthur's "new war" differed basically from the old, nor would he consent to alter his limited objectives. As he relates in his memoirs, he cabled the general on January 13:

. . . pending the build-up of our national strength, we must act with great prudence in so far as extending the area of hostilities is concerned. Steps which might in themselves be fully justified and which might lend some assistance to the campaign in Korea would not be beneficial if they thereby involved Japan or Western Europe in large-scale hostilities.[24]

Thereafter MacArthur, who in December had already begun to complain publicly about the restrictions and limitations that prevented him from acting against the sources of Chinese military strength, became increasingly vocal, and relations between his headquarters and the White House grew more and more strained.

From the President's standpoint, insubordination on MacArthur's part had been evident for some time. In August the general had sent a letter to the head of the Veterans of Foreign Wars which Truman viewed as an attack on his policy toward Formosa. Although MacArthur obeyed his order to withdraw the statement, he did so too late to forestall its publication in a national magazine. The President administered a mild reproof and subsequently journeyed to Wake Island in the mid-Pacific in order to achieve an "understanding" with MacArthur.

Matters drew to a head when, toward the end of March, 1951, Truman and his advisers decided that the major objectives of the Korean action had been won—the aggressor had been repelled; the determination of the United States and the United Nations demonstrated; and the moral and military strength of the West considerably increased. The President was ready to propose truce negotiations, and MacArthur was informed that an announcement to this effect was in preparation. MacArthur, however, on March 24, issued his own invitation and ultimatum. He was prepared, he announced, to meet the enemy commander in the field and discuss "military means" of ending hostilities. Refusal, he implied, might result in an extension of operations to the Chinese coast and homeland. To the President this declaration seemed "open defiance."[25]

Truman felt compelled to exercise his Constitutional powers. Through the JCS he rebuked MacArthur and ordered that any Communist peace feeler be reported to Washington immediately. Scarcely ten days later, he learned of a letter that the General had written to Joseph W. Martin, the Republican leader in the House of Representatives and a bitter critic of the administration. Spread upon the *Congressional Record*, it persuaded Truman that the General could not accept fundamental presidential policies. MacArthur felt "that here we fight Europe's war with arms while the diplomats there still fight it with words; that if we lose this war to Communism in Asia the fall of Europe is inevitable, win it and Europe most probably would avoid war and yet preserve freedom. . . . There is no substitute for victory." Despite a warning from the Secretary of State that he would face the biggest fight of his career, the

President resolved to act. After securing unanimous support from his chief advisers and the JCS, he relieved MacArthur of his commands and replaced him with General Matthew B. Ridgway.[26]

The incidents that led to this climax were not rooted in malice or arrogance, in jealousy or in partisan politics. At the bottom lay misunderstanding, and that by no means wholly on the part of the United Nations commander. For the President and his chief advisers alike failed to comprehend that for MacArthur, isolated in Japan, time had stopped between V-J Day and June 25, 1950. The realities of the United States position in the world, which seemed so obvious to them because they dealt with them daily, they felt should be equally clear to him, especially since the JCS and the army staff were at pains to keep him informed. But teletype conferences and coded messages were at best a highly imperfect means of communication and conveyed only partial understanding to a recipient who thought in a different frame of reference. Even visits to the field, such as those of some of the JCS to Tokyo and Korea, were insufficient to bring the "Big Picture" to a commander who had not seen it for himself. They were insufficient, too, for bringing to light the fact that men were using the same words but meaning different things; hence the "understanding" of Wake Island. Had MacArthur spent six months in a responsible position in the Pentagon between 1948 and 1950, he could not have made the gross miscalculations concerning the President's directives that he apparently made. But the services' policy of rotation in assignment had been suspended for the proconsul and part of his staff. General Ridgway, who went to Korea from the Pentagon, did not have the same difficulty, nor did he make similar mistakes.

Unfortunately for Truman's reputation as commander in chief, his record of quiet courage and integrity is difficult to read in the distracting glare of the MacArthur controversy. The attention of scholars, as well as that of the public, has concentrated on the spectacular dispute between the General and the President, not merely because MacArthur was a hero to two generations, but because of the important questions seemingly raised in the field of civil-military relations and the discussion of the issues of limited versus all-out war. The General never intended to challenge the authority of the Commander in Chief to direct the war, nor did he consider that he had done so. Neither did he advocate an unlimited war in the Far East, despite the inferences that have been read into his phrase, "There is no substitute for victory." MacArthur wished to avoid World War III quite as much as Truman did.

The crux of their disagreement lay in their different answers to two questions in the field of strategy. The first: How great were the risks involved in extending operations beyond the borders of Korea in order to achieve victory on the peninsula? The second: How important to the future security of the United States was such a victory? MacArthur's position, reduced to its simplest terms, was that a U.N.-unified Korea was well-nigh essential in turning back the threat of communism, not only in the Far East, but throughout the world, and that the risks to be run were far from unacceptable. He believed that the measures he considered necessary would not provoke an armed response from the Soviet Union, indeed, would not even result in a full-scale war with Communist China. To Truman, as well as to Marshall and the JCS, these views were the product of the limited outlook of a commander concerned with only one theater. They, who had a world-wide comprehension and responsibility, were better able to understand the hazards inherent in his proposals. In their judgment the possible loss of allies and damage to the system of collective defense, on which they counted so much, as well as the possibility of general war, which they thought much greater than did Mac-Arthur, made the prize not worth the risk.[27]

A disagreement over strategy between the commander in chief and a subordinate of MacArthur's stature was not out of place in Truman's conception of military relationships, as he himself acknowledges in his memoirs. What angered the President and led to his decision to relieve the general was the fact that, as he saw it, MacArthur appealed over his head to the public and, in addition, injected issues of foreign policy that were not in his domain. Furthermore, he believed that he had cautioned the General on several occasions about public statements in a way that a reasonable man could not misunderstand, and he had issued a categorical directive that "No speech, press release, or other public statement" concerning foreign policy be released without State Department clearance and no similar statement on military policy without Defense Department approval.[28] The President apparently could not imagine that this order could be misinterpreted, yet the headquarters in Tokyo did just that, applying it only to public pronouncements and not to communiqués, correspondence, or personal communications with others.[29] Moreover, habits acquired in years of speaking as both the political and the military voice of the United States in Japan seem to have left MacArthur incapable of distinguishing between foreign policy, military policy, and military operations, on the last of which he was free to comment publicly. He therefore saw nothing wrong with his statement of March 24, 1951, or his letter to Congressman Martin, and could find in his own mind no justification for his relief.

The career of MacArthur had been a brilliant one. Its very brilliance, however, led to its end, for because of it he was permitted, during the 1940's, to become more than a soldier. When, in 1950, Truman tried, in a not unkindly way, to lay him in the Procrustean bed of a mere theater commander he could no longer fit, and the President, attributing this to contumaciousness, lopped him off.

The decision to remove MacArthur, like almost all other decisions of the President during the Korean War, can be fitted into two overlapping and inseparable patterns. One pattern is Truman's view of military responsibilities and relationships. The other is that of his war aims. Operating within the first was the commander in chief, head of a military organization dedicated to success on the field of battle. Within the other functioned a president, who knew that there were more things in the philosophy of Clausewitz than were dreamt of in the heaven and earth of the old staff schools.

In his war aims Truman looked far beyond the Korean conflict, both in time and space. Briefly stated, they were: to halt the armed splurge of Communism in Korea and, at the same time, to build up the military power of the West as a deterrent to any further attacks. These aims, of course, had a number of corollaries and extensions. The war had to be limited to Korea. Otherwise there would be no opportunity for the build-up and the United States might be involved heavily with the wrong enemy, China, or the West fighting the whole of Communist power before its defenses were in order. The character of the war as a United Nations' action had to be maintained, since that body was, and might be in the future, a not impotent force against aggression. The nations fighting beside the United States in Korea had to be not pampered but treated as respectable partners, especially because those making the greatest contributions, next to the United States and South Korea, were allies in the North Atlantic Treaty Organization. Formosa had to be protected to prevent a break in United States Pacific defenses. And perhaps above all, World War III had to be prevented.

Within the pattern of these aims, Truman's decisions fell with consistency and integrity, from the first Blair House meeting to the beginning of the truce negotiations and beyond. That he made mistakes is certain, since he was human. What they were, and how great they were, historians can determine only in the future. We stand too close to the events, and too few of the records have been opened, to make any but a preliminary and tentative judgment. But it would seem that on the whole Truman accomplished his objectives. When he left office, the frontier in Korea was at about the same place that it was before June, 1950. The armed forces of the United States were stronger and better prepared for defense of the West. The power of the United Nations to enforce peace had been, to some extent at least, enhanced. The NATO coalition had been stiffened and its strength augmented, and the prestige of the United States, as leader of the West, had not suffered. Finally, the war had been limited to Korea, and the United States could look forward to peace, however uneasy, and time to prepare for a more crucial struggle.

The burden of acting as commander in chief in two major wars fell on one whom many Americans would consider an unlikely candidate for the company of the great wartime presi-

dents—Lincoln, Wilson, and Franklin D. Roosevelt. Yet Harry
S. Truman, sometime farmer, bank clerk, artillery captain,
haberdasher, judge, and Senator, brought to the task at least
as much in experience with military affairs, in dedication to the
security of the United States, and in willingness to make decisions and take the responsibility for them as his more illustrious
predecessors. He also possessed a conception of the rational
organization and working of government, especially in relation
to the military establishment, that others, possessing perhaps
greater qualities of personal leadership, frequently lacked; that
Roosevelt, for one, seems to have consciously avoided. In accordance with this conception, he used his service chiefs and
defense advisers, and his cabinet officers too, much in the
manner in which the modern military commander uses his staff.
As much as anything else, his handling of his top military
advisers by methods to which they themselves had been trained
and with which they felt at ease accounts for the always complete understanding, if not always complete agreement, between the President and the Joint Chiefs of Staff during the
Korean War. It accounts for a rapport so great that, although
nonpolitical, it lent a shadow of verisimilitude to the charge of
Senator Robert Taft that Truman's military chiefs were so
committed to his policies that they should not be retained by
the Republican administration under President Eisenhower.

Furthermore, however harmonious may have been the relationships between the President and the Joint Chiefs of Staff,
Truman never became to any perceptible degree the captive of
his military staff. That he did not do so is owing not only to the
fact that study of history and his own observations had put him
on his guard, but also to what was most characteristic of him
in his performance as commander in chief—the great and un-

flagging energy by which he gained an intimate knowledge of what was going on and held in unrelenting hands the reins of command. Under such an executive there could not develop a Ludendorff or a Moltke or, for that matter, a chief of staff with the power and freedom of action of Marshall in World War II. In more respects than most, Truman was the commander in chief envisioned by the writers of the Constitution.

IX

EISENHOWER
AND AFTER

(1953–   )

ERNEST R. MAY

W E HAVE SEEN that the framers of the Constitution made the president commander in chief so that wartime decisions could be made by someone politically responsible. Some of them also hoped that the result would be to keep military men and military issues out of politics in time of peace. Washington was to control the Society of the Cincinnati while Congress, like the Virginia assemblies which it resembled, could make "a Joke on all military Affars." Noah Webster in his *Examination into the Leading Principles of the Federal Constitution* (1787) assured the apprehensive that "the principles and habits, as well as the powers of the Americans are directly opposed to standing armies; and there is as little necessity to guard against them . . . as to prohibit the establishment of the Mahometan religion."

The more sober of these expectations was realized. From Madison to Truman, presidents successfully made those crucial decisions that Marlborough had made for Queen Anne. For most of a hundred and fifty years, the other hope of the framers was also fulfilled. There were no large peacetime forces, and men in regular uniforms played inconspicuous roles in public life.

But this last changed. After 1940 the American people felt themselves in danger, first from Nazi Germany and then from Communist Russia. New weapons emerged that appeared capable of flying the oceans in minutes and demolishing whole counties in seconds. As Walter Millis remarked in 1956 in *Arms and Men,* the potential character of warfare changed so greatly that the word "war" ceased to define it. Albeit reluctantly, the public, Congress, and the executive concluded that the nation would not only have to stand ready to meet annihilation with annihilation but also maneuver, make alliances, and otherwise conduct itself as if perpetually at war.

One result was that by 1960 peacetime military budgets had risen to the vicinity of $47 billion or roughly ten per cent of the country's gross national product. Another was that representatives of the regular services came to figure much more largely in the nation's life. The Pentagon became one of the best office addresses in Washington, and, though not so acknowledged in hostesses' seating plans, the chiefs of staff came to outrank all but a handful of cabinet secretaries, executive assistants, and congressmen. Writing in *Look* magazine in March, 1952, Justice William O. Douglas declared, "The increasing influence of the military in . . . our affairs is the most ominous aspect of our modern history." In *The Power Elite,* the sociologist C. Wright Mills linked generals and admirals with corporation executives as members of America's ruling class. Though both Douglas and Mills may have exaggerated, the very fact that they could make plausible cases was significant. The relation of military men to society and government had changed as much as that of military policy to national policy.

And no institution felt the impact of these changes more than the presidency. That a general became chief executive was beside the point. As Samuel P. Huntington observed in 1957 in *The Soldier and the State*, Eisenhower's allure resembled Taylor's and Grant's; he was a military hero who looked and acted like a Kiwanis Club president. He put fewer former officers into high civil posts than Truman had, and he cooperated much more closely with fiscal conservatives who sought to trim military expenditures and restore what Harding had called "normalcy." The presidency changed in spite of the fact that a soldier sat in the White House.

What happened was that President Eisenhower, like President Truman, found himself daily in front of issues such as had risen before only in wartime. America stood on the edge of conflict in many theaters: Central Europe, the eastern Mediterranean, the Middle East, India, southeast Asia, Japan, Korea, Africa, and even Latin America. The President was challenged to decide which theater should have priority and what the relative investment should be in readiness at home, in Western Europe, and in peripheral areas like Indo-China, the Formosa Straits, and the Levant, where the stakes were lower but the chances of conflict greater.

These questions involved others, for each threat required a different set of weapons—big bombs, B-52's, missiles, and atom-powered submarines for all-out reprisal; infantry, marines, air transport, cargo vessels, and carriers for limited wars; advisory groups, psychological warfare teams, and economic aid funds for competition short of war. Eisenhower faced the challenge of fixing priorities among arms as well as among theaters.

Both sets of issues were made all the more intricate by the ingenuity of scientists and military technicians. Since development and construction of a given vessel, plane, or missile might take three to seven years, action could not follow immediately upon decision. Weapons in which were invested much time, skill, and money, such as the B-70 bomber and the liquid-fueled Atlas missile, began to appear obsolete even before they were workable. A war game called "Sabre Hawk," enacted in southern Germany in February, 1958, revealed that one of the standing assumptions of American war plans was wrong: warfare with tactical nuclear weapons would require more, not fewer ground troops. Another exercise, "Wintershield," conducted in February, 1960, suggested that revised North Atlantic Treaty Organization plans were still off by a factor of three; thirty days instead of ninety would be the maximum time available to mount defenses against a ground attack.[1] Not only weapons but assumptions, calculations, and definitions proved as changeable as weather. Yet the Commander in Chief was compelled to peer far into the future and to take greater gambles with the people's money and lives than any of his predecessors.

Added to other duties of the presidency, which were also growing, this began to seem too much. Reviewing defense budgets, Congress found increasing evidence that critical decisions had not been made by the executive branch. In May, 1956, for example, a Senate Appropriations Committee subcommittee discovered that the air force and army were developing almost identical ground-to-air missiles—the Talos and the Nike. This was not just an administrative blunder such as congressmen had been delightedly uncovering ever since the executive branch took over budget-making. Nor was it, as in the cases of the Snark, Snipe, and Bomarc missiles, merely another instance of an expensive and unsuccessful gamble. The Secretary of Defense admitted that he knew of the duplication. Air force officers had condemned the Nike system as inadequate, while army officers had been equally critical of the Talos. But no one had been willing to decide between the two.[2] Ultimately, it was the responsibility of the commander in chief to make such choices, and this episode, among others, raised the question of whether this responsibility was being met.

Gnawing at the minds of congressmen and outside observers, this question opened up others. In his State of the Union message for 1954, Eisenhower declared, "The defense program recommended for 1955 . . . is based on a new military program unanimously recommended by the Joint Chiefs of Staff." Subsequently, it developed that General Matthew B. Ridgway, the army Chief of Staff, had not in fact concurred in these recommendations. In his book *Soldier,* published in 1956, he declared that he had been "nonplussed" by the President's statement. Reports made later to Congress and the public carried the same implication—that defense budgets bore the imprimatur of all the professionals in the Pentagon. Yet Ridgway's successor, General Maxwell D. Taylor, also published a book, *The Uncertain Trumpet,* declaring that the budgets of 1955 to 1959 had also been "directed verdicts." Army witnesses appearing before congressional committees proved unable to conceal their belief that preparations for limited war were inadequate. Though the army seemed the most aggrieved service, similar feelings emerged from the testimony of other witnesses. After a Senate Armed Services Committee hearing in 1959, for example, the chairman disclosed to reporters that

Admiral Arleigh A. Burke, the Chief of Naval Operations, had been "very apprehensive about what might happen in the near future." Even the chief of the Strategic Air Command, the best-financed arm of the service with the largest share of the budget, admitted that he believed the balance of massive deterrent power to be precarious at best.[3]

Though this evidence of dissent suggested that the commander in chief was in fact exercising his constitutional powers, the character of the evidence was not such as to quiet apprehension. A special Senate committee in 1956 learned that while the army and marine corps retained a combined combat strength of twenty-three divisions, the air force had been allowed to cut transport facilities so that these divisions could not be sped into action.[4] Difficulties arising when troops were dispatched to Lebanon in 1958 dramatized this deficiency. In December, 1957, another special Senate committee uncovered the fact that the 1956 budget had provided planes for the Strategic Air Command but not sufficient gasoline. General Curtis LeMay admitted that for five weeks in May and June, SAC's bombers had sat on their fields, idle and dry.[5] In January, 1959, the Senate Armed Services Committee received testimony from Admiral Burke that eighty-one per cent of the navy consisted of vessels dating from World War II or before and that, owing to reductions in personnel, both ships and aircraft were undermanned.[6]

Secretary of Defense Charles E. Wilson once admitted commanding the Joint Chiefs to reduce their budget estimates by twenty-five per cent. "I told them," he said, "that the total would represent an unconscionable burden on the American taxpayer and was completely out of the range of the nation."[7] Congressmen, many people within the government, and many outside wondered worriedly if these were the right criteria and if the "range" of the richest nation on earth were really so limited. Especially was this so after the winter of 1959, when even so staunch an administration supporter as Senator Styles Bridges of New Hampshire conceded the U.S.S.R. to be "slightly ahead" in long-range missiles.[8] Evidence such as that of the Talos-Nike duplication raised the question of whether the commander in chief's powers were being employed. Evidence of declining military might and of real alarm among service chiefs raised the question of whether those powers, when used, were rightly used.

And these questions showed concern over something more than the personality or quality or philosophy of President Eisenhower. Much of the comment on lack of coordination among the services came from Democrats, it is true, and so did many of the cries of alarm over America's weakening defenses. The Senate's air power investigation of 1956 was captained by Stuart Symington of Missouri; the missile and satellite investigation of 1957–1958 was led by Senator Lyndon B. Johnson of Texas. The most eloquent arraignment of the administration's military policies came in a speech of August 14, 1958, delivered in the Senate by John F. Kennedy of Massachusetts.[9] And all three, Symington, Johnson, and Kennedy, were open if unavowed candidates for the 1960 Democratic nomination.

But the questions were also asked anxiously by many others. Syndicated journalists such as the Alsop brothers and Walter Lippmann, both of whom had supported Eisenhower against Stevenson, were among the leading alarmists. A panel of scholars and experienced public figures gathered by the Rockefeller Brothers Fund published a volume in 1958 warning of the need for new procedures as well as new appropriations if the Soviet military challenge were to be met. A comparable panel appointed by the administration itself turned in similar recommendations. An Assistant Secretary of the Air Force and a Vice-President of the Convair Corporation, both Republicans, declared that conscience compelled them to speak out in criticism of administration defense policy. It was Nelson Rockefeller, a Republican Governor of New York, who declared on June 8, 1960, "our position in the world is dramatically weaker today than fifteen years ago. . . . our national defense needs great strengthening."[10]

The questions which troubled Democrats and Republicans alike were not only about the President. They were about the presidency itself. And one of the issues to which they went directly was whether, in the second half of the twentieth century, the presidency and the command-in-chief could continue to be united in one man.

Some of the urgency that these questions attained was due to a sense of helplessness that had been growing at least since the Chinese intervention in Korea, perhaps since the collapse of Nationalist China in 1949. Almost from the beginning of his presidency, Eisenhower had seemed to be goaded from crisis to crisis like a bull tormented by picadors. In 1954, when the Viet Minh closed around Dienbienphu, the President spoke as if he meant to deal with Indo-China as a new Korea. He compared the nations of southeast Asia to stacked dominoes and said at a press conference on April 7 that if one fell, all might fall. It is reported that he initialled his "O.K." on an NSC recommendation for limited intervention. Only then did he learn from General Ridgway that there were not the necessary troops or transports and that to carry out the decision would mean national mobilization at least on the scale of 1950–1951.

The President hesitated. While the chairman of the Joint Chiefs, the Vice-President, and others urged him to act, conflicting counsels came from other members of the administration, senators, and representatives of allied governments. Dienbienphu fell, and north Indo-China became Communist territory.[11] America's inaction appeared to be the product, not of a conscious decision, but of procrastination and indecision.

Toward the end of 1954 the Chinese Communists intensified bombardments of Matsu and the Quemoys, tiny barren islands just off the mainland harbors of Foochow and Amoy but still garrisoned by Chiang Kai-shek's troops. By a treaty just negotiated, the United States had committed itself to defend the Nationalist stronghold, Formosa. The question was whether the President would also choose to defend these vulnerable inshore outposts.

Eisenhower himself spoke in such a way as to justify either view. On January 24, 1955, he asked Congress to declare that it would approve "the use of the Armed Forces . . . if necessary to assure the security of Formosa." He did not state clearly whether Communist seizure of the inshore islands would make such action necessary or not. Though senators and members of the House confessed that they did not know why the President made his request, they voted an appropriate resolution 85–3 and 409–3. On March 15, when the Secretary of State was pressed to explain what the administration intended, he told reporters: "the issue is, would an attack on Quemoy, Matsu, perhaps elsewhere, be part of an attack against Formosa . . .? If so, then . . . the President would presumably react with U.S. force. If the President judges that the attack is not related to an attack on Formosa . . . , then neither the treaty nor the law gives him authority to act."[12]

In this instance the result was not disaster, at least not immediately. And it may be that Eisenhower's mind ran much as Lincoln's had in 1864 when faced with the Spanish reoccupation of Santo Domingo. With a choice between acquiescing in a violation of the Monroe Doctrine or provoking Spain and perhaps France to aid the Confederacy, Lincoln felt reminded of a story. As Gideon Welles noted in his diary, he told his cabinet of a Negro preacher who told one of his parishioners how hard it was to achieve salvation: "There are two roads for you, Joe. Be careful which you take. One ob them leads straight to hell, de odder go right to damnation." To which Joe replied, "Josh, take which you please; I go troo de wood." Lincoln added, "I am not disposed to take any new trouble . . . but shall take to the woods."[13] President Eisenhower perhaps made much the same choice. But prudent though his policy may have been, outward appearances resembled 1954. The United States seemed ill prepared and indecisive.

In 1956, in the midst of an election year, came crises in other parts of the world. Ever since the overthrow of King Farouk the State Department had been trying to coax the new government of Egypt into some *de facto* alignment with the West. Negotiations were carried on to provide $1.3 billion for construction of an immense dam at Aswan far up the Nile. The money was virtually promised, but the Egyptian government continued to flirt with Communist states and to barter increasing quantities of cotton for Czech-made arms. On July 19, 1956, Secretary of State Dulles announced that further study showed the proposed dam to be a bad financial risk; the American offer of funds was withdrawn. Egypt retaliated on July 26 by expropriating the Suez Canal and announcing that while British and French stockholders would be compensated, the

Canal's future profits would go into a Nile development fund. Three months later, on October 29, Israeli forces suddenly marched west toward Suez, and the British and French governments delivered ultimatums in Cairo, demanding that Egypt accept a truce with Israel and surrender the Canal. Secretary Dulles had just been on a speaking tour, boasting, among other things, of how the United States had prevented a conflict over Suez. When news first came of Israel's military preparations, the White House seemed to assume that the British and French would join in urging calm. As James Reston of *The New York Times* reported, "Nothing could have caused more dismay in Washington" than the London and Paris ultimatums.[14]

The President seemed to respond in this case with decision and vigor. Henry Cabot Lodge, the American representative on the United Nations Security Council, swiftly introduced a resolution asking for an immediate cease-fire. The White House press secretary let it be known that Eisenhower strongly disapproved of the British-French-Israeli action, and an official release declared, "This Government continues to believe that it is possible by . . . peaceful means to secure a solution."[15]

Only a few days before, a revolt had broken out in Budapest. A large part of the population took up arms against the government, the Hungarian police, and the Russian garrison. A new government came into being, announcing that the Russians were being driven out and appealing to the West for support and aid. Though Radio Free Europe and other propaganda agencies had long been encouraging satellite peoples to rebel, the President felt unable to do more than say, "The heart of America goes out to the people of Hungary," and subsequently offer food and Red Cross supplies. The Soviet Union proposed on October 30 negotiations for mutual withdrawal of forces from Europe. Later analysts have guessed that some show of receptiveness by Eisenhower might at least have delayed a reoccupation. Though the suggestion received the utmost advertising by *Pravda* and the East German *Neues Deutschland,* it was ignored in Washington. There was not even a repetition by the Secretary of State of his earlier declaration that the United States would not seek alliances with liberated satellites. On November 4, while the Suez issue was before the U.N. Security Council, the Red Army marched back across the Hungarian frontier.[16]

The electorate endorsed the Eisenhower administration that November by a majority of ten million, nearly three and a half million votes more than in 1952. Friends of the defeated Democrat, Adlai E. Stevenson, explained the Republican landslide partly in terms of the Hungarian and Suez crises. "T.R.B." remarked acidly in *The New Republic,* "The election had one extraordinary feature. The administration [profited] politically by its own mistakes."[17] Nevertheless, his astonishment at the Suez crisis, coupled with his helplessness before the anguished appeals from Hungary, suggested at the very least that the President had not been prepared for events, that statements about a policy of "liberation" for Eastern Europe had been words signifying almost nothing and that, even within America's strongest alliance, something had come loose.

On October 4, 1957, came the shocking announcement that the U.S.S.R. had fired a satellite, "Sputnik I," into outer space. As commentators like Lippmann and the Alsops hastened to point out, this feat demonstrated that the U.S.S.R. possessed workable rockets capable of throwing hydrogen bombs upon any city in the United States; the Russians appeared to be months if not years ahead of America in developing intercontinental ballistic missiles.

Secretary of Defense Charles E. Wilson sought to minimize the event, dismissing it as "a neat trick" and adding gratuitously, "Basic research is when you don't know what you're doing." Special presidential assistant Sherman Adams said the Russians seemed to be trying for "high score in an outer space basketball game." The President admitted at his press conference that he had not been warned of Russia's rapid progress in missile technology, but he added that "there didn't seem to be any reason for just trying to grow hysterical about it. . . . I don't know what we could have done better. . . . [and] that does not raise my apprehension one iota."[18]

It did, however, raise the apprehension of others. Trevor Gardner, a former Assistant Secretary of the Air Force, spoke out, saying that the United States lagged perilously behind the Soviet Union and would have to hurry even to come abreast. *The Denver Post,* which had previously been able to find little fault with the administration, headed an editorial, "Come Off It, Ike, Who You Kidding?"[19]

In the summer of 1958 a fresh crisis broke over the Middle East. Egypt had absorbed Syria, creating a United Arab Republic that obviously had pan-Arab aspirations and that was suspected in Washington of affiliation with Moscow. Lebanon complained that agents of the new republic were filtering across her borders, reinforcing dissident tribesmen, and threatening Lebanese sovereignty. Secretary of State Dulles suggested publicly that the case might come under the "Eisenhower doctrine," a formula for the Middle East proclaimed by the President in the aftermath of the Suez debacle. Perhaps, the Secretary said, Lebanon could be considered as menaced by "overt aggression from [a] nation controlled by International Communism." If so, then the armed forces of the United States might become available "to secure and protect" Lebanon's "territorial integrity and political independence," for these were the terms of the doctrine. The Lebanese government, unsupported by its own armed forces, hastened to agree with the Secretary of State.[20]

While members of the National Security Council debated whether or not the Eisenhower doctrine applied, Lebanon's larger neighbor, Iraq, experienced a singularly bloody uprising in which the pro-Western monarchy was overthrown and replaced by a junta of relatively little-known army officers. According to *The New York Times* of July 15, this event had been wholly unexpected in Washington. Iraq's capital was the meeting place for members of a Middle East Treaty Organization which the United States had been instrumental in creating, and the plans, codes, and other papers of this organization had not been removed. Coming after the Suez affair and the Sputnik launching, the Iraqi revolt helped to create an image of an administration fixed in an attitude of open-mouthed surprise. This impression was unfortunately not to be erased by later events.

On July 16 the President announced that he and his advisers had found that the Lebanese cause fitted the terms of the Eisenhower doctrine. As a result, marines from the U.S. Mediterranean fleet would land near Beirut. They would not, the President said, trespass on the soil of Iraq or interfere with domestic affairs in that perplexing and unhappy land. They would merely assure democracy in Lebanon against subversion by agents of the Arab Republic or of International Communism.

Though hailed at home as evidence of firmness and resolution, the intervention did not have precisely the expected results. In the first place, the greeting extended by the Lebanese proved surprisingly cool. The Lebanese president evidently had second thoughts about associating himself too closely with a foreign power. He had just succeeded, moreover, in opening negotiations with the chief of staff of the Lebanese army and seemed in prospect of settling his affairs without American help. The marines, as a result, found themselves largely confined to a desolate beach area less diverting and less comfortable than the transports from which they had debarked.

In the second place, the enterprise came to seem morally dubious. The Lebanese ambassador at the U.N., Mr. Charles Malik, had circulated a dossier which seemed irrefutably to prove the United Arab Republic's designs on his country. But a U.N. observer team, after inspecting Lebanese-Syrian border areas, reported that it found little evidence of infiltration. Syrian arms were in the possession of Lebanese rebels, but, so far as the observers could tell, the rebels were Lebanese to a man. An uncomfortable impression spread that, like Wilson in Mexico, Eisenhower had been gulled into protecting one political faction against another.

In the third place, the operation proved to lack vigor and dash. In order to accumulate a landing force of respectable size, the President had to detach forces from commands at home and in Europe. Complaints arose that western Germany was being denuded of defenses. Yet in a period of nineteen days the American government managed to move to Lebanon less than one division. *The New York Times* of August 4 reported that, with the final contingent at last landed, the total force amounted to 13,300 men. Though this bettered by far the

Cuban and Nicaraguan expeditions of the Taft and Coolidge administrations, it fell short of being a terrifying display of strength. Hanson Baldwin remarked with irritation in the *Times* of July 24 that the President had apparently failed to consult his military chiefs before deciding on the intervention.

Finally, the affair proved singularly hard to end. Soviet premier Khrushchev began talking loudly of firing off rockets, of sending Russian volunteers to the Middle East, and of urgent need for a conference between the peace-loving leaders of socialist, African, and Asian states and the warmongers of the West. If President Eisenhower ordered American forces out of Lebanon, he would seem to be yielding before Soviet threats. On the other hand, if he did not, he would run the risk of further affronting Indian Prime Minister Nehru and others who had expressed disapproval of the intervention. Some very complicated exchanges with the Russian government and the Secretary General of the U.N. were required before September 26, when the President felt that he could decently announce the withdrawal of America's marines.

The episode had shown, of course, that the United States would not always appear irresolute and inclined to inaction rather than action. In the upshot, however, it had not been altogether reassuring.

In the winter of 1958 came a fresh challenge at the West's most prominent and most vulnerable outpost—Berlin. Khrushchev declared that West Berlin's status as an island in the midst of Communist East Germany was abnormal and dangerous. He proposed that the entire metropolis be made a free city, threatening that if the West did not agree, the U.S.S.R. would sign a separate peace treaty with the German Communists and give them legal power to encircle, blockade, and absorb Berlin.

Subsequently, he set a six-month time limit, in effect declaring that Russia would turn Berlin over to the East Germans on May 27, 1959.[21]

President Eisenhower eventually made it clear that he meant to defend not only West Berlin's independence but also Western rights of access to that sector of the city. At the same time, he retreated from his earlier refusal to meet Khrushchev in a summit conference, and negotiations began for eventual face-to-face conversations on the issue of Berlin, German reunification, and disarmament.[22] In July, 1959, Vice-President Richard Nixon went to Russia and exchanged words with the Soviet premier. In September the Russian himself came to the United States, made a rapid tour of principal cities, and held long conversations with the President at Camp David, a retreat in Maryland.

According to the Soviet Premier's uncontradicted statement, the President conceded that Berlin's situation was "abnormal." Eisenhower and administration spokesmen subsequently used the term, "unnatural."[23] The public addresses of both American and Russian statesmen began to fill with cautious words about "co-existence" and an "easing of tensions." Newspapers spoke of a new "spirit of Camp David."

Then came the debacle. Arrangements were made for a "summit" conference at Paris between the American, Russian, British, and French heads of government. On April 20, Under-secretary of State C. Douglas Dillon spoke to an A.F. of L.-C.I.O. convention in New York City. He declared that what was "abnormal" was not the situation of Berlin so much as it was the satellite condition of East Germany, and he said plainly: "We will not accept any arrangement which might become a first step toward the abandonment of West Berlin."

These words were answered by Khrushchev himself, speaking at Baku on April 25. The West should understand, said the Soviet premier, that Russia would still sign a separate treaty with East Germany if no satisfactory negotiated settlement were achieved and, moreover, that the signature of such a treaty would mean the termination of all Western rights of access to West Berlin.[24]

Just two weeks before the Paris talks were to open, the Russian Premier announced that an American plane had been shot down over Russian soil. When questioned by reporters, spokesmen for the State Department and the National Aeronautics and Space Agency agreed that it must have been a weather plane operating from a base in Turkey. They suggested that the pilot had probably lost consciousness owing to some failure in his oxygen supply; automatic navigating devices had taken over and propelled the craft beyond its intended course.

Khrushchev then revealed that the plane had not been found on or near the border. On the contrary, it had been brought down near Sverdlovsk, 1,200 miles within Russian territory; it was a U-2, a high-speed, high-altitude reconnaissance craft of advanced and still classified design; it was intact, complete with photographic apparatus and such incidental equipment as a poisoned "suicide needle" for the pilot's use. The pilot himself, said the Russian premier, was "alive and kicking."

Secretary of State Christian Herter, who had just returned from Turkey, held a long, closed-door conference. He emerged with an embarrassed statement that the aircraft was as pictured, that it "probably" had been on an information-gathering mission, but that "there was no authorization for any such flight as described by Mr. Khrushchev."

After a weekend of worried editorials on the cockiness and

independence of the armed services and C.I.A., the Secretary of State clarified his statement. The President had authorized observation flights, he revealed. Indeed, with Mr. Eisenhower's knowledge and approval, they had been going on for several years. The President had simply not concerned himself with their "specific missions."

After this disclosure, the obvious question was whether Eisenhower would continue to sanction such flights. The Secretary of State declared sternly that the government "would be derelict in its responsibilities . . . if it did not . . . take such measures as are possible unilaterally to lessen and overcome [the] danger of surprise attack." He added, "the United States has not and does not shirk this responsibility." Subsequently, when interrogated by a Congressional committee, he remarked that these words had been interpreted as meaning that the flights would continue. "It seems to me," he commented, "it was a pretty far-fetched interpretation."

Both the Vice-President and the President's press secretary seemed guilty of misconstruing Secretary Herter. The latter flatly denied a *New York Times* story that the President had ordered flights suspended. Mr. Nixon, appearing on a New York television program, remarked that people should look at the question reasonably. "Let's suppose . . . the United States will now announce to Mr. Khrushchev: 'Well, since this plane has been knocked down, we're going to discontinue activities of this sort.' Look at the position this puts the United States in."

It was not until the day following this television program, according to later testimony by the Secretary of State, that the President actually made up his mind. The flights, he decided, would be discontinued, but the announcement would not be made until after his arrival in Paris.

There, of course, he found Khrushchev demanding not only an end to reconnaissance flights but also an explicit apology and the punishment of American officials who had been responsible for them in the past. The President's announcement failed to have its intended effect. Indeed, it bore the appearance of an apologetic anticlimax, and since Khrushchev proved unrelenting, the summit conference dissolved before it ever began.[25]

The President did not seem responsible for the collapse of the Paris talks. But the administration had appeared to be ill prepared for the U-2 incident. *Newsweek* magazine, which ordinarily gave the benefit of doubt to the administration, reported in summary: "The news . . . came like the successive shocks of an earthquake . . . , each one worse than the one before." Many Democrats agreed with Senator Kennedy when he spoke on June 14 of the "image of confusion and dissension which our Government presented to the American people and the world" and of "the lack of long-range preparation, the lack of policy-planning, the lack of coherent and purposeful national strategy backed by strength." Many Republicans found themselves in regretful agreement with Governor Nelson Rockefeller of New York, who declared on June 21, "there is something seriously wrong with the working of the decision-making processes of our Government."[26]

The U-2 incident and the unhappy episodes that followed crystallized fears about the presidency and the command-in-chief that had grown out of controversies over the defense budget. The panel of the Rockefeller Brothers Fund had urged that the chairman of the Joint Chiefs of Staff and the Secretary of Defense shoulder more responsibility, the former to act as chief of all the services while the latter controlled research, development, and procurement. Senator Fulbright of Arkansas urged a policy and strategy council having no administrative duties, sitting up above executive departments and between them and the president—men resembling the *genro* of Japan or the wise men of American Indian tribes. President Eisenhower himself was attracted by the notion of having a First Secretary for the executive branch, an official resembling a military commander's chief of staff.[27]

Is the joint burden of the presidency and the command-in-chief so great that it must be divided? When the framers of the Constitution devised the merger of offices, they were looking backward rather than forward. They were thinking of Marlborough and Cumberland, colonial governors, and the experience of the Revolution and Confederation. They certainly did not envision the mid-twentieth century, and reverence for their wisdom need be no bar to change.

Presidents before the 1950's did not face the challenges that have come since. For one thing, commanders in chief now have to know more. Wilson could be content with understanding the tank, the mine, and the Liberty motor; Roosevelt needed little more knowledge of landing craft and planes than that they could beach or fly. But a president today has to discriminate carefully between kiloton and megaton weapons. (The difference is roughly that between Bronx Park and Bronx County.) He must have some technical knowledge of thrust, trajectory, re-entry, and other aspects of rocketry. If he is to judge whether an armored convoy should force the Helmstedt-Berlin autobahn or whether a pentomic division should be dropped into Laos, he requires relatively precise notions of the organization, equipment, and capabilities of such instruments. The commander in chief needs a range of technical knowledge rarely acquired in the normal course of ascent to party leadership and the presidency.

This need not be exaggerated. Even though Lincoln, Wilson, and Roosevelt could do without technical and scientific knowledge, the burdens which they bore should not be underestimated. In Wilson's private files, not his office files, one sometimes finds a whole box of papers for a single day. And Wilson is a useful example because he was a sick man under doctor's orders to work only a few hours a day, to rest, and to attend the theater. He even played golf. But, as one White House functionary observed, he operated "on a pile of papers like a starving man on a pile of flapjacks."[28]

Nevertheless much can be said for dividing the offices. After all, England did relatively well with Marlborough and even with Cumberland. President John Adams, who was at least a peer of most of the framers of the Constitution, was willing to accept such a division. When facing a possible war with France in 1798, he wrote to Washington, who was in retirement, "If the Constitution and your convenience would admit of my changing places with you or of my taking my old station as your Lieutenant Civil, I should have no doubts of the ultimate prosperity and glory of the country."[29] The United States, which so much resembles the Roman republic in other respects, might well devise a Roman form of government, with a president and deputy president like the two consuls, one of whom exercised power inside and the other outside the metropolis.

This will be the effect, probably, if decision-making for the armed forces is concentrated in either a chief of staff or some civilian secretary, for, whatever the title, the command-in-chief lies in fact at the point where responsibility cannot be divided. The president will be commander in chief in name only unless he continues to have at least two competing commanders underneath him bringing their disputes to him for adjudication. That is what an issue is—as Webster defines it, "a point in debate on which the parties take affirmative and negative positions." And without issues, there are no decisions. The burden of the command-in-chief cannot be shared. The question is whether it has become so great that the power must be transferred.

History cannot answer this or any other problem in political science. Insofar as the historical experience is relevant, however, it suggests caution. The character of the man who is president and commander in chief is probably more important than the organization of the office. Roosevelt, after all, worked amid administrative chaos. He frequently appointed two men to do one job, and, as Eliot Janeway remarks, he liked giving a title to one man and its powers to another.[30] Yet Roosevelt filled both his offices with something to spare. And it may be that Mr. Eisenhower lacked the background, the zest for work, and the capacity to make order out of disorder which were characteristics of the great commanders in chief. Perhaps it is that decisions on national priorities can only be made efficiently by men who have learned economy in the allocation of their own resources. Grover Cleveland would not allow any executive business to go unstudied; he sat up late night after night to scrutinize applications for post offices and claims for pensions. Diligent though he was, he would probably have fared badly if forced to act as commander in chief. It may be, in other words, that the fault lay with Eisenhower and not with the office he held. The burdens which seemed too great for the presidency of the 1950's may not seem so in the 1960's. Only the experience of another president will tell.

Even if events continue to suggest that the double load is too great, America's history raises one further caveat. All the presidents who have acted as commanders in chief, even Madison and McKinley, managed never to forget that strategy was the servant of policy. Whether wisely or stupidly, rightly or wrongly, they all waged war as politicians—with a sense of responsibility to public opinion as well as to national interest abstractly conceived. A commander in chief who is not also president and party leader may be under less compulsion to use the country's power as the people want it used. The increasing complexity of the commander in chief's tasks may, in fact, make it all the more important that his choices be those of a politician rather than those of a technician. In retrospect, most Americans probably feel relieved that Truman rather than MacArthur made the decisions in Korea and that Eisenhower rather than Admiral Radford was commander in chief during the Indo-China and Quemoy-Matsu crises. The issue is not only whether one man can stand the double strain of the presidency and the command-in-chief but also whether the nation can stand to have any man except one, the president *and* commander in chief, determine what its fate shall be.

Notes

Chapter I: "The President Shall Be Commander in Chief"

(*There are no notes for this chapter. Nearly everything cited can be located easily through the works listed in the bibliographical note following the footnotes.*)

Chapter II: MADISON

1. James Wilkinson, *Memoirs of My Own Times* (Philadelphia, 1816), III, 359, 367.
2. Henry Adams, *History of the United States* (9 vols.; New York, 1891), VI, 398–99; VII, 34; Sydney Howard Gay, *James Madison* (Boston, 1884), 325–28; Gaillard Hunt, *The Life of James Madison* (New York, 1902),

325; *Dictionary of American Biography* (22 vols.; New York, 1928–1944), XII, 191–92; Abbot Emerson Smith, *James Madison: Builder* (New York, 1937), 308–309; Leonard D. White, *The Jeffersonians, 1801–1829: A Study in Administrative History* (Chicago, 1951), 221; Louis Smith, *American Democracy and Military Power* (Chicago, 1951), 42.

3. The latest volume so far of Irving Brant's biography is *James Madison: The President, 1809–1812* (Indianapolis, 1956). But see his article "Timid President? Futile War?" in *American Heritage*, X (October, 1959), 46–47, 85–89.

4. *Ibid.*, 47.

5. *Debates and Proceedings in the Congress of the United States* (hereafter cited as *Annals of Congress*), *1813–14*, vol. I, 945–46. I have omitted a few commas from these and later quotations.

6. William A. Ganoe, *The History of the United States Army* (New York, 1942), 113.

7. James D. Richardson, *Compilation of the Messages and Papers of the Presidents, 1789–1897* (10 vols.; Washington, D.C., 1907), I, 494.

8. *Annals of Congress, 1811–1812*, vol. I, 441–42.

9. Madison to Jefferson, February 7, 1812, Gaillard Hunt (ed.), *Writings of James Madison* (9 vols.; New York, 1900–1910), VIII, 176; Jefferson to Madison, February 19, 1812, P. L. Ford (ed.), *Writings of Thomas Jefferson* (Federal Edition; 12 vols.; Washington, D.C., 1896), XI, 226.

10. John Armstrong to James Wilkinson, March 12, 1813, quoted in Wilkinson, *Memoirs*, III, 342.

11. James R. Jacobs, *Tarnished Warrior: Major-General James Wilkinson* (New York, 1938), 307.

12. The best-known example of this is Emory Upton, *The Military Policy of the United States* (Washington, D.C., 1904), a piece of special pleading by a regular officer who sought to ram home the lesson that only the regulars had saved America's military honor.

13. *Speech of the Honorable Artemas Ward . . . on the Fifth Day of March, 1814, on a bill making appropriations for the support of the military establishment. . . .* (Washington, D.C., 1814), 18.

14. In the first five years, according to a report of July 8, 1813, only $94,792 out of a total of $1 million was expended by the states. *American State Papers: Military Affairs*, I, 337.

15. Letter of October 16, 1814, *Writings of Jefferson*, XI, 436–37. In his first inaugural address (March 4, 1809; Richardson, *Messages & Papers*, I, 468) Madison had declared his intention "to keep within the requisite limits a

standing military force, always remembering that an armed and trained militia is the firmest bulwark of republics—that without standing armies their liberty can never be in danger, nor with large ones safe. . . ." In subsequent messages (Richardson, I, 486, 494, 519, 538) Madison stressed the need for an improved militia. In his annual message of September 20, 1814 (Richardson, I, 549–50), he recommended "classing and disciplining" the militia.

16. In his second annual message (December 5, 1810; Richardson, I, 486–87) Madison said: "The Corps of Engineers, with the Military Academy, are entitled to the early attention of Congress." He recommended the foundation of a second military academy. "In a government happily without the other opportunities seminaries where . . . the art of war can be taught without actual war, and without the expense of extensive and standing armies, have the precious advantage of uniting an essential preparation against external danger with a scrupulous regard to internal safety." The second academy was not established.

17. Louis Smith, *American Democracy and Military Power*, 309–311; Leonard D. White, *The Jeffersonians*, 539–43.

18. James B. Fry, "The Command of the Army," in *Military Miscellanies* (New York, 1889), 62–146.

19. Richard Rush to Benjamin Rush, June 20, 1812; quoted in Henry Adams, *History of the United States*, VI, 229.

20. *Ibid.*, 419–26.

21. James B. McMaster, *A History of the People of the United States* (8 vols.; New York, 1883–1913), IV, 50, 53.

22. February 25, 1813, S. M. Hamilton (ed.), *Writings of James Monroe* (7 vols.; New York, 1898–1903), V, 244–45. Daniel C. Gilman, *James Monroe* (Boston, 1892), 108, gives the date of this letter as July 25, 1813.

23. April 22, 1813, Henry Adams (ed.), *The Writings of Albert Gallatin* (3 vols.; Philadelphia, 1879), I, 538–39.

24. Winfield Scott, *Memoirs* (New York, 1864), I, 35.

25. November 24, 1813, *American State Papers: Military Affairs*, I, 480.

26. September 22, 1813, *Writings of Gallatin*, I, 582–83.

27. Jefferson to William Duane, October 1, 1812, *Writings of Jefferson*, XI, 268–69; Gallatin to Jefferson, December 18, 1812, *Writings of Gallatin*, I, 530–31.

28. Speech in House of Representatives on the invasion of Canada, January 5, 1813, Edmund Quincy (ed.), *Speeches of Josiah Quincy* (Boston, 1874), 407.

Notes

29. *Ibid.*, 405–06.
30. *Writings of Monroe*, V, 264–65.
31. August 30, 1813, William C. Bruce, *John Randolph of Roanoke* (New York, 1922), I, 397.
32. Letter to William Wirt, September 30, 1813, *Writings of Madison*, VIII, 262–63.
33. *Ibid.*, VIII, 264.
34. Kenneth L. Brown, "Mr. Madison's Secretary of the Navy," *U.S. Naval Institute Proceedings*, LXXIII (1947), 967–75.
35. *Writings*, VIII, 286–87; Madison, *Letters and Other Writings* (1865 edition), II, 603–06 (to Benjamin W. Crowninshield, June 12, 1815).
36. Madison, *Letters*, III, 384 (comments made in 1824).
37. In addition to Wilkinson's *Memoirs*, see John Armstrong, *Notices of the War of 1812* (2 vols.; New York, 1836–40), and the report on the causes of failure on the northern frontier, *American State Papers: Military Affairs*, I, 439–88.
38. *Annals of Congress, 1813–14*, vol. I, pp. 1112–1113.
39. *Ibid.*, January 1814, vol. I, p. 1065.
40. Ingersoll, *Historical Sketch of the Second War Between the United States . . . and Great Britain* (Philadelphia, 1845), I, 262.

Chapter III: POLK

[Leonard D. White, *The Jacksonians, A Study in Administrative History, 1829–1861* (New York, 1954), Chapter III, "The President as Commander in Chief," pp. 50–66. Reprinted with the permission of The Macmillan Company.]

1. *The Diary of James K. Polk During His Presidency, 1845 to 1849* (4 vols., Milo Milton Quaife, ed., Chicago: A. C. McClurg and Co., 1910), I, 427–28 (May 25, 1846). Shields went out to Illinois and became brigadier general of Illinois volunteers, was badly wounded at Cerro Gordo, but survived to serve a term in the U.S. Senate (1849–55) and to fight in the Civil War as a brigadier general of volunteers. See William Henry Condon, *Life of Major-General James Shields* (Chicago: Blakely Printing Co., 1900); *Dictionary of American Biography*, XVII, 106.
2. Polk, *Diary*, II, 355–56 (Jan. 25, 1847).
3. The course of events as seen by General Winfield Scott is ably described

Notes

by Major Charles Winslow Elliott, *Winfield Scott: the Soldier and the Man* (New York: Macmillan, 1937).

4. Polk, *Diary*, I, 9–10 (August 29, 1845); *ibid.*, I, 12 (August 30, 1845).

5. *Ibid.*, I, 400 (May 14, 1846).

6. *Ibid.*, I, 403–4 (May 16, 1846).

7. *Ibid.*, I, 443 (June 2, 1846).

8. *Ibid.*, II, 16–17 (July 8, 1846). The instructions, under date of July 9, 1846, are found in House Ex. Doc. 60, 30th Cong., 1st sess., pp. 155–58. They are of primary importance, stressing the desirability of conciliating the Mexican people, keeping open a channel of communication with the Mexican army, and encouraging a separatist movement in the northern provinces.

9. Scott to R. P. Netcher (June 5, 1846), in Ann Mary Butler Coleman, ed., *The Life of John J. Crittenden* (2 vols., Philadelphia: J. B. Lippincott, 1871), I, 244–46.

10. Senate Doc. 378, 29th Cong., 1st sess., p. 5 (May 21, 1846).

11. Polk, *Diary*, I, 415–16 (May 21, 1846).

12. *Ibid.*, I, 424 (May 25, 1846). Marcy's reply to Scott's accusations was thought so important that Polk called a special meeting of the Cabinet to consider and approve it. Scott was *persona non grata* whether in Washington or elsewhere. Just before the episode related above, Polk had discovered that Scott intended not to go to the front until September, 1846. The President told Marcy that Scott would proceed "very soon" or be superseded in his command. Marcy replied that Scott was embarrassing him by his schemes, constantly talking and not acting. Polk told Marcy "to issue his orders and cause them to be obeyed." *Ibid.*, I, 407–8 (May 19, 1846). Held in Washington by the Cabinet decision of May 25, he continued, according to Polk, to be a problem. "Gen'l Scott is of no aid to the Department, but his presence at Washington is constantly embarrassing to the Secretary of War. I will observe his course, and if necessary will order him to some other post." *Ibid.*, II, 151 (Sept. 22, 1846).

13. Polk wrote in his diary, "He is evidently a weak man and has been made giddy with the idea of the Presidency. . . . I am now satisfied that he is a narrow minded, bigotted partisan, without resources and wholly unqualified for the command he holds." *Ibid.*, II, 249–50 (Nov. 21, 1846). The break became complete when a critical letter from Taylor to General Gaines (then in disgrace) was published with Gaines' connivance. *Ibid.*, II, 353–55 (Jan. 25, 1847).

14. *Ibid.*, II, 236 (Nov. 14, 1846).

15. Elliott, *Winfield Scott*, p. 437.
16. Polk, *Diary*, II, 148–49 (Sept. 21, 1846).
17. *Ibid.*, I, 412–13 (May 21, 1846). He appointed Colonel Clarkson, a Whig, to the office of paymaster at the request of Whig Senators Crittenden and Morehead. "I was gratified myself that I had it in my power promptly to meet the wishes of these gentlemen, and thus to prove to them that I was not proscriptive in my appointments." *Ibid.*, II, 6 (July 2, 1846).
18. *Ibid.*, II, 382–83 (Feb. 19, 1847).
19. Library of Congress, William L. Marcy, Private Letter Book, 1845–1849, pp. 20–21 (Sept. 2, 1845).
20. Polk, *Diary*, III, 31 (May 19, 1847).
21. *Ibid.*, II, 384–86 (Feb. 20, 1847).
22. *Ibid.*, III, 158–59 (Sept. 3, 1847).
23. *Ibid.*, I, 14–15 (Sept. 2, 1845).
24. *Ibid.*, II, 103–4 (August 29, 1846); II, 117–18 (Sept. 5, 1846).
25. *Ibid.*, II, 146–47 (Sept. 20, 1846).
26. *Ibid.*, II, 118 (Sept. 5, 1846). Polk had received a tip from an informant in New Orleans, *ibid.*, II, 86–87. Jesup might have recalled that he had been given specific instructions by General Scott on May 15, 1846, to investigate the relative value of wagons or pack mules. House Ex. Doc. 60, 30th Cong., 1st sess., p. 546.
27. Polk, *Diary*, II, 430–41 (March 20, 1847).
28. *Ibid.*, I, 14–15 (Sept. 2, 1845).
29. *Ibid.*, II, 117 (Sept. 5, 1846).
30. *Ibid.*, II, 431 (March 20, 1847); cf. *ibid.*, II, 439 (March 24, 1847); *ibid.*, III, 24 (May 13, 1847).
31. Library of Congress, William L. Marcy Papers, Vol. 12, No. 34,862 (Nov. 8, 1846).
32. *Ibid.*, Vol. 12, No. 34,911 (Dec. 25, 1846).
33. Polk, *Diary*, II, 151 (Sept. 22, 1846); II, 154 (Sept. 24, 1846).
34. *Ibid.*, III, 26 (May 14, 1847).
35. See White, *The Jacksonians*, ch 4.
36. Polk, *Diary*, III, 125–47, *passim* (August, 1847).
37. *Ibid.*, II, 204 (Oct. 22, 1846).
38. *Ibid.*, II, 388 (Feb. 20, 1847).
39. Examples recur in the diary from September 15, 1846 (*ibid.*, II, 139), to May 18, 1847 (*ibid.*, III, 29–30), sometimes before the President, sometimes before the Cabinet.
40. *Ibid.*, II, 150 (Sept. 22, 1846); *ibid.*, III, 24 (May 13, 1847).

41. *Ibid.*, II, 16–17 (July 8, 1846).
42. *Ibid.*, II, 420–21 (March 12, 1847).
43. *Ibid.*, III, 80 (July 10, 1847).
44. After a long march the initial expedition against this city was abandoned. Later it was taken, almost by accident. See Oliver Lyman Spaulding. *The United States Army in War and Peace* (New York: G. P. Putnam's Sons, 1937), pp. 190–91, 197–98.
45. Polk, *Diary*, II, 429–30 (March 20, 1847).

Chapter IV: LINCOLN

[T. Harry Williams, *Lincoln and His Generals* (New York, 1952), Chapter I, "The Pattern of Command," pp. 3–14. Reprinted with the permission of Alfred A. Knopf, Inc.]

1. Winfield Scott to Simon Cameron, October 31, 1861, *War of the Rebellion . . . the Official Records of the Union and Confederate Armies*, Ser. 3, I, 611. Hereafter cited as *Official Records;* unless otherwise noted, all citations are to Ser. 1.
2. Frederick W. Seward, *Reminiscenses of a War-Time Statesman and Diplomat, 1830–1915*, 167–168.
3. Henry M. Flint to Frederic Hudson, September 10, 1862, James Gordon Bennett MSS.
4. Charles W. Elliott, *Winfield Scott: The Soldier and the Man*, 718.
5. Arthur Latham Conger, "President Lincoln as War Statesman," *Wisconsin Historical Publications, Proceedings*, 1916, 12; Jacob Dolson Cox, *Military Reminiscences of the Civil War*, I, 177–180.
6. Henry W. Halleck to D. C. Buell, February 13, 1862, *Official Records*, VII, 609; B. H. Latrobe to Frederick W. Lander, January 4, 1862, Lander MSS.; George B. McClellan, *McClellan's Own Story*, 253–264; Emerson Gifford Taylor, *Gouverneur Kemble Warren . . .* , 106–107.
7. Herman Haupt to Lincoln, January 16, 1864, the Robert Todd Lincoln Collection of the Papers of Abraham Lincoln, vol. 138. Hereafter cited as Lincoln MSS.
8. Karl von Clausewitz, *On War*, 599, Modern Library Edition.
9. Colin R. Ballard, *The Military Genius of Abraham Lincoln: An Essay*, 2–3, 6, 28–29, 239; John C. Ropes, *The Story of the Civil War*, I, 111.

10. Sir Frederick Maurice, "Lincoln as a Strategist," *Forum*, LXXV, 1926, 164.
11. Sir Frederick Maurice, *Statesmen and Soldiers of the Civil War*, 95–96.
12. Lincoln to Simon Cameron, June 20, 1861, John G. Nicolay and John Hay (eds.), *The Complete Works of Abraham Lincoln*, VI, 294. Hereafter cited as *Works of Lincoln*.
13. James Harrison Wilson, *Under the Old Flag*, I, 349.
14. George W. Julian, *Speeches on Political Questions, 1850–1868*, 202–204; Senator Henry Wilson in *Congressional Globe*, 2 Sess., 38 Cong., pt. 1, 164; P. A. Ladue to Lincoln, January 6, 1862, Lincoln MSS.; Joseph Medill to Lincoln, February 17, 1864, *ibid.*
15. Fred Harvey Harrington, *Fighting Politician, Major General N. P. Banks*, 54–56.
16. Allen Thorndike Rice (ed.), *Reminiscences of Abraham Lincoln by Distinguished Men of His Time*, 391–392.
17. Memorandum, April, 1861, Lincoln MSS., vol. 44.
18. Memorandum, August 23, 1862, *ibid.*, vol. 85.
19. MS. Journal of Samuel P. Heintzelman, entry of June 22, 1862. There are no quotation marks around the spoken statements in Heintzelman's account.
20. Carl Schurz to Lincoln, November 8, 1862, Lincoln MSS., vol. 92.
21. Lincoln to Schurz, November 24, 1862, *Works of Lincoln*, VIII, 84–87.

Chapter V: McKINLEY

1. See Walter Millis, *The Martial Spirit* (New York, 1931), chapters I–VI; Richard Hofstadter, "Manifest Destiny and the Philippines," in Daniel Aaron (ed.), *America in Crisis* (New York, 1952); and Margaret Leech, *In the Days of McKinley* (New York, 1959), chapter VII. I rely also on material gathered for a book in progress tentatively entitled *America Becomes a Power*.
2. Elting E. Morison *et al.* (eds.), *The Letters of Theodore Roosevelt* (8 vols.; Cambridge, Mass., 1951–1954), I, 685–686; John D. Long, *The New American Navy* (2 vols.; Boston, 1903), I, 182; U.S. Department of State, *Papers relating to the Foreign Relations of the United States . . . 1898* (Washington, D.C., 1901), 769–770; U.S. Department of the Navy, *Appendix to the Report of the Chief of the Bureau of Navigation, 1898: Naval Operations of the War with Spain* (Washington, D.C., 1898), 67.
3. Leech, *In the Days of McKinley*, 198; Russell A. Alger, *The Spanish-Ameri-*

can War (New York, 1901), 8–9, 11, 16–18; *Foreign Relations, 1898,* p. 770.

4. McKinley's recourse to the globe is related in H. H. Kohlsaat, *From McKinley to Harding* (New York, 1923), 68; *Naval Operations,* 97–98; see Nathan Sargent (comp.), *Dewey and the Manila Campaign* (Washington, D.C., 1947).

5. Again, McKinley's remark is recounted by Kohlsaat, *McKinley to Harding,* 68; Alger, *Spanish-American War,* 326, says the decision to send troops to the Philippines had been made even before news arrived of Dewey's victory.

6. Nelson A. Miles, *Serving the Republic* (New York, 1911), 272–273; Lawrence S. Mayo (ed.), *America of Yesterday, As Reflected in the Journal of John Davis Long* (Boston, 1923), 192.

7. U.S. War Department, *Correspondence relating to the War with Spain* . . . (2 vols.; Washington, D.C., 1902), II, 643–678; the warning appeared in Oscar S. Straus to McKinley, May 12, 1898, Private Papers of William McKinley, Manuscripts Division, Library of Congress, Washington, D.C.

8. Hengelmüller to Goluchowski, June 5, 1898, Liasse XX (Spanien), Box 70, Austrian Foreign Ministry Archives, Haus-, Hof-, und Staatsarchiv, Vienna; Cambon to Hanotaux, May 30, 1898, Espagne: Cuba, vol. X, French Foreign Ministry Archives, Quai d'Orsay, Paris; London *Times,* May 29, May 31, 1898.

9. Hay to Day, May 8, 1898, Great Britain: Despatches, vol. 192, U.S. Department of State Archives, National Archives, Washington, D.C.; Day to Hay, June 3, 1898, Great Britain: Instructions, vol. 32, *ibid.;* Springfield *Republican* quoted in *Public Opinion,* XXIV (May 12, 1898), p. 583.

10. Hay to Day, June 5, 1898, McKinley Papers; Day to Hay, June 7, 1898, Private Papers of John Hay, Manuscripts Division, Library of Congress.

11. Day to Hay, June 14, 1898, *ibid.;* cf. Alfred L. P. Dennis, *Adventures in American Diplomacy, 1896–1906* (New York, 1928), 99; 55th Congress, 3rd Session, *Senate Document 62,* Part III (*Correspondence of the Department of State with Consuls in the Orient*), pp. 341ff.

12. War Department, *Correspondence,* I, 29–30.

13. Lodge to Henry White, May 5, 1898, Private Papers of Henry White, Manuscripts Division, Library of Congress; New York *Tribune,* May 16, 1898; Chicago (Baptist) *Standard,* May 21, 1898.

14. War Department, *Correspondence,* I, 30–31.

15. *Ibid.,* 31–50.

16. Bascom N. Timmons (ed.), *A Journal of the McKinley Years by Charles G. Dawes* (Chicago, 1950), 186; War Department, *Correspondence*, I, 89–90; *Naval Operations*, 607–614.
17. Miles, *Serving the Republic*, 282; War Department, *Correspondence*, I, 116; Charles S. Olcott, *William McKinley* (2 vols.; Boston, 1916), II, 49–50.
18. War Department, *Correspondence*, I, 119–156; Olcott, *McKinley*, 50–51.
19. Miles, *Serving the Republic*, 274; War Department, *Correspondence*, I, 261–262; New York *Tribune*, July 2, 1898; French E. Chadwick, *The Relations of the United States and Spain: the Spanish-American War* (2 vols.; New York, 1911), II, 267.
20. Patenôtre to Hanotaux, July 12, July 16, 1898, Espagne: Cuba, vol. XX, French Foreign Ministry Archives; Dubsky to Goluchowski, July 14, 1898, Liasse XX, Box 70, Austrian Foreign Ministry Archives; Blanco to Moret, July 14, 1898, Legajo 2423, Spanish Foreign Ministry Archives, Ministerio de Asuntos Exteriores, Madrid; Almodovar to León y Castillo, July 14, 1898, Legajo 2417, *ibid.; Foreign Relations*, 1898, pp. 819–830.
21. Dawes, *Journal of the McKinley Years*, 145–149; Harry Thurston Peck, *Twenty Years of the Republic* (New York, 1906), 462.

Chapter VI: WILSON

1. Arthur S. Link, *Wilson: The New Freedom* (Princeton, 1956), 298–299.
2. Frederick Palmer, *Bliss, Peacemaker* (New York, 1934), 106–107.
3. Ray Stannard Baker, *Woodrow Wilson: Life and Letters* (8 vols.; New York, 1927–1939), VI, 76.
4. Frederick Palmer, *Newton D. Baker: America at War* (2 vols.; New York, 1931), I, 152.
5. *Ibid.*, 170–172, 180.
6. Baker, *Wilson*, VII, 211–212.
7. *Ibid.*, 50–51, 146–147; Sims to Daniels, April 18, 1917, U.S. Department of State, *Papers relating to the Foreign Relations of the United States . . . 1917, Supplement 2*, vol. I, pp. 28–29.
8. U.S. Department of the Army, Historical Division, *United States Army in the World War, 1917–1919: Policy-forming Documents, American Expeditionary Forces* (Washington, D.C., 1948), 17, 133; Palmer, *Newton D. Baker*, I, 371; Peyton C. March, *The Nation at War* (Garden City, New York, 1932), 356ff.; diary of the White House Usher, Private Papers of

Woodrow Wilson, Manuscripts Division, Library of Congress, Washington, D.C.

9. Charles Seymour (ed.), *The Intimate Papers of Colonel House* (4 vols.; Boston, 1926–1928), III, 188.

10. David Lloyd George, *War Memoirs* (6 vols.; London, 1933–1936), IV, 518–524.

11. House to Wilson, Nov. 13, 1917, Wilson Papers; Baker, *Wilson*, VII, 354, 361.

12. *Ibid.*, 417–418, 449–450; *Policy-forming Documents, A.E.F.*, 132.

13. Baker, *Wilson*, VII, 361.

14. *Ibid.*, 457–458.

15. Charles G. Dawes, *A Journal of the Great War* (2 vols.; Boston, 1921), I, 221.

16. Wiseman to Balfour, Feb. 3, 1918, *Intimate Papers of Colonel House*, III, 431–432.

17. *Policy-forming Documents, A.E.F.*, 336–337.

18. Palmer, *Bliss*, 206.

19. *Policy-forming Documents, A.E.F.*, 274–277.

20. *Ibid.*, 380–381.

21. Baker, *Wilson*, VIII, 122.

22. *Policy-forming Documents, A.E.F.*, 399.

23. March, *Nation at War*, 49–50.

24. *Policy-forming Documents, A.E.F.*, 558; George F. Kennan, *Soviet-American Relations, 1917–1920: The Decision to Intervene* (Princeton, 1958), 266–271.

25. *Ibid., passim.* Kennan cites the enormous literature on this subject, and it is unnecessary to multiply citations here.

26. *Policy-forming Documents, A.E.F.*, 541–542.

27. Wilson to House, July 21, 1917, Private Papers of E. M. House, Yale University Library, New Haven, Connecticut; cf. Charles Seymour, *American Diplomacy during the World War* (Baltimore, 1934), 270.

28. Baker, *Wilson*, VIII, 549.

29. See Harry Rudin, *Armistice: 1918* (New Haven, 1944), 100–104.

30. *Intimate Papers of Colonel House*, III, 188; Baker, *Wilson*, VII, 359.

Chapter VII: F.D.R.

[In somewhat different form, this essay appeared in *Military Affairs*, XXII, IV, (Winter, 1958–1959), and the author wishes to express his appreciation to the editor of that journal and to the American Military Institute for their courtesy in allowing him to publish it here in revised form.]

1. Ray S. Cline, *The War Department: Washington Command Post: the Operations Division* (Washington, D.C., 1951), 45 f.
2. Eliot Janeway, *The Struggle for Survival: a Chronicle of Economic Mobilization in World War II* (New Haven, 1951), 44 ff.
3. Mark S. Watson, *The War Department: Chief of Staff: Prewar Plans and Preparations* (Washington, D.C., 1950), 79–84, 97–104.
4. *Ibid.*, 89–94.
5. 79th Congress, 1st Session, *Senate Hearings on S. 84*, p. 521; 79th Congress, 1st Session, *Report to Hon. James Forrestal, Secretary of the Navy on Unification of the War and Navy Departments* [The Eberstadt Report] (Washington, D.C., 1945), pp. 70–71, 76, 86–87.
6. Janeway, *Struggle for Survival*, 51.
7. Watson, *Chief of Staff*, Chapter V. See also Wesley Frank Craven and James Lea Cate, eds., *The Army Air Forces in World War II* (6 vols.; Chicago, 1948–1955), VI, 8–10.
8. Watson, *Chief of Staff*, 127, 131.
9. Robert Payne, *The Marshall Story* (New York, 1951), 111–112.
10. At the time that Roosevelt issued his demand for 50,000 airplanes, Air Corps planners had just completed staff studies of a proposal to increase first line combat aircraft strength from 1900 to 2700, this increase to be accomplished within the framework of the previously established 5500 plane program. 50,000 planes approximated the total American aircraft production since the Wright brothers took to the air at Kitty Hawk in 1903: Craven and Cate, *Army Air Forces*, VI, 264, 271.
11. Janeway, *Struggle for Survival*, 80.
12. Watson, *Chief of Staff*, 360–366.
13. Winston Churchill, *Closing the Ring* (Boston, 1951), 346.
14. Frederick Morgan, *Overture to Overlord* (London, 1950), 207–208. General Morgan was suitably impressed by this remark and went away strengthened, no doubt, in his opposition to Churchillian projects of strategy. The historian—alas!—must record the fact that the general had been ushered into Roosevelt's office by Harry Hopkins!
15. Watson, *Chief of Staff*, 308.
16. *Ibid.*, 111–113. In their Joint Estimate of June 22, 1940, the chiefs said that "to release to Great Britain additional war material now in the hands of the armed forces will seriously weaken our present state of defense

and will not materially assist the British forces." They recommended that no further commitments be made. The President's reaction was typical. He said, "In general, yes," but in further remarks he qualified his agreement so extensively that in the final draft the relevant recommendation was "nonbelligerent support of the British Commonwealth and China." See also Maurice Matloff and Edwin M. Snell, *The War Department: Strategic Planning for Coalition Warfare, 1941–1942* (Washington, D.C., 1953), 13–21.

17. Watson, *Chief of Staff*, 116–118.

18. Matloff and Snell, *Strategic Planning, 1941–1942*, 25–28.

19. *Ibid.*, pp. 28–31; Watson, *Chief of Staff*, 119–125.

20. For the Joint Board's opposition to the oil embargo, see 79th Congress, 1st Session, *Joint Committee on the Investigation of the Pearl Harbor Attack, Hearings* . . . (Washington, D.C., 1946), Part V, pp. 2381–2384. For the incidents and effects of General MacArthur's appointment, see Watson, *Chief of Staff*, 397, 424–425, 434–439, 494–496, and Matloff and Snell, *Strategic Planning, 1941–1942*, 63–67. Cf. Louis Morton, *The War in the Pacific: The Fall of the Philippines* (Washington, D.C., 1953), 14–18.

21. *Pearl Harbor Hearings*, Part I, 401–402; Part V, 2122–2123.

22. William L. Langer and S. Everett Gleason, *The Undeclared War, 1940–1941* (New York, 1953), 898–900.

23. *The Diary of Henry L. Stimson*, Sept. 25–26, 1940 (Yale University Library).

24. *Ibid.*, Aug. 4 and Apr. 2, 1941.

25. Watson, *Chief of Staff*, 388.

26. *Ibid.*, 5–7.

27. The definitive study of the U.S. army staff during World War II is Ray Cline's *Washington Command Post*, a detailed analysis of the workings of the Operations Division of the War Department. No similar study of the navy planners has been completed.

28. John Ehrman, *Grand Strategy*, vol. VI: *October 1944–August 1945* (London, 1956), 344.

29. Robert E. Sherwood, *Roosevelt and Hopkins* (New York, 1948), 446, 615, 948.

30. Samuel P. Huntington, *The Soldier and the State* (Cambridge, Mass., 1957), 329.

31. Matloff and Snell, *Strategic Planning, 1941–1942*, 382.

32. Robert Sherwood argues that Roosevelt's concern over Churchill's "powers of emotional endurance . . . after six months of mortification" was a

weighty element in his later decisions on the issue of TORCH: *Roosevelt and Hopkins,* 601–602. On the weakness of the Churchill government see the war narrative of one of Churchill's military staff: John Kennedy, *The Business of War* (London, 1957), 194–195.

33. The implied threat of a transfer of American forces to the Pacific theater had been present in the BOLERO plan from its inception. As General Eisenhower, then Chief of the Operations Division, wrote General Marshall in March, 1942, ". . . unless this plan is adopted as the eventual aim of all our efforts, we must turn our *backs* upon the Eastern Atlantic and go full out, as quickly as possible, against Japan!" Matloff and Snell, *Strategic Planning, 1941–1942,* 182.

34. The full draft of the President's final instructions to the Hopkins-Marshall mission is printed in Sherwood, 603–606. Cf. the War Department's draft instructions, which Roosevelt edited and altered, in Matloff and Snell, *Strategic Planning, 1941–1942,* Appendix B, pp. 384–385.

35. Cf. the President's outline instructions of July 15 to General Marshall and the somewhat divergent draft instructions drawn up in the War Department: *ibid.,* p. 273.

36. Samuel E. Morison, *Strategy and Compromise* (Boston, 1958), 38.

37. Secretary Stimson and General Marshall never ceased to mourn the passing of BOLERO and the mounting of TORCH in 1942. On reflection, some of the officers of the OPD (Operations Division of the War Department General Staff) most closely associated with the development of the BOLERO plan, as their historian reveals, "were not so sure that it represented the wisest strategic course that could have been charted. Rather . . . they strongly felt the need of *some* central strategy and the BOLERO plan was their solution at the time." Cline, 145, n. 3.

38. *Ibid.,* 315–317.

39. A good appreciation of Leahy's influence is to be found in John Ehrman, *Grand Strategy,* VI, 340–341.

40. Matloff and Snell, *Strategic Planning, 1941–1942,* 379–382. See also Gordon A. Harrison, *The European Theatre of Operations: Cross-Channel Attack* (Washington, D.C., 1951), 37–38.

41. Quoted from the diary of Brigadier Ian Jacob in Arthur Bryant, *The Turn of the Tide* (New York, 1957), 561.

42. Cline, 236.

43. See Robert Ross Smith, "Luzon versus Formosa," in Kent R. Greenfield, ed., *Command Decisions* (New York, 1959). The President's dramatic trip to meet General MacArthur and Admiral Nimitz at Pearl Harbor was proba-

bly not unconnected with the 1944 election campaign. Despite this trip it does not appear that the President intervened in the controversy between the army and navy staffs and their leaders over the question of whether to invade or to "by-pass" the Philippines. Some army planners, however, had at the time the distinct impression that a presidential intervention might have been likely had the decision gone for Formosa, as the navy planners had argued, rather than for the Philippines, General MacArthur's preferred objective.

44. Henry L. Stimson and McGeorge Bundy, *On Active Service in Peace and War* (New York, 1947), 438.
45. *Ibid.*, 443.
46. Department of State, *Foreign Relations of the United States, Diplomatic Papers: The Conferences at Malta and Yalta, 1945* (Washington, D.C., 1955), pp. 106–108. In this document the Joint Chiefs argue that the United States should at all costs avoid the appearance of an Anglo-American *entente* in Europe and that "our basic national policy . . . should seek to maintain the solidarity of the three great powers."
47. Samuel I. Rosenman, *Working with Roosevelt* (New York, 1953), 504, 526–527, 539. Rosenman argues that Roosevelt was puzzled and upset by Stalin's actions in the spring of 1945 but that he was in some ways no less suspicious of Churchill's postwar intentions than he was of Stalin's.
48. Quoted in Sherwood, *Roosevelt and Hopkins,* 948.
49. Herbert Feis, *Churchill-Roosevelt-Stalin* (Princeton, 1957), 212, 451.
50. Maurice Matloff, *Strategic Planning for Coalition Warfare, 1943–1944* (Washington, D.C., 1959), 491.
51. Feis, *Churchill-Roosevelt-Stalin,* 270.
52. Gordon Harrison, *Cross-Channel Attack,* 92, n. 27.
53. Feis, *Churchill-Roosevelt-Stalin,* 621; Matloff, *Strategic Planning, 1943–1944,* 341, 493, 511.
54. Huntington, 315; Hanson Baldwin, *Great Mistakes of the War* (New York, 1950), 26.
55. William D. Leahy, *I Was There* (New York, 1950), 106.

Chapter VIII: TRUMAN

1. Harry S. Truman, *Memoirs,* vol. I (Garden City, N.Y.: Doubleday and Co., 1955), pp. 10, 55.

2. *Ibid.*, p. 12.

3. *Ibid.*, pp. 328–329.

4. Public Law 253, 80th Congress, 1st session.

5. Public Law 216, 81st Congress, 1st session.

6. *Ibid.*

7. See extract of Department of Defense Directive 5100.1, March 16, 1954, reprinted in Timothy W. Stanley, *American Defense and National Security* (Washington, D.C.: Public Affairs Press, 1956), pp. 176–188.

8. Public Law 216, 81st Congress, 1st session.

9. Department of Defense Directive 5100.1, March 16, 1954.

10. See Ernest R. May, "The Development of Political-Military Consultation in the United States," *Political Science Quarterly*, vol. LXX, No. 2, June, 1955, pp. 161–180.

11. *Military Situation in the Far East,* Hearings before the Committee on Armed Services and the Committee on Foreign Relations, U.S. Senate, 82nd Congress, 1st session [hereinafter: Hearings], p. 1067.

12. Truman, II, p. 59.

13. *Ibid.*, pp. 334–336.

14. *Ibid.*, p. 338.

15. *Ibid.*, pp. 342–343.

16. Hearings, pp. 326–327, 582–583.

17. Hearings, p. 1067.

18. Hearings, pp. 10, 14, 326–327.

19. See Major Lawrence J. Legere, USA, *Unification of the Armed Forces* [unpublished doctoral dissertation (Harvard University)], pp. 307–313, 333 ff.

20. Hearings, pp. 2594–2595, 2618.

21. Hearings, pp. 379, 523.

22. Hearings, pp. 324–327, 735–738.

23. General Mark W. Clark, *From the Danube to the Yalu* (New York: Harper and Brothers, 1954), p. 27.

24. Truman, II, pp. 435–436.

25. *Ibid.*, pp. 440–442.

26. *Ibid.*, pp. 443–448.

27. Hearings, pp. 75, 81, 103, 324–325, 351–352, 729–742, 894, 897, 1021; Truman, II, pp. 415–416, 446.

28. Truman, II, pp. 443–446; Hearings, p. 3536.

29. See statement by Major General Courtney Whitney in Hearings, p. 3552.

Notes

Chapter IX: EISENHOWER and after

1. *New York Times,* March 15, 1958, February 1–11, March 30, 1960.
2. 84th Congress, 2nd Session, *Hearings before the Subcommittee of the Senate Committee on Appropriations: Department of Defense Appropriations for 1957* (Washington, D.C., 1956), pp. 86 ff.; *New York Times,* May 21–22, July 7, November 27, 1956.
3. Testimony of Secretary of the Army Brucker, 85th Congress, 2nd Session, *Hearings before the House Armed Services Committee: Investigation of National Defense Missiles* (Washington, D.C., 1958), pp. 4212 ff.; *New York Times,* January 27, 1959, April 5, 1960.
4. 84th Congress, 2nd Session, *Hearings before the Subcommittee on the Air Force of the Senate Committee on Armed Services: Study of Airpower* (Washington, D.C., 1956), pp. 498–499.
5. 85th Congress, 1st and 2nd Sessions, *Hearings before the Subcommittee on Preparedness of the Senate Armed Services Committee: Satellite and Missile Programs* (3 vols.; Washington, D.C., 1958), vol. II, pp. 917–918.
6. *Ibid.,* III, pp. 1925 ff.
7. *New York Times,* August 8, 1956.
8. *Ibid.,* January 26, 1959.
9. John F. Kennedy, *The Strategy of Peace* (New York, 1960), 33–45.
10. *International Security, The Military Aspect: Report of the Panel II of the Special Studies Project, Rockefeller Brothers Fund* (New York, 1958). On the Gaither committee's report, see Drew Pearson and Jack Anderson, *U.S.A.—Second Class Power?* (New York, 1958), 12–16. (The authors claim to have read the still classified report.) The Assistant Secretary of the Air Force is Mr. Trevor Gardner; the Convair Vice-President, Mr. Thomas Lamphier. Rockefeller's speech is in the *New York Times,* June 9, 1960.

    In fairness to President Eisenhower, it should be pointed out that he essayed a beginning of a fundamental reform when in 1959 he sent in a budget arranged by categories rather than by service projects. He was immediately assailed by Representative Carl Vinson of Georgia, a power on the House Armed Services Committee, for attempting to usurp prerogatives of Congress! *New York Times,* January 30, 1959.
11. Robert J. Donovan, *Eisenhower: the Inside Story* (New York, 1956), 259–268; Matthew B. Ridgway, *Soldier* (New York, 1956), 275–278; Chalmers

M. Roberts, "The Day We Didn't Go to War," *The Reporter*, XI (September 14, 1954), 31–35.

12. *New York Times*, March 16, 1955.
13. *The Diary of Gideon Welles* (3 vols.; Boston, 1911), I, 519–520.
14. Dulles' speech in Dallas, *The Department of State Bulletin*, XXV (November 5, 1956), 695–699; *New York Times*, November 1, 1956. See Sir Anthony Eden, *Memoirs: Full Circle* (London, 1960), 419–559.
15. State Department *Bulletin*, XXXV (November 12, 1956), 747–756.
16. *Ibid.*, 764; *New York Times*, October 26, November 1, 1956. Dulles' declaration was in his Dallas speech cited above, footnote 14.
17. *New Republic*, CXXXV (November 12, 1956), p. 2.
18. *New York Times*, October 5, 7, 8, 1957.
19. *Ibid.*, October 12, 1957; *Denver Post* quoted in the *New Republic*, CXXXVII (November 4, 1957), p. 3.
20. Dulles' press conference of June 17, 1958, State Department *Bulletin*, XXXIX (July 7, 1958), 8; *New York Times*, June 20, 1958. What follows is largely based on the *Times* and on accounts in Charles W. Thayer, *Diplomat* (New York, 1959), and Richard P. Stebbins, *The United States in World Affairs, 1958* (New York, 1960).
21. *New York Times*, November 11, 28, December 1, 1958.
22. *Ibid.*, March 17, 1959.
23. President's press conference, *New York Times*, September 29, 1959; Andrew H. Berding, "Reflections on the Khrushchev Visit," State Department *Bulletin*, XLI (October 19, 1959), 545.
24. *New York Times*, April 21, 25, 1960.
25. *Ibid.*, May 2–17, 1960; testimony by Secretary Herter before the Senate Foreign Relations Committee, *ibid.*, May 28, 1960; Douglass Cater, "A Chronicle of Confusion," *The Reporter*, XX (June 9, 1960), 15–17.
26. *Newsweek*, LV (May 16, 1960), 27; Kennedy in *New York Times*, June 15, 1960; Rockefeller, *ibid.*, June 22, 1960.
27. Press conference of July 15, *New York Times*, July 16, 1959. See Samuel P. Huntington, "Strategic Planning and the Political Process," *Foreign Affairs*, XXXVIII (January, 1960), 295 ff.
28. Edmund W. Starling, *Starling of the White House* (Chicago, 1946), 36.
29. John Alexander Carroll and Mary Wells Ashworth, *George Washington*, VII: *First in Peace* (New York, 1957), 517.
30. Eliot Janeway, *The Struggle for Survival* (New Haven, 1951), 42–43.

Acknowledgments

As INDICATED IN the chapter notes, I am indebted to the Macmillan Company for permission to reprint the chapter from Leonard D. White's *The Jacksonians* and to Alfred A. Knopf, Inc., for permission to reprint the chapter from T. Harry Williams' *Lincoln and His Generals*. My essay on Wilson and Professor Emerson's on F.D.R. were originally papers presented at a meeting of the American Historical Association, and we both have obligations to the American Military Institute, which sponsored the panel and to Dr. Maurice Matloff of the Department of the Army, Mr. Walter Millis of the Fund for the Republic, and Professor Louis Morton of Dartmouth College, who offered comments on our papers. Professors Bernard Bailyn and Robert G. McCloskey of Harvard read Chapter I, and I deeply appreciate their help and suggestions. I also have a very heavy obligation to the John Simon Guggenheim Foundation and the Social Science Research Council; their fellowships in support of another project gave me the time to do this book on the side. Nancy Caughey May, my wife, has been typist, editor, and guardian of time, and I owe her more than I can say.

Bibliographical Notes

Chapter I: "The President Shall Be Commander in Chief"

The principal sources are Max Farrand (ed.), *The Records of the Federal Convention* (4 vols.; New Haven, 1911–1937), Jonathan Elliot (ed.), *The Debates in the Several State Conventions on the Adoption of the Federal Constitution* (4 vols.; Washington, D.C., 1836), pamphlets and letters written during these debates, such as *The Federalist Papers*, Paul Leicester Ford (ed.), *Pamphlets on the Constitution of the United States Published during its Discussion by the People, 1787–1788* (Brooklyn, 1888) and *Essays on the Constitution of the United States Published during its Discussion by the People, 1787–1788* (Brooklyn, 1892), and the published correspondence of Washington, Madison, John Adams, Jefferson, and others.

On the American background of the commander-in-chief clause, some important works are John F. Burns, *Controversies between Royal Governors and Their Assemblies* (Boston, 1923), Clarence E. Carter, "The Office of Commander-in-Chief: A Phase of Imperial Unity on the Eve of the Revolution," in Richard B. Morris (ed.), *The Era of the American Revolution* (New York, 1939), Evarts B. Greene, *The Provincial Governor in the English Colonies of North America* (Cambridge, Mass., 1898), Merrill Jensen, *The New Nation: A History of the United States during the Confederation, 1781–1789* (New York, 1950), and Leonard W. Labaree, *Royal Government in America* (New Haven, 1930).

On the English experience also in the background, see G. M. Trevelyan, *England under Queen Anne* (3 vols.; London, 1930–1934), Winston S. Churchill, *Marlborough: His Life and Times* (6 vols.; London, 1933–1938), and Evan Charteris, *William Augustus, Duke of Cumberland* (London, 1913).

Bibliographical Notes

On other aspects, see C. A. Berdahl, *War Powers of the Executive* (Urbana, Illinois, 1922), Edward S. Corwin, *The President. Offices and Powers* (4th edition; New York, 1957) and *Total War and the Constitution* (New York, 1947), Clinton Rossiter, *The Supreme Court and the Commander in Chief* (Ithaca, New York, 1951), and Charles Warren, *The Making of the Constitution* (Boston, 1928).

Chapter II: MADISON

The best account of the period is still in Henry Adams, *History of the United States during the Administrations of Jefferson and Madison* (9 vols.; New York, 1891). Irving Brant has a biography in progress, but the latest volume, *James Madison: The President, 1809–1812* (Indianapolis, 1956), only comes up to the outbreak of war. Theodore Roosevelt, *The Naval War of 1812* (2 vols.; Boston, 1882), does not hold up as well as Adams' *History*, but it is still surprisingly valuable. Neither F. F. Beirne, *The War of 1812* (New York, 1949), nor Glenn Tucker, *Poltroons and Patriots* (2 vols.; Indianapolis, 1954), is a distinguished contribution.

The major sources are the *Annals of Congress, American State Papers: Military Affairs,* and the papers and writings of participants, especially Gaillard Hunt (ed.), *The Writings of James Madison* (9 vols.; New York, 1900–1910), P. L. Ford (ed.), *The Writings of Thomas Jefferson* (10 vols.; New York, 1892–1899), S. M. Hamilton (ed.), *The Writings of James Monroe* (7 vols.; New York, 1898–1903), and Henry Adams (ed.), *The Writings of Albert Gallatin* (3 vols.; Philadelphia, 1879). James Wilkinson, *Memoirs of My Own Times* (3 vols.; Philadelphia, 1816), and John Armstrong, *Notices of the War of 1812* (2 vols.; New York, 1835–1840), are important, and so are the biographies of Wilkinson: James R. Jacobs, *Tarnished Warrior* (New York, 1938), and T. R. Hay and M. R. Werner, *The Admirable Trumpeter* (New York, 1941), and Henry Adams, *Albert Gallatin* (Philadelphia, 1879), and the sketch of William Jones by Kenneth L. Brown, "Mr. Madison's Secretary of the Navy," *U.S. Naval Institute Proceedings,* LXXIII (1947), 967–975.

Chapter III: POLK

Polk as war president has received even less attention than Madison. An excellent biography of him by Charles G. Sellers, Jr., is in progress, but only one volume has thus far been published: *James K. Polk, Jacksonian, 1795–1843* (Princeton, 1957). The standard work, E. I. MacCormac, *James Knox Polk: A Political Biography* (Berkeley, 1922), is relatively uninformative about his work as commander in chief, while Martha M. Morrel, *'Young Hickory': The Life and Times of President James K. Polk* (New York, 1949), is sprightly but very thin.

Justin H. Smith, *The War with Mexico* (2 vols.; New York, 1919), still tells more about the subject than any other work, though many of the military details have been brought up to date in Robert S. Henry, *The Story of the Mexican War* (New York, 1950), and there is an excellent short narrative in Otis Singletary, *The Mexican War* (Chicago, 1960). There is also information in Winfield D. Scott, *Memoirs, Written by Himself* (New York, 1864), Charles W. Elliott, *Winfield Scott, The Soldier and the Man* (New York, 1937), Brainerd Dyer, *Zachary Taylor* (Baton Rouge, 1946), Holman Hamilton, *Zachary Taylor* (2 vols.; New York, 1941–1951), Ivor D. Spencer, *The Victor and the Spoils, A Life of William L. Marcy* (Providence, 1959), M. A. DeWolfe Howe, *The Life and Public Services of George Bancroft* (2 vols.; New York, 1908), and Allan Nevins, *Frémont, Pathmarker of the West* (New York, 1939).

A major source is Milo M. Quaife (ed.), *The Diary of James K. Polk during his Presidency, 1845 to 1849* (4 vols.; Chicago, 1910), which has been edited and abridged by Allan Nevins as *Polk: The Diary of a President, 1845–1849* (New York, 1952). The official correspondence is in Congressional documents, the most important of which is 30th Congress, 1st Session, *House Executive Doc. 60: The Mexican War.*

E.R.M.

Chapter IV: LINCOLN

Far the best study of Lincoln as commander in chief is the book from which this essay is excerpted: T. Harry Williams, *Lincoln and His Generals* (New York, 1952). Two earlier works are Francis V. Greene, "Lincoln as Commander-in-Chief," *Scribner's Magazine,* XLVI (July, 1909), 104–15, and Colin R. Ballard, *The Military Genius of Abraham Lincoln: An Essay* (London, 1926).

The number of Lincoln biographies touching on his work as commander in chief is legion. John Hay and John G. Nicolay, *Abraham Lincoln: A History* (10 vols.; New York, 1904), is the indispensable narrative by his two secretaries. J. G. Randall and Richard N. Current, *Lincoln the President* (4 vols.;

New York, 1945–1955), is the most solid of recent large-scale works. David Donald, *Lincoln Reconsidered* (New York, 1956), is the most important recent re-evaluation. Some treatments of aspects of Lincoln's life that are relevant here are David H. Bates, *Lincoln in the Telegraph Office* (New York, 1907), and Robert V. Bruce, *Lincoln and the Tools of War* (Indianapolis, 1956). Some relevant monographs not directly on Lincoln are Alexander H. Meneely, *The War Department, 1861* (New York, 1928), Fred A. Shannon, *The Organization and Administration of the Union Army, 1861–1865* (2 vols.; Cleveland, 1928), James M. Merrill, *The Rebel Shore: The Story of Union Sea Power in the Civil War* (Boston, 1957), and Richard S. West, Jr., *Mr. Lincoln's Navy* (New York, 1957).

The principal sources are, first of all, U.S. War Department, *The War of the Rebellion: A Compilation of the Official Records of the Union and Confederate Armies* (69 vols.; Washington, D.C., 1880–1900), U.S. Department of the Navy, *Official Records of the Union and Confederate Navies in the War of the Rebellion* (30 vols.; Washington, D.C., 1894–1922), and Roy P. Barber *et al.* (eds.), *The Collected Works of Abraham Lincoln* (8 vols.; New Brunswick, New Jersey, 1953). There are also diaries, autobiographies, and biographies of many civilians and military and naval men who worked with Lincoln. Among the more important are Adam Badeau, *Military History of Ulysses S. Grant* (3 vols.; New York, 1868–1881), Tyler Dennett (ed.), *Lincoln and the Civil War in the Diaries and Letters of John Hay* (New York, 1939), David Donald (ed.), *Inside Lincoln's Cabinet: The Civil War Diaries of Salmon P. Chase* (New York, 1954), George C. Gorham, *The Life and Public Service of Edwin M. Stanton* (2 vols.; Boston, 1899), Warren W. Hassler, *General George B. McClellan: Shield of the Union* (Baton Rouge, 1957), George B. McClellan, *McClellan's Own Story* (New York, 1887), George Meade, *The Life and Letters of George Gordon Meade* (2 vols.; New York, 1913), Russell F. Weigley, *Quarter Master General of the Union Army: A Biography of M. C. Meigs* (New York, 1959), *The Diary of Gideon Welles* (3 vols.; Boston, 1917), and Kenneth P. Williams, *Lincoln Finds a General* (5 vols.; New York, 1949–1959).

Three works dealing with the command-in-chief on the Confederate side are Hudson Strode, *Jefferson Davis: Confederate President* (New York, 1959), Frank E. Vandiver, *Rebel Brass: The Confederate Command System* (Baton Rouge, 1956), and Joseph T. Durkin, *Stephen R. Mallory: Confederate Navy Chief* (Chapel Hill, 1954).

E.R.M.

Chapter V: McKINLEY

The basic sources for McKinley's command-in-chief are U.S. War Department, *Correspondence relating to the War with Spain* . . . (2 vols.; Washington, D.C., 1902), and U.S. Department of the Navy, *Appendix to the Report of the Chief of the Bureau of Navigation, 1898: Naval Operations of the War with Spain* (Washington, D.C., 1898). Some additional information crops up in 57th Congress, 1st Session, *House Doc. 485: Report of the Proceedings of a Court of Inquiry in the Case of Rear-Admiral Winfield S. Schley, U.S. Navy* (2 vols.; Washington, D.C., 1902), 56th Congress, 1st Session, *Senate Doc. 221: Report of the Commission Appointed by the President to Investigate the Conduct of the War Department in the War with Spain* (8 vols.; Washington, D.C., 1900), and U.S. Department of State, *Papers relating to the Foreign Relations of the United States . . . 1898* (Washington, D.C., 1901).

Charles S. Olcott, *William McKinley* (2 vols.; Boston, 1916), prints excerpts from McKinley's private secretary's diary and draws on interviews with many men who worked with McKinley. Russell A. Alger, *The Spanish-American War* (New York, 1901), is a pedestrian narrative by the Secretary of War. John D. Long, *The New American Navy* (2 vols.; Boston, 1903), is a similar work by the Secretary of the Navy. Long's journal has been published twice, once as Lawrence S. Mayo (ed.), *America of Yesterday, As Reflected in the Journal of John Davis Long* (Boston, 1923), and again, with both additions and deletions, as Margaret Long (ed.), *The Journal of John D. Long* (Rindge, New Hampshire, 1956). His correspondence is in Gardner Weld Allen (ed.), *Papers of John Davis Long, 1897–1904, Collections of the Massachusetts Historical Society,* vol. 78 (Boston, 1939). Nelson A. Miles, the Commanding General, wrote *Serving the Republic* (New York, 1911); John D. Miley, an aide to Shafter, wrote *In Cuba with Shafter* (New York, 1899); Admiral William T. Sampson contributed to W. A. M. Goode, *With Sampson Through the War* (New York, 1899); his rival, Admiral Winfield S. Schley, published *Forty-five Years under the Flag* (New York, 1904). Admiral George Dewey wrote an *Autobiography* (New York, 1913), and there are several works about him: Albert M. Dewey, *The Life and Letters of Admiral Dewey* (Akron, Ohio, 1899), Laurin H. Healy and Luis Kutner, *The Admiral* (Chicago, 1944), and Nathan Sargent (comp.), *Admiral Dewey and the Manila Campaign* (Washington, D.C., 1947). Richard S. West, Jr., *Admirals of American Empire* (Indianapolis, 1948), is a composite biography of Dewey, Mahan, Schley, and Sampson.

Bibliographical Notes

Margaret Leech, *In the Days of McKinley* (New York, 1959), is the most up-to date narrative, though it does not entirely replace Walter Millis' *The Martial Spirit* (New York, 1931) as a literary account of the war or French E. Chadwick, *The Relations of the United States and Spain: The Spanish-American War* (2 vols., New York, 1911), as a recital of events. By far the best short treatment is the text in Frank Freidel's pictorial history, *The Splendid Little War* (Boston, 1958).

Chapter VI: WILSON

The most important source is volumes VII and VIII of Ray Stannard Baker, *Woodrow Wilson: Life and Letters* (8 vols.; New York, 1927–1939). These two volumes consist almost entirely of documents, including nearly everything of importance from the vast collection of Wilson manuscripts in the Library of Congress. Additional material is in U.S. Department of the Army, *United States Army in the World War, 1917–1919* (17 vols.; Washington, D.C., 1948), 66th Congress, 2nd Session, *Hearings before the Subcommittee of the Senate Committee on Naval Affairs: Naval Investigation* (2 vols.; Washington, D.C., 1920), and U.S. Department of State, *Papers relating to the Foreign Relations of the United States . . . Supplement: the World War, 1917 and 1918* (5 vols.; Washington, D.C., 1932–1933) and *Supplement: Russia, 1918* (3 vols.; Washington, D.C., 1931–1932).

Among important autobiographies and biographies are Frederick Palmer, *Newton D. Baker: America at War* (2 vols.; New York, 1931) and *Bliss, Peacemaker* (New York, 1934), Peyton C. March, *The Nation at War* (Garden City, New York, 1932), John J. Pershing, *My Experiences in the World War* (2 vols.; New York, 1931), Josephus Daniels, *Our Navy at War* (New York, 1922) and *The Wilson Era* (2 vols.; Chapel Hill, 1944–1946), William S. Sims, *The Victory at Sea* (New York, 1920), Elting E. Morison, *Admiral Sims and the Modern American Navy* (Boston, 1942), Frank Freidel, *Franklin D. Roosevelt: The Apprenticeship* (Boston, 1952), and Charles Seymour (ed.), *The Intimate Papers of Colonel House* (4 vols.; Boston, 1926–1928).

There is astonishingly little writing that deals directly with Wilson as commander in chief. The first three volumes of Arthur S. Link's *Wilson* (Princeton, 1947–   ) only reach the autumn of 1915. Arthur G. Walworth, *Woodrow Wilson: A Biography* (2 vols.; New York, 1958), and other shorter biographies tend to slight the period between April, 1917, and November, 1918. Charles

Seymour, *American Diplomacy during the World War* (Baltimore, 1934), has a chapter on "The Diplomacy of Co-ordination," which deals with Wilson and the Supreme War Council. Warner R. Schilling, "Civil-Naval Politics in World War I," *World Politics*, VII (July, 1955), pp. 572–591, is a fascinating article foreshadowing a book on Wilson and his navy.

Thomas G. Frothingham, *The American Reinforcement in the World War* (New York, 1927), is probably still the best account of operations on land.

Chapter VII: F.D.R.

The best general works on Franklin Roosevelt's war presidency are William L. Langer and S. Everett Gleason, *The Challenge to Isolation, 1937–1940* (New York, 1952), and the same authors' *The Undeclared War, 1940–1941* (New York, 1953), covering the prewar period, and Herbert Feis, *Churchill-Roosevelt-Stalin* (Princeton, 1957), which deals with the diplomacy of the war. Walter Millis, Harvey C. Mansfield, and Harold Stein, *Arms and the State* (New York, 1958), treats generally of civil-military relations during the 1930's and 1940's, and Samuel P. Huntington, *The Soldier and the State* (Cambridge, Mass., 1957), contains a valuable chapter on American participation in World War II. American strategy during the war is covered in greatest detail in the U.S. Army's official history, *The U.S. Army in World War II*. The volumes most closely dealing with grand strategy are: Mark S. Watson, *Chief of Staff: Prewar Plans and Preparations* (Washington, D.C., 1950), Ray S. Cline, *Washington Command Post: The Operations Division* (Washington, D.C., 1951), Maurice Matloff and Edwin M. Snell, *Strategic Planning for Coalition Warfare, 1941–1942* (Washington, D.C., 1953), and Maurice Matloff, *Strategic Planning for Coalition Warfare, 1943–1944* (Washington, D.C., 1959).

Among the memoirs of Roosevelt's war presidency the most useful are Robert E. Sherwood, *Roosevelt and Hopkins* (New York, 1948), and Samuel I. Rosenman, *Working with Roosevelt* (New York, 1953). From the organizational point of view, the Senate hearing on the unification of the armed forces after World War II provides the most revealing sources; these are 79th Congress, 1st Session, *Hearings before the Committee on Military Affairs: S. 84, a Bill to Provide for a Department of the Armed Forces* (Washington, D.C., 1945), and *Report to Hon. James Forrestal, Secretary of the Navy, on Unification of the War and Navy Departments* [The Eberstadt Report] (Washington, D.C., 1945).

Bibliographical Notes

Chapter VIII: TRUMAN

Far and away the most important source of information concerning the commander in chief in the Korean War is: 82nd Congress, 1st Session, *Hearings before the Committee on Armed Services and the Committee on Foreign Relations, U.S. Senate: Military Situation in the Far East* (5 vols.; Washington, D.C., 1951), commonly termed the "MacArthur Hearings." Contained in its three thousand and some pages of testimony are many details of the military organization that served the President. Supplemented by Truman's memoirs and Major General Courtney Whitney's *MacArthur: His Rendezvous with Destiny* (New York, 1956), it provides the best picture of the Commander in Chief likely to be available until the army's historians, whose works have permitted us to see the wartime Roosevelt so clearly, complete their Korean volumes.

Compared to the three just mentioned, other sources for the Korean period are of minor importance. They include memoirs, such as General Mark W. Clark's *From the Danube to the Yalu* (New York, 1954) and General Matthew B. Ridgway's *Soldier* (New York, 1956), quasi-memoirs such as *MacArthur, 1941–1951* (New York, 1954), by Major General Charles A. Willoughby and John Chamberlain, and psychological travelogues such as John Gunther's *The Riddle of MacArthur* (New York, 1951). Scholarly works have been written, for the most part, by political scientists, who have been chiefly interested in the problems of civil-military relations and limited and general war. They have rushed in where the historians, although no more angelic, have feared to tread owing to the unavailability of the official military records. The most thorough of these works is the one by John W. Spanier, *The Truman-MacArthur Controversy and the Korean War* (Cambridge, Mass., 1959).

For the World War II period and the between-wars development of the office of the commander in chief, much of the information has been derived from Truman's memoirs; Leahy's *I Was There* (New York, 1950); *The Forrestal Diaries* (New York, 1951), edited by Walter Millis; Henry L. Stimson and McGeorge Bundy, *On Active Service in Peace and War* (New York, 1950); and an unpublished doctoral dissertation by Major Lawrence J. Legere, Jr., entitled *Unification of the Armed Forces*.

Liberal use had been made throughout of various news publications, popular and professional journals, and numerous records of the hearings before several committees of Congress.

Bibliographical Notes

Chapter IX: EISENHOWER and after

The sources available for so recent a subject are mainly documents and reports in *The New York Times, The Department of State Bulletin,* and congressional hearings. Of the latter, two are unusually valuable: 84th Congress, 2nd Session, *Hearings before the Subcommittee on the Air Force of the Senate Committee on Armed Services: Study of Airpower* (Washington, D.C., 1956), and 85th Congress, 1st and 2nd Sessions, *Hearings before the Subcommittee on Preparedness of the Senate Armed Services Committee: Satellite and Missile Programs* (3 vols.; Washington, D.C., 1959). Matthew B. Ridgway, *Soldier* (New York, 1956), and Maxwell D. Taylor, *The Uncertain Trumpet* (New York, 1959), are documents by former army chiefs of staff. Robert J. Donovan, *Eisenhower: The Inside Story* (New York, 1956), is enlivened by some excerpts from cabinet records.

Walter W. Rostow, *The United States in the World Arena* (New York, 1960), is a careful analysis written with perspective and insight. Walter Millis, Harvey Mansfield, and Harold Stein, *Arms and the State* (New York, 1958), examines defense administration. Richard P. Stebbins's annual *The United States in World Affairs* is invariably a judicious and informed narrative. Among the many works on issues in defense policy in these years, perhaps the most significant are Samuel P. Huntington, *The Soldier and the State* (Cambridge, Mass., 1957), William R. Kintner *et al., Forging a New Sword: A Study of the Department of Defense* (New York, 1958), Robert E. Osgood, *Limited War: The Challenge to American Strategy* (Chicago, 1957), Henry Kissinger, *Nuclear Weapons and Foreign Policy* (New York, 1957), James M. Gavin, *War and Peace in the Space Age* (New York, 1958), and Oskar Morgenstern, *The Question of National Defense* (New York, 1959).

Index

About the Contributors

ERNEST R. MAY is Associate Professor of History at Harvard University. During the Korean War he served with the Pacific Fleet and with the Historical Section of the Joint Chiefs of Staff. He held a Guggenheim Fellowship in 1958–1959, and he is now a Faculty Research Fellow of the Social Science Research Council. His book *The World War and American Isolation, 1914–1917* was awarded the George Louis Beer Prize of the American Historical Association as the best work of 1959 in European international history. He has also written articles for *The American Scholar, Frontier, The New Republic,* and various scholarly journals.

MARCUS CUNLIFFE is Professor of American History and Institutions at the University of Manchester. Educated at Oriel College, Oxford, he was a Commonwealth Fellow at Yale, 1947–1949, Fellow at the Center for Advanced Study in the Behavioral Sciences, Stanford, California, 1957–1958, and Visiting Professor in American History at Harvard, 1959–1960. His books on America include *The Literature of the United States* (1954); *George Washington: Man and Monument* (1958); and *The Nation Takes Shape, 1789–1837* (1959). He is presently making a study of American military attitudes, 1775–1865.

LEONARD D. WHITE (1891–1959) was Burton Distinguished Professor of Public Administration at the University of Chicago and author of an outstanding series of volumes on the administrative history of the United States: *The Federalists, The Jeffersonians, The Jacksonians,* and *The Republicans.* He was recipient of a Bancroft Award for distinguished historical writing, and he had been President of the American Political Science Association.

T. HARRY WILLIAMS is Boyd Professor of History at Louisiana State University, author of *Lincoln and the Radicals, Lincoln and his Generals,* and *P. G. T. Beauregard,* co-author (with Frank Freidel and Richard N. Current) of a *History of the United States,* and editor of *The Selected Writings and Speeches of Abraham Lincoln.* He also serves on the Historical Advisory Commission of the Department of the Army.

WILLIAM R. EMERSON is Assistant Professor of History at Yale University, where he teaches European and American military history. He was an officer in the Army Air Force in World War II. He has contributed to many scholarly journals.

WILBER W. HOARE is a historian trained at the University of Chicago. He served as an Army officer during World War II and in the Korean War. For the past seven years he has worked as a historian in the Department of Defense.